The Mexican Revolution 1914-1915

The Mexican Revolution

1914 - 1915

The Convention of Aguascalientes

R O B E R T E. Q U I R K

I N D I A N A U N I V E R S I T Y P R E S S

Bloomington

Acknowledgment

I SHOULD LIKE TO RECORD A DEBT OF GRATITUDE
to the Social Science Research Council and to
the Graduate School of Indiana University for
timely grants which made possible the research
for this book.

Contents

The Mexican Revolution 1914-1915

1

Winds of Revolution

IN SEPTEMBER 1910 MEXICO CELEBRATED THE HUN-
dredth anniversary of Father Miguel Hidalgo's "Cry of Dolores"
which launched the war of independence against Spain. It was
a magnificent occasion, with honored guests present from many
countries. There were public speeches, banquets, and grand
official receptions for the foreign visitors, the higher clergy, and
the diplomats. Money seemed no object as the government of
Porfirio Díaz demonstrated the wealth and good fortune of
Mexico. And there were many reasons for celebration. Mexico
was prosperous, more so than at any time in the previous hundred
years. The budget was balanced; Mexican currency was solidly
on the gold standard. The money of foreign capitalists was safe
and returned comfortable dividends to those wise enough to
buy agricultural lands, oil properties, and mining or railroad
stocks. It was indeed a golden age, and Díaz was understandably
proud of what had been accomplished since he became president
more than a quarter of a century before. To the casual visitor, to
the investor abroad, Mexico presented an imposing façade. All
seemed well in the best of all possible worlds.

The façade of prosperity was a cruel illusion, however, for
the Mexican economy was basically weak. Most outsiders re-

mained blissfully unaware of the extreme disparity between the wealthy few and the masses of the poor. A balanced budget meant little to an Indian agricultural worker whose standard of living plummeted while the national income rose. Real wages were lower than they had been a century earlier under Spanish rule. With the approval of the government of Díaz the Indian pueblos were despoiled of their lands, and where fields were once held and worked in common by villagers, large estates now kept the workers tied to the soil as effectively as had medieval feudalism. By 1910 less than five per cent of Mexico's population owned almost all of the arable land. And no escape seemed possible for the landless peasant who tilled the soil for the master of an hacienda. To flee from his debts and obligations was virtually impossible, for the government maintained rural guards to run down and return those who sought to escape. In any event, a family was made responsible for the debts of its head, so that even death provided no relief for the perpetual indebtedness of the peasant classes. In the cities the industrial workers labored for little pay under hazardous and unsanitary conditions. Strikes were repressed by the army with extreme brutality. Nor did the government seem inclined to remedy the inequities of the system. The philosophy of positivism, which dominated the thinking of the chief members of the regime, sanctioned the worst excesses, and malcontents were silenced by imprisonment or exile.

Despite the constitution, which recognized all of the traditional freedoms and rights of the Mexican people, the government was a dictatorship. There was no semblance of popular rule, as opposition parties had long been discouraged, and voting procedures were rigged to insure the election and re-election of Díaz, his legislators, and his state officials. The national regime intervened in elections at all levels to keep loyal officials in power everywhere in the Republic. And as a check on governors and municipal presidents Díaz built an elaborate system of *jefes políticos* (political chiefs), which throttled local initiative or independence. Among the members of the middle and upper classes, Mexico's politically effective population, the dictatorship found much support. The positivists taught that the masses—more than eighty per cent of the Mexicans were illiterate—were not, perhaps would never be capable of self-government. Owners of property, even those who might be liberal-minded in principle, preferred the dictatorship with its guarantees of peace and the protection of property to the unrest and civil war which had characterized the first half century of independence. Most critics of the regime hoped that any necessary reforms could be carried out peacefully and without recourse to revolution or bloodshed. It was a vain, if pious, hope.

In the presidential election of 1910, as farcical as any which had preceded it, Díaz was opposed by Francisco I. Madero, a member of a rich, landowning family from the northern state of Coahuila. Madero had entered national politics in the expectation that the president would at last permit democratic rule. The government of Díaz showed its attitude toward free elections by jailing Madero until after the balloting had been concluded. When the results of the elections were announced few were surprised to learn that Díaz and his unpopular vice president, Ramón Corral, had been chosen again for another six-year term. Madero went into exile in the United States.

Madero abhorred revolution. In his book, *The Presidential Succession of 1910,* which he had published two years earlier, he made it clear that changes in Mexico should come through orderly and legal processes. He was a Liberal of the nineteenth-century variety, who believed in a well-regulated, middle-class-directed, limited democracy. With an abiding faith in laws and education, he rejected social reforms unless they should come through the natural course of events. But seeing his dreams of a free election shattered on the rocks of the dictatorship, he turned, however reluctantly, to armed revolt. In October 1910 he published his Plan of San Luis Potosí, denouncing the election of Díaz as a fraud. Madero himself laid claim to the presidential office. He made no mention of economic or social reform; with his conservative nature it would have been strange had he done so. Yet men such as Pascual Orozco and Francisco Villa in the North and Emiliano Zapata in the South read into his plan more than Madero intended, and his call to revolution met with a quick and remarkable response throughout Mexico. Armed resistance grew at a rate which alarmed members of the government, and the army seemed unable to contain the revolution. Only the president, who was now over eighty years of age, seemed oblivious of the dangers which threatened his regime.

José Limantour, a positivist and Díaz' Minister of the Treasury, took the lead in negotiating a settlement with Madero. At the border city of Ciudad Juárez—across the Rio Grande from El Paso, Texas—an agreement was made providing for the elimination of the president. Francisco de la Barra, the chief of Díaz' cabinet, would serve as interim president until elections could be held in the fall of 1911. Reluctant and protesting to the last, Díaz left the country to take up a life of exile in Europe. He did not return.

The downfall of Porfirio Díaz marked the beginning of a new era in Mexican history. Since 1910 Mexico has lived in the shadow of Madero's revolution, and more than forty years later the official party still bears the name of that revolution. For good or for bad the concept of change through armed revolt has been indelibly stamped on the soul of the Mexican people. Mexico has remade itself in the image of the ideals of 1910. Yet this was not the intention of Madero when he proclaimed his Plan of San Luis Potosí. He did not foresee the years of trouble ahead when he untied Aeolus' bag of revolution. The winds of rebellious unrest swept him to his destruction and drove his country through a decade of angry, intestine warfare. Great battles were fought, more bloody, more terrible than any in Mexican history. Mexican slew Mexican; some because they wished to preserve the Liberal ideals of the nineteenth century, others because they felt that Mexico needed more radical reform than the free elections and "effective suffrage" promised by Madero. And still others would destroy the revolution completely, would return to the halcyon days of the dictatorship and military rule in Mexico. The significance of this decade, and especially of the years 1914–15, was that the people were offered a choice of ideologies. The answer was given on the field of battle, in parliamentary debate, and in revolutionary proclamations. The constitution which was forged in 1917 at Querétaro demonstrated conclusively that Madero's philosophy was outmoded. The future belonged to the radicals.

Yet Madero was elevated to the presidency in a mood of optimism. His election was without doubt the freest in Mexican history. And the new administration seemed in 1911 and early 1912 to promise Mexico peaceful but gradual progress toward the political, social, and economic level achieved by the United States and Great Britain. Madero offered Mexico an end to dictatorship and a return to the pre-Porfirian days of Mexican Liberalism, the era of Benito Juárez and Sebastián Lerdo de Tejada. The touchstones of Madero's political philosophy were secular education, free elections in a federal system of government, and separation of church and state. He was moderate and well intentioned, but as president he soon proved himself bumbling and inept as well. He was an idealist, a dreamer, not a man of action. He did not recognize that his country needed more than free elections, that his Liberal principles were hopelessly out of date. Above all, he failed to see the need for genuine economic and social reform. Madero might have succeeded in restoring stable government to the Republic had the times been less critical. As it was, his hopes for peace, and those of Mexico, were dashed as the storms of revolution broke, venting their fury on idealists.

In the North of the Republic, in the state of Chihuahua, Pascual Orozco rebelled against him, alleging that the president had withheld funds from his Colorado troops. Madero was forced to call upon the federal army to put down his fellow-revolutionaries. In Veracruz Félix Díaz, nephew of the erstwhile dictator, sustained a short-lived *cuartelazo*. Captured and brought to the capital, where he was lodged in the penitentiary, Díaz continued to conspire against Madero with Bernardo Reyes, an ex-Porfirista, who was also imprisoned in Mexico City, and Manuel Mondragón, an officer in the federal army. In the South, in the mountains and valleys of Morelos, Emiliano Zapata's Liberating Army defied

Madero as it had Porfirio Díaz, flouting the president's demand that all irregular troops surrender their arms to the government. The Zapatistas distrusted Madero and his vague promises of social reform. Moreover, Madero showed no inclination to end the noxious institution of the *jefatura política* and insisted on naming a governor for the state of Morelos who was completely unacceptable to Zapata and his followers. So far as the men of the South were concerned, there had been no revolution at all, and they continued to demand, and to fight for, land reforms based on the seizure and partition of large estates. It was this which the middle-class Madero was not prepared to accept. In November 1911 Zapata proclaimed his own Plan of Ayala in support of Pascual Orozco. And he continued to confiscate haciendas regardless of the attitude of the federal government.

Within his government Madero faced the perennial dilemma of revolutionary heads of state—whether to sweep out the hold-overs from the old regime and risk chaos or to keep them in their positions and risk the sabotaging of his program. In choosing the latter, Madero alienated many of those who had initially supported his revolt against Díaz. The federal army, nominally loyal to the president, was also an Achilles' heel of treason, and it could be used against the Zapatistas, Orozquistas, and Felicistas only with great peril to Madero himself. The senate, which was not renewed in the congressional election of 1912, was largely Porfirian in its allegiance, while in the Chamber of Deputies the Maderista majority was hopelessly split by factional disputes. The sizable Catholic party was actively, if not vociferously, in opposition to the president and his Liberal program. And the ambassador of the United States to Mexico, Henry Lane Wilson, was an unrelenting enemy of Madero, seeking to undermine his position in unfavorable dispatches to the American Secretary of State, Philander C. Knox. Meanwhile, Madero's freedom of the press permitted scurrilous attacks on him, his family, and his government in the conservative newspapers in the capital.

Madero proved incapable of weathering the rebellions raised

against him. In the end, however, it was the federal army which broke him. When Félix Díaz and Bernardo Reyes were traitorously released from their prison cells on February 9, 1913, to march upon the National Palace, Madero, in calling upon General Victoriano Huerta for protection, erred grievously. Though Huerta had earlier served Madero well in the campaigns against Orozco and Zapata, he now plotted with his ostensible enemy, Díaz, the overthrow of Madero's government. It was under the aegis of Henry Lane Wilson—a fact Mexico's historians will not forget—that Huerta and Díaz agreed to end the bombardment in Mexico City and to depose the unfortunate president. On the night of February 22 Madero, having been forced to resign his office, was shot to death by officers of General Huerta. Victoriano Huerta, the "bloody usurper" in Mexico's revolutionary tradition, assumed the provisional presidency while the martyred Madero gained a popularity in death which he had never achieved in life. He became the symbol for the continued struggle against military dictatorship, was canonized and enrolled in the hagiology of the revolution as its first "apostle."

Many responsible citizens hailed the return of a vigorous central government with exquisite relief, weary of the two years of unrest since the deposition of Porfirio Díaz. And responsible and irresponsible citizens alike descended upon Mexico City like harpies. Francisco de la Barra had no compunctions about joining the cabinet of Huerta. Pascual Orozco, once defeated by Huerta, now made his peace with the new president and ranged his Colorado troops alongside the federal forces of Huerta. The army was, of course, solidly behind him, and the majority of the state governors placed expediency above their loyalty to the legally constituted government of Madero. Though many of the Maderista deputies opposed the usurpation, Huerta countered by forcibly dispersing his enemies in the 26th Legislature and imprisoning many of its members. The Catholic Party forsook its forward-looking program of Social Action and took refuge in the lap of reaction. In the capital's cathedral a *Te*

Deum was sung to celebrate the supposed pacification of Mexico. The central government was now completely conservative and frankly military in character.

Yet Huerta was not master of all the Republic. In the mountains half ringing the capital to the south and west, Zapatista Mexico was as inflexible in its opposition to the new president as it had been against Madero and Porfirio Díaz. Zapata's Plan of Ayala was emended to take into account the *coup d'état* of Huerta and the defection of Orozco. Although his movement was still confined primarily to the small state of Morelos, Zapata now claimed the leadership of the entire revolution. But his knowledge of the rest of Mexico was extremely limited. He was a national leader only in his own mind and in the minds of his exuberant peasant lieutenants. The forces of Zapata were illequipped and without discipline, and the commanders, including Zapata, possessed only the rudiments of military science. Although the Plan of Ayala was broad in conception, in that it called for land for the landless everywhere in Mexico, in reality the Zapatistas had no concern for areas other than their own. The revolution of Zapata was not a national movement and was powerless to defeat Huerta without help from chiefs in other parts of Mexico.

The real threat against the new regime came from the North, where the followers of Madero refused to accept Huerta. In the state of Coahuila the governor, Venustiano Carranza, and the state legislature stood like a dike against the inundation of Mexico by resurgent militarism. Revolutionary bands, following the lead of Carranza, took up arms again as they had in earlier times for Madero's Plan of San Luis Potosí. Moreover, Woodrow Wilson, taking office just ten days after the assassination of Madero, refused to be pressed into a hasty acceptance of Huerta's seizure of power. By making recognition contingent upon popularly elected government in Mexico, President Wilson probably contributed more to the downfall of Huerta than any other one person.

On March 26, 1913, at the Hacienda de Guadalupe in the

state of Coahuila, Venustiano Carranza dictated to his private secretary, Alfredo Breceda, a revolutionary plan for the projected rebellion against Huerta. It must be apparent that this Plan of Guadalupe, formulated by a small group of conspirators, had no more authority than that with which the brute force of military revolution could endow it. (The document was signed by Breceda, by Jacinto B. Treviño, and Lucio Blanco, and by others of lesser subsequent importance in the revolution, none of the signers with higher rank than lieutenant colonel in an irregular revolutionary band.) But it became the banner for the Constitutionalist cause because it gained acceptance by most revolutionaries. Its very vagueness made it palatable to men of all stripes, and initially few but the Zapatistas saw fit to question its principles.

This plan, promulgated in Coahuila, denied recognition to Huerta as Mexico's legal president and designated in his place Venustiano Carranza as the "First Chief of the Constitutionalist Army in charge of the Executive Power." Significantly, Carranza did not specifically lay claim to the presidency, since constitutionally he could not become president without an election. The revolutionaries led by Carranza were above all else constitutionalists. It is probable that at this early date, at least, Carranza aspired to the interim presidency, and a hint of this aspiration is provided in Article 6 of the plan, which noted that a provisional president would assume office when the revolutionary armies reached Mexico City. But against the wishes of many of his most powerful generals, Carranza never did exchange the role of the First Chief for that of an interim or provisional president. He came to prefer the extra- or pre-constitutional informality of decreeing laws and reforms without a cabinet, a congress, or courts of law. He thought this an especially good means of dealing with Huerta and the "criminals" who supported him.[1]

Carranza was a man of property, of middle-class mentality like the dead president. Tall, taciturn, with an Olympian beard, his person was the hallmark of respectability and legality in the Constitutionalist revolution against Huerta. He was the living proof of the revolutionary claim to the inheritance of the Liberal traditions of Gómez Farías, Juárez, Lerdo, and Madero. He was aloof, usually approachable only through intermediaries, men such as Isidro Fabela, Félix Palavicini, Rafael Zubarán Capmany, and the rest of the Carrancista clique of lawyers, engineers, and educators who grouped themselves around their First Chief. He could be admired or hated; he was too detached from his fellow citizens to be loved. He was impeccably honest and insufferably conscious of his own rectitude. If Carranza had a developed, well-thought-out political philosophy it was not apparent, for he expressed himself only in platitudes. His speeches were uninspiring, long-winded, and dull. He was quite content to allow others to give mouth to his political inclinations. José Natividad Macías wrote his constitution; Ciro B. Ceballos and Heriberto Barrón edited his newspapers and propagandized for the Constitutionalist revolution. The First Chief said, wrote, perhaps even thought, little that was important or worth remembering. He was bourgeois mediocrity incarnate.

Throughout his revolutionary career Carranza insisted stubbornly that Mexico's government must be civilian, that militarism and pretorianism were endemic evils to be extirpated upon the success of his revolution. Because of his stubbornness he precipitated a break with Francisco Villa in 1914 and threw his country into a sanguinary civil war. When, at the instance of Woodrow Wilson, he might have compromised with his enemies, he refused, insisting upon the integrity of his course of action. And he died in 1920, an assassin's victim, because he believed, rightly or wrongly, that Mexico needed another civilian's hand at the helm, a nonmilitary president like himself.

The regime of Huerta in 1913 and 1914 was no house of cards to be toppled by any gust, even from the North. Zapata was unable, or did not care, to hazard an attack on the capital. Carranza had no army to match the federals, even though many of the soldiers of Huerta were unreliable victims of the Porfirian *leva*. Musketry and horsemanship, the nineteenth-century levelers of Mexican armies, no longer sufficed to win battles. Against heavy cannons, machine guns, grenades, and barbed wire irregular troops stood little chance. Until his enemies had modern weapons in sufficient quantity and a regular supply of ammunition Huerta was safe—so long, that is, as the army remained loyal. Woodrow Wilson's decision to ban shipments of arms to Huerta, even to the extent of seizing the port of Veracruz, insured his ultimate defeat, for the Constitutionalists continued to be supplied through ports of entry along the Texan border. At El Paso and elsewhere organized smuggling was carried on by respectable American firms during periods when arms were embargoed, and winked at by the American customs officials.

Through 1913 the gains made by the Constitutionalists were minimal. In Coahuila the First Chief lost ground and was finally ejected from his own state completely. It was a tedious and disheartening period dedicated to the formation of armies, the training of troops, and the accumulation of weapons, ammunition, and supplies. Until midsummer operations of the Constitutionalist government were confined to the territory in the north of Coahuila between Monclova and Piedras Negras. A federal garrison in Saltillo denied Carranza access even to his own capital. Yet he looked beyond the relatively small scope of his authority at that time to decree on May 14 the revival of Juárez' law of January 25, 1862 (against the armed intervention of the French). The First Chief fixed the death penalty or other "appropriate punishments" for Huerta and "all others who officially or privately" had recognized or aided that regime.[2]

In other isolated pockets of the mushrooming rebellion against Huerta revolutionary chiefs tentatively adhered to the First Chieftaincy of Carranza. In Zacatecas the state capital fell to General Pánfilo Natera, the first capital to pass from federal hands. Although nine days later the revolutionaries left the city as a large federal army approached under General Joaquín Maass, Natera and other chiefs roamed at will through the state. Their movements were not so swift or efficient as those of Huerta's troops, however, since the latter continued to hold control of the railroads. As early as February 1913, Eulalio Gutiérrez, the municipal president of Concepción del Oro in the state of Zacatecas, had withdrawn recognition from the governor and had associated himself with Carranza.[3] Concepción del Oro was a mining center, connected by rail with Saltillo, and had little affinity to its own state capital, from which it was isolated. Gutiérrez, joined by his brother Luis, raised a small band of revolutionaries, hopefully designated it an army, and began operations against the government of Huerta in the triangle between Concepción del Oro, Saltillo, and San Luis Potosí.

In the state of Chihuahua the revolution coalesced around the person of Francisco Villa. Born Doroteo Arango, Villa has been one of the most romanticized and controversial figures in the Mexican revolution. Unable to read or write until he was an adult, and then only partly literate, he was in his heyday Mexico's mightiest *caudillo*. Villa lived outside the law for most of his life. He fashioned his own personal code of behavior, whether as a youthful Robin Hood, avenging a ravished sister, or a mature general of world renown. With no higher law to gainsay his will he took what he pleased, whether it was a herd of cattle, a human life, or a beautiful woman. Fanatically loyal to his friends, he was an implacable enemy to those who crossed him, rarely forgetting or forgiving a slight. He was all that Carranza was not: virile (in Mexico *muy macho*), earthy, passionate, given to emotional outbursts. He could ruthlessly threaten death in one moment and embrace his would-be victim with protestations of affection and esteem in the next. He inspired love and loyalty, fear and loathing. Villa was peon Mexico as Carranza was her educated, city-dwelling middle class. Each came to distrust, hate, and contemn the other.

Francisco Villa was a poor subordinate. His lack of military discipline had once brought him close to death before a firing squad, as he disobeyed orders of Victoriano Huerta when both were fighting for Madero against the Orozquistas in Chihuahua. At the last moment his life had been spared through the intervention of Emilio and Raúl Madero with their brother. The president ordered Villa brought to the penitentiary in the Federal District to await trial. While in prison he met Gildardo Magaña, a Zapatista, who told him of the Plan of Ayala and, according to Villa's own account, began to teach him to read and write. From this chance meeting of two prisoners came subsequently the ill-starred alliance between the generals of North and South. Transferred to the military prison of Santiago, Villa eluded his guards and escaped from the capital, ultimately to make his way to safety and exile in the United States. He never wavered in his loyalty to Madero, although he was invited by Huerta and Díaz to join the *cuartelazo* which deposed the president.[4]

In El Paso Villa learned of the death of Madero and found it easy to cast his lot with the revolution against Huerta. He recrossed the frontier at Columbus, New Mexico, to raise the standard of revolt in the state of Chihuahua. There he joined Rosalío Hernández, who operated from Santa Rosalía; Maclovio Herrera and Manuel Chao, in control of Parral; and Tomás Urbina, who dominated the territory around Jiménez. Chosen as their leader by these revolutionary *caudillos,* Villa by the fall of 1913 had welded their irregular forces into a respectable Division of the North, controlling the whole state, except for the arterial railway line from Torreón to Ciudad Juárez.[5]

The strategy of Huerta's commanders, as the revolution spread from state to state, was to hold a limited number of key fortified cities on the trunk rail lines from the northern border to the capital, and thus to inhibit rebel troops from advancing to the South. President Huerta, at the same time, maneuvered diplomatically to gain recognition from the United States and other foreign nations. Strong federal garrisons were maintained at Torreón, Zacatecas, Chihuahua, Saltillo, Monterrey, Tampico, San Luis Potosí, and Guadalajara, while outposts in the Federal District fended the Zapatistas from Mexico City. The exigencies of twentieth-century Mexican warfare, the movement of large numbers of troops and heavy equipment, together with the federal control of the principal cities, forced the revolutionaries, as well, to conform their strategy to the railway net of Mexico. Indeed, strategy is a word perhaps too grandiose to apply to the battle plans of the Constitutionalists. The refusal of the federals to wage war in the open virtually destroyed the element of surprise for the revolutionaries. There were no battlefields in the war. Rebel bands or armies attacked towns or cities and either were repulsed or succeeded in capturing the fortified point, with the federals fleeing along a railroad to the next town.

There were three principal routes to Mexico City available to the Constitutionalists: the first, from Piedras Negras, Saltillo, and Monterrey, by way of San Luis Potosí, ran over the lines of the Internacional Mexicano and the Nacional; the second, through the center of the Republic from Ciudad Juárez and Chihuahua by way of Torreón and Zacatecas, was the important Central Mexicano; and the third, along the west coast from Nogales and Hermosillo, passed through Culiacán and Guadalajara. The western tracks, those of the Southern Pacific Railroad and the Ferrocarril de Sonora, ran directly only as far as Tepic, where there was a gap of over fifty miles to be negotiated through the Sierra Madres before an army might pick up train transportation again through Jalisco to Mexico City. Although Parral, Durango, and Hermosillo were in revolutionary hands, the possession of these cities availed nothing since all the ways to the federal capital were effectively blocked by forces of Huerta at the railroad junctions. Rebel bands might cut the lines and tear up tracks or blast locomotives, but the Constitutionalists could not win the war unless these cities were captured.

Although Villa and the Division of the North had gained some success in Chihuahua by the summer of 1913, Carranza found his own position in Coahuila untenable. Driven from Saltillo, he had established his headquarters at Cuatro Ciénegas, at the tip of a railway spur of the Internacional Mexicano west of Monclova. But here the First Chief was in a blind alley, for he could get no supplies from the United States, and he risked his life and the entire cause of the Constitutionalists if a sudden sally of the Huertistas in Monclova should entrap him. In

August Carranza decided to make a bold gamble to save his crumbling authority. He would move his government from Coahuila to Sonora, where Huerta had never exercised any control at all. Entrusting the military command in the Northeast to his subordinate, Pablo González, a timorous general, but always an ardent revolutionary, the First Chief retreated to the West. He was determined to stay in Mexican territory rather than risk internment in the United States. He refused, therefore, to cross the frontier to use American communications even to make his journey more comfortable and swift. Partly by horseback, partly by train, Carranza traversed the embattled Republic from Cuatro Ciénegas to Parral, now held by Maclovio Herrera and Manuel Chao, and Durango, controlled by the Arrieta brothers, Domingo and Mariano. He was careful to skirt the northern cities which were still in federal hands.[6]

Carranza's reasons for crossing to the West Coast were twofold. He could find haven there for his fugitive government; and he hoped to organize a force in Sonora capable of pushing to Mexico City. In late 1913 there were only a few weak federal garrisons between Hermosillo and Guadalajara. After conferring with the revolutionary chiefs in the center of the Republic, the First Chief, with the members of his staff, pushed on by train from Durango to Santiago Papasquiaro, where the rail line ended. Walking or riding they made their way slowly through the rough mountainous terrain of the Sierra Madres, arriving on September 12 at Chinabampo in the Pacific state of Sinaloa. Shortly thereafter they reached their destination safely, the state capital of Sonora, Hermosillo.[7]

Carranza's government remained in Hermosillo for five months, protected by the armies of Alvaro Obregón, Benjamín Hill, and José M. Maytorena, the latter the constitutional governor of the state. But at the end of the five months Carranza was no closer to the presidential chair than when he had come to Sonora. Although he had dubbed the troops of Sonora an Army Corps of the Northwest and, on September 19, had designated Obregón its chief with the rank of brigadier general, it soon became apparent that Obregón's was not the quickest or easiest way to Mexico City. There was little possibility of organizing an important offensive in the Northwest. Perhaps the greatest handicap was the lack of through railroad communications to Mexico City, with the gap between Tepic and Orendáin. Further, the area of the Northwest produced no rich source of export for financing the purchase of munitions, such as the cotton of Torreón, the oil of Tampico, or the cattle or copper of Chihuahua. Most of Mexico's exportable wealth lay in territory controlled by the federals or in which the Division of the North was operating. Obregón's army was neither so large nor so well equipped and supplied as Villa's. In the first month of 1914 Carranza could see that, unless he recrossed the Sierra to Chihuahua, he might be among the last to reach Mexico City, whenever Huerta should capitulate. The Division of the North was beginning to achieve success at arms matched nowhere else among the Constitutionalist forces. And Villa was carving out for himself a bailiwick almost completely independent of the First Chief. To forestall Villa and to take advantage of his victories, Carranza left Hermosillo on February 23, 1914, on the long, difficult trek to Chihuahua.[8]

With Carranza went his civilian coterie, escorted by the troops of Felipe Angeles, an ex-federal officer who had deserted Huerta to join the Constitutionalist revolution. Carranza's informal cabinet now included Rafael Zubarán Capmany, Secretary of *Gobernación* (Interior); Isidro Fabela, in charge of Foreign Affairs; Ignacio Bonillas, in charge of Communications; and General Angeles, the Sub-secretary of Defense. Obregón accompanied the column as far as Naco before returning to Hermosillo to initiate the long delayed advance on Mazatlán and Tepic. While the entourage paralleled the American border —Carranza still would not set foot in the United States—word came from Villa requesting that Angeles be permitted to take charge of the artillery of the Division of the North which Villa was fast accumulating. Carranza immediately relieved Angeles of his responsibilities as a cabinet member and acceded to Villa's wish. Angeles crossed the international frontier to take a train to El Paso and Ciudad Juárez. The column of the First Chief continued its slow march overland into Chihuahua.[9]

Francisco Villa, whose hegemony in Chihuahua had been confirmed by Carranza while the government of the First Chief was still in Hermosillo, was fast mopping up federal resistance in his state preparatory to moving on Torreón. Indeed, he had earlier gained possession of that military and cotton center on October 1, 1913, but had evacuated it soon after, preferring first to consolidate his hold on his own state. From Torreón he turned north as though to assault Chihuahua, feinted there, and then circled the city to capture Ciudad Juárez in a surprise move.[10] The importance of his holding this port city cannot be overemphasized, for he could now freely import supplies and ammunition, paid for with confiscated cotton and cattle. The legitimate owners had no recourse but a discreet, if fearful, silence if Mexican, or a vociferous, though unavailing, plaint if they were Americans. From the beginning of the revolution the government of Wilson was always unaccountably tolerant of Villa's illegality, and his depredations against American property owners brought no official reaction in Washington.

By the end of November 1913 the federal garrison in Chihuahua City was completely isolated. On December 3, unable to go either north or south on the rail line, the troops of Huerta struck out over the desert to Ojinaga, across the Rio Grande from the Texan town of Presidio. Villa dispatched General Pánfilo Natera to run the fugitives down, but when Natera proved unable to break the tight ring of desperate troops around Ojinaga, Villa, with characteristic lack of patience, determined to take the town himself. On January 10, 1914, as Villa approached, the federals yielded their positions, after taking the precaution of crossing the river to be interned by the United States army. The irregular Colorados of Orozco, who had fought beside the troops of Huerta in Chihuahua and Ojinaga, dispersed into the desert to continue their opposition against Villa. By the end of January, except for small bands of Orozquistas, the state was entirely in revolutionary hands.[11]

The First Chief arrived in Chihuahua City with his government as Villa was preparing to move on Torreón once more. It would seem that from the first each of the two leaders was disposed to suspect the other. Although Villa acknowledged his nominal allegiance to Carranza and the Plan of Guadalupe, he preferred the First Chief to be anywhere but in Chihuahua. He also viewed with misgivings the civilians around Carranza, for, to him, too many of them were men of property and education, unmilitary slackers, untrustworthy, and certainly not genuine revolutionaries. On his part, Carranza demanded obedience from his military subordinates and insisted on the competency of his civilian government to handle all nonmilitary matters. It was this last which Villa would not concede in his own domain. There was not room in Chihuahua for two *caudillos*.

Villa's own account of their first meeting, as related many years later to Ramón Puente, may have been charged with Villa's rancor toward Carranza after their complete rupture.[12] Nevertheless, it has the ring of authenticity. Villa reminisced: "I embraced him energetically, but with the first few words we spoke my blood turned to ice. I saw that I could not open my heart to him. As far as he was concerned, I was a rival, not a friend. He never looked me in the eye and during our entire conversation emphasized our differences in origin, pointing out to me that he had been everything from municipal president, *jefe político,* governor, and senator to First Chief. And he lectured me on things like decrees and laws which I could not understand. . . . There was nothing in common between that man and me. . . ." If these were in truth his first impressions of Carranza, Villa dissimulated reasonably well. He manifested his loyalty to Carranza and addressed him as "my chief." For Villa there were matters of greater immediacy than his relationship with the Constitutionalist leader. The time had come for a drive toward Mexico City. Happily he pushed aside the problem of the continued presence of the First Chief in Chihuahua and turned to military considerations. Villa was always in best spirits in planning or conducting a campaign. He loved the life of the soldier.

The city of Torreón lay athwart the lines of the Central Mexicano nearly 300 miles distant from Chihuahua. From this important railroad junction lines radiated to Parral, to Saltillo and Monterrey in the East, and Zacatecas and Mexico City to the South. It dominated the Comarca Lagunera, the rich cotton-producing area of north central Mexico. For more than three months Torreón had been occupied by federal troops under General José Refugio Velasco, and the soldiers of Huerta were now strongly entrenched. Velasco had placed federals and Colorados throughout the surrounding terrain to guard the approaches to the city. A cavalry unit under Benjamín Argumedo, an Orozquista general, occupied Bermejillo twenty-seven miles out, the most northerly point in the defensive system of Torreón. The hills in the more immediate vicinity were crisscrossed with trenches, while cannons and Gatling guns were dug into the slopes. Velasco openly boasted that the city of Torreón was impregnable to rebel attack. The Constitutionalists could not suffer Velasco to remain in Torreón, however, for its possession by the federals blocked off Carranza from Saltillo and both Villa and Carranza from Mexico City. In the middle of March Villa perfected plans for a swift advance on the Jewel of the Laguna.[13]

The commander of the Division of the North threw a veil of secrecy over his operations. He suspended train service north and south of Chihuahua and banned travel of any nature from the city. Telegraph and telephone communications were interrupted, and mounted troops picketed the countryside so no one could reach Ciudad Juárez by automobile, on horse, or afoot to give warning to the federals in Torreón of the impending attack. On March 16 his trains and wagons began to move south. Now under the command of Villa were the troops of Maclovio Herrera, José Trinidad Rodríguez, Eugenio Aguirre Benavides, Toribio Ortega, and Rosalío Hernández. Felipe Angeles was in charge of the division's artillery. The trains moved forward rapidly, and within a day the advance forces had reached Yermo, only 70 miles from Torreón. There they dismounted to prepare for the attack. Villa was unaccountably missing, however, and he was not seen by his men for nearly four days. During this time the army remained restlessly alerted for battle. On March 20 Villa appeared in Yermo, as John Reed wrote for the *New York World,* "all frowsy and bedraggled." Quixotically, he had left the column at Camargo to act as best man at the marriage of an old companion. While his troops waited, he had been dancing at the interminable festivities that accompany Mexican weddings.[14]

Early on the morning of the twentieth the march was resumed, as the men of Villa formed columns on either side of the railroad tracks. A repair train, with a mounted cannon and two armored cars, and provision trains kept slow pace with the marching soldiers as the fingers of the Division of the North penetrated the outer defenses of the federal stronghold. For more than forty miles there was no opposition until the advance guard reached Bermejillo, garrisoned by the detested Orozquistas. Within Bermejillo, Argumedo had already sighted huge clouds of dust and black smoke on the northern horizon which marked Villa's detraining operations, and he had telegraphed Velasco in Torreón asking for instructions. The federal commander ordered Argumedo to send out scouts to the north, but these were rounded up by Villa's men before they could report back to Bermejillo. As a result, Villa's forward parties caught Argumedo unawares—he was, at best, a poor general—and the Colorados were fortunate in escaping and avoiding certain death at the hands of the vengeful Villa. His hatred for the men of Orozco knew no bounds, for these had been the first to rebel against Madero and now continued to dispute with Villa the control of his own state of Chihuahua.[15]

In Bermejillo the Villistas found the hasty departure of the Orozquistas had left communications with Torreón intact. In the railroad station there was a telephone, and Villa, perhaps

still merry from the post-nuptial celebrations, asked Felipe
Angeles to put through a call to General Velasco, demanding the
surrender of the city. According to Roque González Garza, who
was present in the station, Angeles actually talked to the federal
commander, relaying Villa's message.[16] Velasco refused to yield
to Villa without a try at arms, however. He was not amused and
curtly terminated the conversation. A moment later the telephone
in Bermejillo rang, and Villa, himself, picked up the receiver.
It was an unnamed official in Gómez Palacio, a large town five
miles from Torreón. With exaggerated courtesy and evident
sarcasm Villa invited the federal officer to visit them in Bermejillo. "But if you don't want to disturb yourselves we are coming
there anyway. For I've covered a lot of territory just to see you
fellows!" he said.

The voice asked, "Are there many of you up there?" And Villa
replied, "No, not many. Just two regiments of artillery and ten
thousand *muchachitos* to entertain you." "Good," said the
official, "here we come to blast you." "You must be some kind
of old fool that we don't see around here any more!" shouted
Villa, suddenly losing his patience. He put an end to the tom-
foolery by jamming down the receiver without waiting for a
reply to his parting sally. The time had come for the more sober
thought of the impending battle.

Within the single day of March 20 Villa's troops rolled over
the federal outposts at Mapimí and Tlahualillo, inflicting heavy
losses on the retreating enemy. About eight miles north of
Torreón was the small station of Noé. There the Huertistas had
removed the tracks, and Villa's trains and marching columns
came to an abrupt halt. While his repair crews labored feverishly
to lay new tracks or repair the old, Villa dispatched units to
mop up any enemy forces in the surrounding villages and to
complete the investment of the cities of Gómez Palacio and
Torreón. Aguirre Benavides was ordered to cut to the east and
to take Sacramento on the rail line from Torreón to Paredón
and Monterrey, in order to prevent the escape of Velasco's troops
in that direction. On March 22, as Villa readied an assault on

Gómez Palacio, his force was augmented by the fortunate arrival of Constitutionalist troops from Durango.[17]

As the general advance began, Villa took personal charge of the center of his line. Here he committed his first grievous error, for, tied down in the center, he was unable to give over-all direction to the attack. Instead there were a series of unco-ordinated movements by Villa and his various subordinates, which dissipated the force of the division. But Villa loved the scene of battle too much to stay in the rear. Joyfully he led his men into their first great engagement—he in a "slouch hat" and a dirty, disheveled suit of clothes, with no tie or collar on his shirt; they in ill-fitting, ragged uniforms, many wearing the sandals and serape of the Mexican peasant, and carrying old Springfield rifles with bandoliers of ammunition slung from their shoulders. Laughing and jesting with those around him, Villa rode his horse into combat. They appeared for all the world like an army of tatterdemalions going off to do make-believe battle. But beside Villa as he rode and between the columns of marching men was a large cannon, mounted on a flat car. Its ugly snout silhouetted against the clear sky was proof enough that the war would soon be real.[18]

Merriment shortly gave way to despair, for the first attack upon Gómez Palacio was a dismal failure. Many of the artillery shells, which Villa had carefully husbanded for this moment, proved to be faulty. These shrapnel shells had been manufactured in Mexico by the Constitutionalists themselves, and the greater number fell uselessly as duds. Villa's infantry, which had expected to be supported by cannon fire, wavered as emplaced machine guns decimated their ranks, then fell back to flee in panic. Had the federals cared to leave their positions, they might have inflicted a severe defeat on the overly rash Villa. As it was, the revolutionary losses were high, though the reluctance of the enemy to come out gave Villa's troops a respite to reform their lines.[19]

For three days Villa flung his men recklessly against the federal positions, while the rival artillery batteries exchanged shots. On the night of March 25 foot soldiers of Tomás Urbina and Calixto Contreras attempted to scale a hill to the west of the city where a strong force protected Gómez Palacio. Losses on both sides were severe, and Villa's troops failed to take the position even after seven heroic assaults. John Reed of Harvard, probably the best, and certainly the most venturesome, of the American correspondents in Mexico, has left a poignant account of the valor of the men of the North and the federals alike. Soon after the battle he wrote for the *New York World:* "Seven windrows of men I counted, where seven successive charges failed. The trenches were choked with the bodies of the defenders." A federal relief column had been sent out from Torreón under General Javier de Moure, but it never reached the beleaguered garrison in Gómez Palacio. When word arrived at Gómez Palacio of Moure's defeat at the hands of the rebels, the disheartened Huertista and Colorado troops decided to fall back to Torreón, yielding their positions to the Division of the North. On the night of March 26, Villa's troops entered the city. Before them lay the much more formidable garrison in Torreón.[20]

The two contending forces fought at close quarters for five days. It was city fighting at its deadliest, as Villa's inexperienced troops inched through Torreón, block by block, only to be thrust back again and again by savage counterattacks by the defenders. The men of Villa paid dearly for each small success. On the first day of April the most furious assault of the Villistas carried troops of the Division of the North into the heart of Torreón, but once more the federals ejected them. Seeing, however, that the men of Huerta could not long hold out, George C. Carothers, the American consul in Torreón, proposed to Villa that the city be spared further destruction and that Velasco be permitted to withdraw unmolested. But Villa now scented victory, and he refused to give the enemy any quarter. Instead he redoubled his efforts to dislodge the federals. Fighting raged unabated throughout the fifth day of battle as Velasco made plans to escape.

On the afternoon of April 2, the federal artillery laid down a heavy barrage on the rebel positions north and west of the city. Thinking this concerted fire heralded a counterattack in that direction, Villa hastily and thoughtlessly drew in his troops from the east to meet this new danger. As Velasco had hoped, this maneuver of the Constitutionalists gave him his opportunity to escape the city. Fortune smiled doubly upon the federal commander in his moment of defeat, for a sudden dust storm, typical in that dry area, blew up to mask his movements from the eyes of the Villistas. As his artillery continued its fire until the moment of withdrawal, Velasco's trains, covered by a rear guard of Colorado cavalry, pulled out of Torreón unmolested. They headed east on the lines of the Coahuila and Pacific Railroad toward Saltillo. But the city of Torreón was now in Villa's possession. He had won his greatest victory.[21]

With the capture of Torreón Villa was no longer the *guerrillero* of small-scale skirmishes. He was a successful general, the famed commander of thousands of troops. Most revolutionaries in the North were now willing to acknowledge his leadership. In the United States, as well, his name took precedence over that of Venustiano Carranza as a rebel leader. John Reed, who had fallen in love with him, wrote jubilantly: "Villa . . . is without . . . doubt the greatest leader Mexico has ever had. His method of fighting is astonishingly like Napoleon's." [22] However rudimentary his knowledge of military science may appear in hindsight, he had defeated professional generals, trained in the military college of Chapultepec. In the battle of Torreón the revolutionaries of the North demonstrated what could be done by spirited troops, though untrained and poorly led, against an enemy which was well dug in and better trained, but lacking in the will to fight to the death. Had Velasco's troops not eluded Villa, the Division might have proceeded with impunity to Mexico City. There was no garrison between Torreón and the capital strong enough to halt the Villistas. As it was, Villa could not afford to continue south and leave the federal troops behind him so close to his supply line. Tarrying but briefly in Torreón, the division turned east to run down the fugitives.[23]

The army of Velasco reached Viesca, forty-five miles east of Torreón in the heart of the cotton country, only to find that the rail lines had been severed beyond that town. Because of the inhospitable desert terrain ahead, the Huertista commander decided to halt in order to give his tired and disheartened troops a rest. Meanwhile, the relief column under General Joaquín Maass had arrived at San Pedro de las Colonias too late to save the situation at Torreón. San Pedro, forty-eight miles north of Viesca, was an important railway junction with a population in 1914 of about ten thousand. On April 4 Villa ordered simultaneous attacks against the two federal garrisons. For more than a week the troops of the Division of the North battered both positions, but stubborn resistance and sharp counterattacks by the Huertistas nullified any temporary successes by the revolutionaries. By April 11, Velasco's troops in Viesca had virtually exhausted their ammunition and food supplies. Despite the efforts of Villa to prevent a juncture of the two forces, Velasco broke through the ring of besiegers which surrounded Viesca and, protected by the horsemen of Benjamín Argumedo, reached San Pedro de las Colonias with heavy losses.

In anger Villa learned of the escape of Velasco. He came from Torreón to San Pedro to take personal charge of the attack and gathered his entire force to encircle the city. For two days the Division of the North probed the federal positions. Early on the morning of April 14 Villa commenced an all-out assault on San Pedro. Despite the fury and perseverance of the attack, the Huertistas remained steadfast. Villa was unable either to penetrate their lines or to expel them from their positions. In his moment of need, however, luck came to the aid of the rebel commander. Within the city a rift developed between the two federal generals. Velasco and Maass were of equal rank, each being a general of division, and the two quarreled bitterly as to which took precedence. In a pique, Velasco decided to abandon Maass to his fate, and on the morning of April 15 he pulled out to the East, still accompanied by the Colorados of Argumedo. Villa increased his efforts against the remaining enemy troops, and later the same day Maass, too, decided to give up his positions. He followed Velasco in disastrous retreat toward Saltillo. Casualties on both sides were extremely heavy with Villa probably losing more men killed or wounded than the Huertistas. But the double federal defeat at Viesca and San Pedro, following on the heels of the loss of Torreón, made the men of Huerta more dispirited than ever. Many now made no attempt to reach Saltillo, where Velasco and Maass hoped to regroup their forces. They deserted the column, in hopes of reaching their homes or of joining the victorious armies of the Constitutionalists. Abandoned weapons and equipment gave mute testimony to their headlong flight.[24]

Although Villa's victory at San Pedro never received the publicity of the capture of Torreón, and Barragán Rodríguez, in his history of the Constitutionalist army, gives no details of the battle, it was actually the greater achievement for the revolutionaries. Velasco had escaped from Torreón with his army almost intact. But at Viesca and San Pedro de las Colonias Villa had cut up two major federal forces, virtually assuring the ultimate defeat of Huerta. Only the necessity of resting his men and replenishing his store of supplies and ammunition held up Villa's uninterrupted march south. Back in Torreón Villa was a revolutionary cock of the walk. He ignored Carranza, who remained with his stepsister government in Chihuahua. Villa sent his own agents to El Paso to obtain supplies, issued his own currency, and confiscated cattle, cotton, and ores to pay for the needs of his army. He made no pretense of accounting to the First Chief for his actions. As early as April 9 Carothers in Torreón had told the American Secretary of State that Carranza had "not assumed control of anything so far." [25]

Relations between Francisco Villa and his chief became increasingly strained as Villa's prestige mounted and his insouciance grew more intolerable to Carranza. Although there was no hint in their official dispatches of an impending break, all of Villa's messages being respectfully addressed to "my chief," the actions of both revolutionary leaders, during and after the battle of Torreón, boded ill for continued harmony. Villa had expected to become military governor of Chihuahua, but Carranza had instead designated Manuel Chao, one of Villa's officers, to that office. In the midst of the hostilities at Torreón, when every man was needed, Villa ordered General Chao to report for military duty with his troops. But the governor, after consultation with Carranza, refused to heed Villa's command. Incensed at this breach of discipline on the part of a subordinate, Villa directed that Chao be captured and summarily shot. The governor was seized and narrowly avoided a quick execution when Carranza ordered his release. Villa grudgingly complied with the wishes of the First Chief, but he did not forget the incident.[26] When the commander of the Division of the North returned to Chihuahua in late April to organize a new campaign and at the same time to protect his interests in his own state, the proximity of the two chiefs bred further discord. Carranza did not take lightly the growth of the cult of *Villismo* or the popular acclaim for the victor of Torreón. Villa, for his part, expressed himself sarcastically about the pompous First Chief. He refused to attend banquets at which Carranza harangued his listeners with vague promises of social reform. Villa said that he would not "fool around with pantywaists" like Carranza.[27]

Although not as spectacularly successful as Villa's Division of the North, Pablo González and the Army Corps of the Northeast now began to achieve victories against the Huertistas in Coahuila, Nuevo León, and Tamaulipas. General Francisco Murguía defeated the federals at Monclova and Piedras Negras; Jesús Carranza, bewhiskered brother of the First Chief, isolated the garrison at Nuevo Laredo; and on April 24 Monterrey, the largest city in the North of the Republic, was occupied by the troops of González.[28] In the last week of March the Constitutionalists in Tamaulipas had begun a drive on Tampico calculated to pry that valuable port city from the Huertistas. It was during the attack on Tampico that the untoward arrest of American sailors by a federal commander brought the active intervention of the United States and the military occupation of Veracruz. The American intervention held up the campaign in Tamaulipas, and it was not until May 13 that Tampico passed into revolutionary hands. Carranza now had a seaport through which to import arms and supplies. And most important, the Constitutionalist government controlled the oil fields near Tampico and possessed a rich source of dollar exchange. By the middle of May 1914 the entire North of Mexico, except for Saltillo, Zacatecas, and San Luis Potosí, was under revolutionary domination.

In the first days of May Villa returned to Torreón with his chiefs to begin his campaign against Zacatecas. Felipe Angeles, upon whom Villa relied heavily for advice, wished to clear the federal garrison from Zacatecas before Obregón could cross the mountains between Tepic and Jalisco. Once in Guadalajara, Obregón could move swiftly on the capital, arriving there before the Division of the North, Angeles feared. Villa's generals made no attempt to consult Carranza as they planned their strategy. The First Chief, nevertheless, refused to be shunted aside. Though uninvited, he followed Villa to Torreón. Ostensibly his mission was to coordinate the projected operations against Huerta, but actually he meant to thwart Villa and prevent his arriving in Mexico City before the forces of Obregón or González. As the chiefs met, presided over by Carranza, Villa signified his intention of moving on Zacatecas before Huerta had time to reinforce his garrison there. But Carranza demurred, insisting that Saltillo be the next objective for the Constitutionalist armies. He pointed out that the federal troops from Torreón, Monterrey, and Monclova had all collected in the Coahuila capital, posing a threat to "our left flank." [29]

In an effort to conciliate Carranza, Felipe Angeles proposed that the Division of the North take Zacatecas first and then return to liberate Saltillo. Although Pablo González was now in Monterrey, only fifty miles from Saltillo, and would have been the logical choice for an attack upon that city, Carranza remained adamant. He did not trust Villa, fearing that he would move on to Mexico City after the capture of Zacatecas, rather than return north to Coahuila. After a heated and lengthy discussion, in which Carranza was unmoved by the arguments of Villa and Angeles, Villa, with characteristic impetuosity, suddenly capitulated and said: "Well, we'll do it to please the Chief." Carranza had won his point and had diverted the Division of the North long enough, he hoped, to let someone else win the race to the capital. He was intent upon demonstrating that Villa was not indispensable to the success of the Constitutionalist revolution.[30]

From Torreón Carranza traveled to Durango to visit Pánfilo Natera, revolutionary chief in the state of Zacatecas. Carranza now planned to entrust to Natera the task of capturing the city. Natera expressed confidence in his ability to take Zacatecas, if the First Chief would give him reinforcements of men and materiel. Before he left Durango for the North, Carranza arranged that Natera, Martín Triana, and the Arrieta brothers should cooperate in the assault on this last bastion between the Constitutionalists and the federal capital.[31] For a month Natera gathered his forces for the battle. But all his preparations and protestations of self-confidence proved to be in vain. For three days the rebels battered fruitlessly at the strongly implaced enemy. Natera and his associates were forced to recognize that they were impotent to effect the capture of Zacatecas without further aid—aid which could come only from Villa.[32]

While the Constitutionalists bogged down at Zacatecas, the powerful Division of the North captured Saltillo for Carranza with comparative ease. From Torreón Villa crossed over to Coahuila on the rail line through San Pedro de las Colonias. In Paredón a federal garrison protected the approaches to Saltillo, but it was too small to hold off Villa's forces for any length of time. After two hours of fighting, the troops of Huerta, their morale gone, fled from the town. Villa entered Saltillo without a contest on May 21. The remnants of the federal garrisons in Coahuila straggled toward San Luis Potosí to the South, marching afoot because Eulalio and Luis Gutiérrez had cut the railroad below Saltillo. Villa now had two courses of action open to him: he could turn south from Coahuila and push through San Luis Potosí to Mexico City; or he could return to Torreón or Chihuahua. He rejected the first alternative because his lines of communications, running back through Torreón to the state of Chihuahua, would be too tenuous. More than that, he did not trust Pablo González, who was completely loyal to Carranza, behind him menacing his supply line. He resolved, therefore, to go back to Torreón to await the developments in the unsuccessful Constitutionalist campaign in Zacatecas.[33]

When it became apparent to Carranza that Natera and the two Arrietas could not capture Zacatecas unaided, he was in a quandary. Villa was willing to take the city, but his demeanor since returning to Torreón was more insubordinate than ever. He concerned himself increasingly with the civil administration in Chihuahua and Durango, a matter the First Chief held to be the province of his civilian government. And on May 30 Villa brusquely demanded of Carranza that Obregón and González, whom he considered laggards, should coordinate their movements with his. Significantly he addressed Carranza as "Señor General," not "Chief" and signed himself "general-in-chief," a rank he did not hold, since he was only a divisional commander with the grade of brigadier.[34] Obregón was indeed dallying. By the middle of May he had only reached Tepic, and it took him another month to cross the Sierra. On June 17 the Army Corps of the Northwest was still a hundred miles from Guadalajara, which was guarded by a strong federal force at Orendáin. Obregón could not take Mexico City before Villa unless the Division of the North were restrained. Carranza tried to escape from his quandary by breaking up Villa's command.

The First Chief was in Saltillo when he received word from the Constitutionalists outside Zacatecas that they were unable to oust the federal garrison. On June 11 he sent a message to Villa at Torreón, ordering him to send Natera five thousand men under General José Isabel Robles. Villa refused, preferring to keep his forces intact. He was confident that he could soon take the city himself. When Carranza remained obdurate and repeated his demand that Robles leave for Zacatecas immediately, Villa asked for a telegraphic conference with the First Chief. On June 13, 1914, the two men came to the railway stations in Torreón and Saltillo. In each station, surrounded by subordinates, the two chiefs dictated messages to the telegraph operators. The atmosphere in both rooms was tense. All knew that this was a showdown between Carranza and Villa.

Villa again balked at sending troops to Zacatecas as Carranza had requested, alleging that he must wait at least five days. Robles was ailing, he said, and was at that moment confined to his bed. Carranza would not be put off, however. He countered that if Robles were ill, Villa might send Aguirre Benavides, Ortega, or Contreras. But he insisted that five thousand troops be sent at once. Villa turned and twisted and placated his chief, but finally, in complete frustration before Carranza's unwillingness to yield, he impulsively tendered his resignation as commander of the Division of the North. Carranza, after a mock show of reluctance, quickly accepted it. He had fortunately, if unexpectedly, eliminated a dangerous rival to his civilian government and a recalcitrant military subordinate.[35] The First Chief had reason to be pleased with this new turn of events. George C. Carothers, who had come to Saltillo to seek a reconciliation between Villa and Carranza, later recalled his conversation with the Constitutionalist leader: "I urged him the necessity of patching up the break, but he appeared to be overjoyed that the breach had come, and he would not listen to my reasoning." [36]

There was no cause for joy in the railroad station in Torreón. Felipe Angeles had not attended the conference, and he was still abed when a messenger entered his sleeping quarters to summon him to Villa. In the telegraphic office he found his chief and a number of Villista officials and railroad employees all milling about with grave countenances. Angeles heard José Trinidad Rodríguez say inconsolably: "I'm going up and eat roots in the mountains!" All felt that this marked the end of the career of their valiant division.[37]

At Angeles' behest the chiefs of the division met the following day to draft a message to Carranza, asking him to reconsider his decision to accept Villa's resignation. But having achieved his aim, Carrenza refused and ordered the generals to designate from among themselves a successor for Villa. Carranza's reply placed the lieutenants of Villa in a difficult position. They were forced to choose between disloyalty to their chief and rebellion against the Constitutionalist leader. Led by Angeles, they elected the latter, informing Carranza that they were unable to heed his request. On June 15 they telegraphed the First Chief to justify their actions. "We are well aware," they said, "that you have been looking for an occasion such as this to extinguish a sun which dims your light. . . . But above your interests are those of the Mexican people, and for them the famous and victorious sword of Villa is indispensable." Carranza was told that they would seek to prevail upon their leader to continue in command of his forces.[38] Villa, if he ever took seriously his resignation, was easily convinced. Without a word of explanation to Carranza, the Division of the North, on June 17, began its belated march on Zacatecas, in open defiance of the Constitutionalist First Chief. When he heard that Villa had resumed command of his troops, Carranza took care to inform the rest of the revolutionary chiefs of the insubordination of Villa and his officers. From Obregón, from González, and from other commanders, Carranza received affirmation of their continued loyalty to him.[39] A dangerous crack was beginning to cleave the ranks of the revolutionaries. And Huerta was still not defeated.

By June 20 the Division of the North had reached Vetagrande, an old silver mining town which overlooked Zacatecas. From its heights Villa's men could see that Zacatecas was protected by two well defended ridges. It had been these positions which had held up Natera, Triana, and the Arrietas. Although the rainy season was now upon Mexico and a heavy downpour retarded Villa's progress, an assault was launched against the federal defenses on June 23. Aguirre Benavides, Gonzalitos, and Raúl Madero were placed in the center, flanked to the left by José Trinidad Rodríguez and the old *guerrillero,* Rosalío Hernández. Villa took personal charge of troops on the right against Guadalupe, where a troop of Orozquistas under Benjamín Argumedo guarded the approaches to Zacatecas. Against heavy small-arms fire and well-defiladed artillery, the division ground forward inexorably. Once more Villa's losses were heavy as he followed the tactic which had gained him victory at Torreón, the prodigal expenditure of masses of men. The capture of Guadalupe by Villa—though Argumedo again escaped unscathed—and of the strongly fortified height of La Bufa by Gonzalitos and Severino Ceniceros made the federal position in Zacatecas untenable. General Luis Medina Barrón, Huerta's governor in the state of Zacatecas and military commander of the city, gave orders to evacuate. At noon of the twenty-third the troops of Argumedo and Pascual Orozco began to pull out. The federals retreated toward Aguascalientes, tearing up sections of track behind them to impede the pursuit by the Villistas. Villa was satisfied to have captured Zacatecas, and he made no move to catch up with the fleeing enemy. On June 24 his troops entered the now deserted city.[40]

As earlier, after the battles of Torreón and San Pedro, there was little to keep Villa from advancing on Mexico City but a lack of coal for his trains and ammunition for his troops. The torn-up rails south of Zacatecas could be re-laid. There were not enough federal troops between Zacatecas and the capital to hinder his progress measurably. But the situation was serious enough for Villa. His division had completely exhausted its supply of ammunition in the wasteful assaults on Torreón, San Pedro, Paredón, and Zacatecas, and it was necessary for Villa to return to Torreón or Chihuahua to replenish his stores. Perhaps hoping to pacify Carranza, Villa sent a long account of the capture of Zacatecas and protested his regard for the person of the First Chief.[41] But Carranza was not to be humored by such protestations of loyalty. He saw Villa still as an insubordinate, and he was determined to prevent any movement south by the division until Obregón and González should come together and block off Villa from the capital. Reinforcements had been sent to Obregón, who was now on the outskirts of Guadalajara, and his Army Corps of the Northwest was ordered to proceed swiftly toward Mexico City. Further, in what proved to be one of the most decisive acts of the revolution, Carranza shut off shipments of coal and ammunition to Villa's forces. To punish Villa for his defiance of superior authority, the First Chief would immobilize the Division of the North.[42]

Most of the coal used by the Constitutionalists was mined at Muzquiz in the northern part of the state of Coahuila and in territory now controlled by Carranza. Munitions for the revolutionary armies were now imported principally through Tampico. Although Villa had been accustomed to obtain fuel and supplies from the United States by way of El Paso and Ciudad Juárez, the recent heavy summer rains had washed out two railroad bridges between Juárez and Chihuahua.[43] Villa, unfortunately for his division, was entirely dependent upon Carranza for his supplies. It was clear that Carranza's order was an act of hostility against Villa and the Division of the North. Though an open clash between Villa and Carranza was avoided at that time, there never was, thereafter, a reconciliation between the two chiefs. In a real sense the Convention, which met at Aguascalientes several months later in an attempt to heal the revolutionary schism, was the outgrowth of the *mésalliance* between Francisco Villa and Venustiano Carranza.

2

Seeds of Discord

THE GOVERNMENT OF THE UNITED STATES HAD NEVER recognized the seizure of the Mexican presidency by General Victoriano Huerta. In order to manifest his distaste for this military *coup d'état,* Woodrow Wilson recalled the American ambassador, Henry Lane Wilson, leaving diplomatic matters in the hands of a chargé d'affaires, Nelson O'Shaughnessy. By midsummer of 1914 the Constitutonalists were not sufficiently successful to warrant being awarded American recognition, yet the Secretary of State and the President felt the need to keep a diplomatic finger on the revolutionary pulse. They therefore commissioned a number of special agents, with diplomatic status, but without the regular titles which would give official sanction to relations between the United States and the Constitutionalists. After O'Shaughnessy was expelled from Mexico City following the American seizure of Veracruz, the affairs of the United States in the capital were handled by J. M. Cardoso de Oliveira, Brazilian minister to Mexico. Consular agents were left at their posts in several cities (e.g., Veracruz, Mazatlán, Hermosillo, Monterrey, and Chihuahua), as well. But it was the special agents who were primarily responsible for the information and recommendations upon which the mercurial Mexican policies of the United States were based.

William Bayard Hale, a trusted political adviser of the President, and John Lind, former governor of Minnesota, were the first of many amateur diplomatists dispatched to Mexico by Wilson or Bryan to assess the troubled political and military situation under Huerta and the succeeding revolutionary regimes. But neither Hale nor Lind knew much about Mexico, and their usefulness to the United States, despite their close relationship with the President, was limited. Moreover, they were birds of passage. They could not stay long enough to learn anything of real value. Much more important to the United States were the permanent agents, who were attached to the revolutionary headquarters, who spoke Spanish, and who were thoroughly conversant with Mexican affairs. George C. Carothers, a former grocer and the American consul in Torreón, was assigned to accompany Villa, while Leon J. Canova, a newspaperman with some experience in Cuba, was sent by Bryan to keep an eye on Carranza in particular and the revolution in general.

On July 1, 1914, Canova and Carothers were granted an extensive interview with the First Chief, who had just come to Saltillo after a short visit to Monterrey. To Woodrow Wilson, intent upon bringing about the collapse of the Huerta government, the falling out between Carranza and Villa was vexatious, the more so since the success of the revolution had seemed so imminent. On the last day of June Bryan telegraphed Carothers, calling the estrangement "most unfortunate" and asking his agent to talk with both chiefs about the "restoration of peace." This dispatch hinted at subsequent American policy in Mexico, for Bryan intimated that he would work for a provisional government which would eliminate both Huerta and Carranza.

Canova had been in Monterrey with the First Chief, and he came up to Saltillo on the same train. Writing to Bryan, Canova expressed surprise over the lack of popular enthusiasm for the governor of Coahuila. "When Carranza boarded the rear platform of the train at Monterrey," he wrote, "there was some applause, but not to the degree one would expect from the [people] towards one of their heroes. At . . . Ramos Arizpe, enroute, the train stopped for a few minutes. A crowd gathered, and Carranza stepped out on the rear platform. I expected to hear *vivas* and applause, but a deep hush prevailed. Carranza got down and went into the group, shaking hands and exchanging a few quiet words with probably three or four. They stood regarding each other with that dumb expression on their faces like so many cattle. . . ." [1]

General Carranza, never a popular figure, had gained little public support for his rude break with Villa. Since the fall of Zacatecas and Carranza's cutting off of coal supplies to Villa, the two revolutionary chiefs had been as indignantly pugnacious as two gamecocks. Although each was honestly convinced of his own rectitude in the affair, both were loath to make the breach complete, hoping for an honorable way out. A solution to the impasse was offered in late June by Pablo González, commanding general of the Army Corps of the Northeast, who bade Villa's Division of the North designate a commission to meet in Torreón with representatives of his own forces. Villa complied by appointing Dr. Miguel Silva, Manuel Bonilla, and General José Isabel Robles to join González' delegates, Generals Cesáreo Castro, Luis Caballero, and Antonio I. Villarreal, during the first week of July. [2] It was concerning this proposed conference that Canova and Carothers asked to speak to the First Chief on July 1.

Although many Mexicans were waiting to see Carranza when the American agents arrived, Canova and Carothers were immediately brought to his quarters. It is worth while to quote at some length from Canova's account of their interview because in it Carranza made clear his position regarding Villa and his insistence upon discipline and subordination from the Division of the North. [3] After some polite small talk, Carothers, who bore the burden of the conversation, broached to Carranza the subject of the impending meeting at Torreón. "Then it is sure, General," he said, "that the commission of generals you are sending will go tomorrow?"

Carranza denied that the commission was being sent by him. He replied to Carothers: "The generals composing it are going of their own initiative to learn if it is possible to re-establish concord." Carothers expressed the hope that the conferees would succeed, "for if they do not, I fear very serious trouble will result. I have been instructed by Secretary Bryan to use my good offices in this matter and assure you that we are here to assist in every manner."

The First Chief thanked the Americans for their solicitude and agreed that there could be "serious trouble." He launched into a long tirade against the contumacious Villa: "Obedience and discipline are absolute requisites to our success and must be exacted. We can arrive at no satisfactory ends if Villa, or any of the others, do just what they please, independent of the other forces, or the general plan of the campaign. When I sent for his generals to come here, they placed themselves in open rebellion by refusing to come when there was a chance of our arriving at a satisfactory settlement of the matter. . . . The trouble with Villa is that while I am directing my efforts toward the establishment of internal order and good foreign relations, he is working along very contrary lines. While I am supreme chief of the Constitutionalist Army this condition cannot be tolerated. . . . Villa thinks that he is indispensable to the Constitutionalist cause. Well, he is mistaken. No individual who defies the constituted authorities is indispensable, for he who manifests such a spirit today, and is allowed to have his way, will be a very dangerous man for us to deal with tomorrow."

"Just review the conduct of Villa," he continued. "All of the trouble we have had has originated in Villa's territory. It was he who was responsible for the Benton and Bauche affairs. Had it not been for the delay caused us by the Benton affair we would probably have now been in possession of Mexico City. . . . The trouble with him is that he will not try to curb his passions. . . . However, I trust he will listen to reason and that the commission will be able to arrange the matter amicably."

Carothers then asked the First Chief if there would be any

particular incident to be settled at Torreón, or would the conference deal with the matter of the future conduct of Villa. "Has
Villa to apologize or humble himself in any manner, or will the
efforts of the commission be to wipe out the past and pave the way
for good relations hereafter?"

Carranza denied that either humiliation or an apology was
required from Villa. "All I wish is obedience and discipline. I do
not wish to make the arrangement difficult, but Villa has been
taking altogether too much upon himself." He charged that Villa
had been given five million pesos in Constitutionalist currency to
redeem an equal amount of spurious paper issued in his territory.
Instead of calling in the bad currency, Villa had spent the good,
so that ten million pesos were outstanding without any accounting to the First Chief's government. It did not seem to concern
Villa, he said, that the whole country would be responsible for
the currency he was printing so freely. Carranza asked rhetori-
cally: "Does he think that the cause [of the Constitutionalists]
can prosper when sacrificed to every abandoned whim of his? I
think not. . . ."

Carranza had remained seated during most of the interview,
but, as he gave vent to his irritations toward Villa, he rose and
emphasized his points with forceful gestures. He concluded by
assuring Carothers and Canova of his friendship for their country, despite unfavorable criticism in the American press, charges
that he was too haughty or unfriendly in his dealings with the
United States. Canova wrote to Bryan that while Carranza denied vehemently that he was sending the generals to Torreón,
"it is a fact that they go with his consent to treat with Villa."

It is probably true that Carranza assented to González' sending
a commission to Torreón to meet with the Villistas. At least he
placed no obstacles in the way of an accord, if that accord were
consonant with his own view of relations between himself and
his subordinates. But it is clear from his subsequent demeanor
that he felt himself in no way bound by the decisions made at
Torreón by six men, none of whom represented him. In any
event, Carranza hoped that Obregón would soon be in Mexico

City, so that Villa's actions would be of little concern to him. Obregón's Army Corps of the Northwest, which tarried between Ixtlán del Río and Guadalajara for the last two weeks of June, finally reached its penultimate objective. On July 7, the Constitutionalist forces from Sonora defeated the federal garrison at Orendáin, and on the next day they marched into Mexico's second largest city. From Guadalajara the road to Mexico City was clear.[4]

While Obregón stormed the approaches to Guadalajara the delegates from Villa and González were meeting in Torreón. Carothers, at Bryan's instruction, came over from Saltillo with González' generals, as Canova remained with the First Chief in his capital. The train carrying Carothers and the representatives of the Northeast arrived at Torreón on July 3, and informal discussions were held that afternoon and the following morning. Carothers met with Villa and found him apparently well disposed toward a settlement and aware that a definitive break with Carranza would be disastrous for the Constitutionalist cause. But Villa poured out to Carothers his grievances toward the First Chief, exclaiming that Carranza was bending every effort to minimize the victories of the Division of the North. Carranza was trying to surround him with obstacles, prompted, Villa thought, by personal jealousies. He conceded that Carranza might have been right in principle on some points, but maintained that in times of war many things were done which would be unacceptable in ordinary times. Villa told Carothers that he held it his duty as a revolutionary to clean out the reactionary enemies, confiscating their properties for the use of the revolution. He felt that unless there was a division of the lands of the *hacendados,* another revolution would surely succeed this one.

Villa made it plain to Carothers, however, that he considered this conciliation of Carranza a temporary expedient. He said the Constitutionalist armies were beginning to realize that Carranza was not the leader to save the country, that sooner or later they would be forced to choose another. When the fighting against Huerta was concluded, Villa predicted, the victorious chiefs would assemble and elect some one else in Carranza's place. He told the American agent that Carranza was "surrounded with politicians, who are feathering their nest [sic] and laying the foundation for a more despotic government than ever before." [5]

That Villa was not truly sanguine about the success of the Torreón commission is indicated by a telegraphic conversation he conducted with General Hugh Scott, who was commander of the Southern Department of the United States Army, with headquarters at San Antonio. On July 6, while the conferences were in session, Villa asked Scott what the attitude of the American government would be in the event of a definite rupture with Carranza. Scott refused to commit himself, saying he had no authority to speak for Washington. Instead he told Villa: "I find it indispensable that you come to an understanding with General Carranza, and that you advance as quickly as possible towards Mexico City, and once in Mexico City it would be easy to arrange then what you deem most convenient." He intimated that the United States might recognize a national government organized by Villa and the other Constitutionalist chiefs and then turn over Veracruz to that government.[6]

By July 8, the pacification commission had worked out an agreement which they hoped would settle the difficulties between Carranza and Villa. The Division of the North would continue to recognize Carranza as First Chief of all the Constitutionalist armies, while Villa would retain his command of the division. Carranza should furnish Villa with coal and ammunition, while leaving him freedom of action in administrative and military matters in his own area. Villa would report his acts to Carranza, however, for "rectification or ratification." The representatives of the Division of the North and the Army Corps of the Northeast drew up a list of persons, about equally divided between Villistas and Carrancistas, from which Carranza would form his cabinet when he became, under the Plan of Guadalupe, Mexico's interim president. The names offered for the First Chief's consideration included Fernando Iglesias Calderón, Luis Cabrera, Antonio I. Villarreal, Miguel Silva, Manuel Bonilla, Alberto J. Pani,

Eduardo Hay, Ignacio L. Pesquiera, Miguel Díaz Lombardo, José Vasconcelos, Miguel Alessio Robles, and Federico González Garza.[7]

In the Pact of Torreón the delegates laid the basis for the subsequent calling of the Revolutionary Convention of Aguascalientes when they agreed that, upon assuming the office of interim president, Carranza would summon a convention to discuss and determine the date for elections and "the plan of government to be put into practice by the officials who shall have been elected, and other topics of national interest." The convention was to be a preconstitutional device for achieving revolutionary reforms and would not be chosen in a regular election. Instead it would be drawn from the victorious Constitutionalist armies—one delegate would be allowed for each one thousand men in the ranks. Moreover, in the elections which were to follow the holding of the convention, no member of the Constitutionalist armies could be a candidate for the presidency, nor could a provisional official seek permanent office.

Perhaps at the insistence of Villarreal, a radical Carrancista and an early affiliate with the Flores Magón party, and certainly with the acquiescence of the Villistas, a provision was made in the Pact of Torreón for agrarian reform. Article 8 promised land division for the peasants and social legislation for the urban proletariat. By means of a convention of military men applying the principles of this article, the delegates at Torreón demonstrated their intention of converting the purely political revolution of Carranza and his Plan of Guadalupe into a social and economic revolution, into a movement of the masses against the classes.[8]

Informally the delegates agreed that Villa should release some forty prisoners whom he had sent to Torreón against the wishes of Carranza and that Villa should recall from circulation the paper money which, according to Carranza, he was issuing illegally. The railroads of the North would continue under the charge of Eusebio Calzada, Villa's man, despite the First Chief's desire that he be removed and replaced by a Carrancista. The coal fields at Muzquiz were to be transferred to Calzada's control in order to insure Villa an adequate supply of fuel. Finally, the Villistas demanded that their leader be accorded the rank of general of division, since both González and Obregón had recently been advanced to that grade by Carranza.[9]

Except for the temporary restoration of relations between Villa and Carranza, the conference at Torreón had few immediate results. When the pact was submitted to Carranza for his consideration he rejected it, maintaining that "matters of such great importance cannot be discussed or approved by such a small group of persons." [10] Most distasteful to him was the apparent attempt to sidetrack him from the constitutional presidency, with the ban against provisional officials' standing for election at the conclusion of the preconstitutional period. Nor did he think it within the province of these six men to determine his cabinet or to fix the qualifications for any revolutionary assembly. In rejecting most provisions of the pact, Carranza was consistent in holding that questions of reform and elections must be decided by civilians, not by the military. And concerning Article 8 Carranza said: "I must insist that such matters . . . have no relation to the incident which motivated the conferences." [11] He steadfastly opposed extra-legal social reforms and excluded them from his revolutionary plans. When, at the end of the year, he issued his famous Veracruz decrees,[12] it was solely to gain support for a cause which seemed doomed to failure. In July of 1914 he would not compromise with his antagonists on any point. He would not, even as a gesture of conciliation, accede to Villa's wish to become a general of division. On July 14 Canova interviewed Carranza and was assured that the difficulties with Villa were now definitely settled, so far as Carranza was concerned. He told Canova that if another rupture occurred, "it will be through some act of Villa. . . ." [13]

As an apparent peace settled upon the revolutionary armies in the North, Villa was busily building up his strength for the anticipated showdown with Carranza. He seemed more concerned with confronting Carranza with the overpowering might of the

Division of the North than in accomplishing the speedy defeat of Huerta. He continued through July to recruit men for his division and scoured the countryside for horses and livestock—the horses for his cavalry and the cattle to sell in Texas. On July 25, the American consul at Chihuahua, Marion T. Letcher, informed Bryan that "nobody here doubts the purpose of his activity." [14] When on July 20 Villa came to Ciudad Juárez, ostensibly to meet with American army officials about border problems, it was in reality to arrange for a large shipment of arms. Hardware dealers in El Paso shipped ammunition into Mexico freely, and the United States customs officials made only a perfunctory examination, if any, of the goods. General Tasker H. Bliss reported to General Scott that coal, oil, dynamite, arms, and other supplies were readily obtainable by Villa in El Paso, despite the American embargo.[15] And Bliss wired the Secretary of War, Lindley M. Garrison, asking if the Department of the Treasury could not order its customs employees to halt this illegal traffic in materials of war with Villa.[16] The large-scale business activities of Villa are demonstrated by the report of Zacharay L. Cobb, the customs collector at El Paso, to Bryan that Villa had sold 35,000 unbranded Chihuahua cattle to "Garrett of Corpus Christi" for five hundred thousand dollars.[17] But neither the Department of State nor Wilson took seriously Villa's seizures of property or tried to close the border to his agents. It is not surprising that on July 26 Carranza informed Obregón in Guadalajara that "Villa is acting very suspiciously." At the same time, he ordered Obregón to hurry to Mexico City to accept the surrender of the federal government and the army, for Huerta had finally resigned the presidency and had fled the country.[18]

In July 1914 Francisco Villa had made few plans beyond the military occupation of Mexico City before Obregón or González could reach the capital. Carranza, on the other hand, was much more cognizant of the problems that now confronted him as the leader of the Constitutionalist revolution and prospective chief of the Mexican government. He had to gain control of all of the territory of the Republic to the south and east of the capital—

Puebla, Veracruz, Tlaxcala, and Oaxaca—and at the same time to secure the dissolution of the federal army, which, despite defeats and defections in the North, probably still numbered as many as 40,000 men. Politically he had to deal with the remnants of the Huerta regime still in Mexico City and gain the support and recognition of Zapata. In international matters Carranza must now deal with the American State Department to secure recognition as *de facto* head of Mexico's government and, at the same time, to persuade the United States to turn over to him his country's chief port, Veracruz, now occupied by American troops.

In retrospect it must be acknowledged that the Tampico affair, which led to the seizure of Veracruz, resembled nothing so much as an Italian *opera buffa,* were it not for the loss of life to Americans and Mexicans and the loss of prestige by the United States and its president. Beginning with the accidental, but explicable, arrest of American sailors in Tampico on April 9 and the consequent demands by the naval authorities for an apology and a salvo of salute to the flag of the United States, the farce ran its course to its logical, but ludicrous, conclusion—the landing of troops at Veracruz. Once the American navy and Woodrow Wilson took a stand for American honor, there was no place to stop, short of actual military intervention in Mexico. Although Wilson was glad of the opportunity to back down gracefully, without appearing to do so, when a conference of Latin American states met at Niagara Falls, Ontario, to mediate the dispute, he was adamant about what was now to him the principal point in the controversy. He refused to withdraw the troops from Veracruz until a decision was made for the elimination of Huerta. In Veracruz the Americans could choke off supplies from Huerta's government and the federal army and force Huerta to give up the Mexican presidency. This policy had been, after all, Wilson's chief diplomatic preoccupation from his inauguration in March 1913.

Since Francisco Villa was from the North and had no real concern for Veracruz and because his knowledge of political and international matters was rudimentary, he readily acceded to the

American occupation. On April 23 he expressed to Carothers his warm friendship for the United States. So far as he was concerned, Villa said, the United States could "keep Veracruz and hold it so tight that not even water could get in to Huerta." [19] Bryan found Villa's attitude "gratifying" and, in all seriousness, told Carothers that Villa showed "a largeness of view and a comprehension of the whole situation which is greatly to his credit." [20] Carranza was of a different stripe, however. He was an experienced politician, a man with expert civilian advisers, and, above all, he had the spirit of an overloaded burro rebelling at the goad. He would not be moved by Wilson to do anything he did not desire to do. In Carranza, who resembled Wilson in many respects, the American president met his match.

Although the First Chief might have been expected to be pleased at this aid by the United States, he stubbornly refused to acquiesce in an infringement on Mexican sovereignty, even though the American occupation might redound to his benefit. Moreover, he refused to send delegates to Niagara Falls, maintaining that Mexico's internal problems were her own concern, to be solved by Mexicans alone, without foreign intermeddling. When the United States and the ABC powers (Argentina, Brazil, and Chile) met in May at Niagara Falls to propose that Carranza and Huerta agree on a provisional president and end the hostilities in Mexico, Carranza replied that this would be "tantamount to compounding a felony," that it could only insure another revolution. He pointed to the evil consequences of the *arreglos* of Ciudad Juárez, when Madero in 1911 had consented to de la Barra's becoming provisional president. The First Chief informed the United States that the reforms for which the revolutionaries had taken the field could come only through an informal government "in a pre-constitutional stage under a revolutionary, military rule." He would not end the revolution on the basis of a deal with the Huertista regime.[21]

From April to July, despite the dangerous cleavage in the revolutionary ranks caused by the wrangling between Villa and Carranza, the military position of Huerta deteriorated. The victories of Obregón at Orendáin and Villa at Torreón and Zacatecas, coupled with the American occupation of Veracruz, had tightened a noose around Huerta in the capital. As Pablo González' and Eulalio Gutiérrez' troops neared San Luis Potosí and threatened to join with revolutionary bands operating in the north of the State of Veracruz, it behooved Huerta to leave Mexico City while there was still an exit to the Caribbean. Yet only a week before his precipitous flight from the presidency, he had gone through the motions of holding a "national" election. It was a strange election with no parties, no announced candidates, and no campaigning. On the day of the balloting, July 5, 1914, the newspapers in the capital made no mention of any candidates for the presidency or the vice-presidency. And on the day following the "election," *El Sol* announced that almost no one had troubled himself to go to the polls. The consensus was that whatever votes there were had been cast for Huerta and General Aurelio Blanquet.[22]

By these elections Huerta was probably the president, but the president of nothing. He no longer had a government and possessed little authority throughout the Republic. He had been running away from the bitter truth, finding solace in countless bottles of cognac. In the second week of July his imaginary flight no longer sufficed to save him from the consequences of his usurpation. He faced certain and ruthless death at the hands of the Constitutionalist avengers of Madero. On July 9 he named as his Secretary of Foreign Relations Francisco S. Carbajal, a jurist and a man of honor, but also the Huertista chief of the supreme court of Mexico. This was correctly interpreted in the capital as the first step toward the formation of an interim government, for Carbajal was now next in line for the presidency.[23]

Unaware of Huerta's intentions, the American State Department continued its pressure on Carranza to find some means of agreement between the president and the Constitutionalists that would end the revolution. Bryan instructed Canova to invite Carranza to commission representatives to the United States to meet with the delegates Huerta had sent to the unsuccessful Niagara

Falls conference. On July 10, Canova and John R. Silliman, formerly vice-consul at Veracruz, were received by Isidro Fabela, in charge of foreign affairs in the informal cabinet of the First Chief. While Fabela expressed his and Carranza's polite appreciation for the offers of mediation, he firmly rejected any peaceful overtures toward Huerta. When Silliman earnestly requested that Fabela at least convey some expression of their intentions to Huerta's representatives, Fabela acquiesced to a meeting with the Huertistas in Washington, but insisted that the Constitutionalists would treat with them only on the basis of unconditional surrender. Because the United States and the ABC powers had been working to get the contending parties to accept a provisional government agreeable to both parties, Silliman expressed his surprise, though Carranza's intentions should have been clear by that time, that the Constitutionalists did not desire such an interim regime.[24]

After his meeting with Fabela, Silliman telegraphed Bryan: "The reforms considered necessary will be made by a government consisting of Governor Carranza, in his character of First Chief, and his associates. It will be a military government, and it will continue for such a term as is necessary until constitutional order is re-established. When it is considered opportune, elections will be held." [25]

Huerta submitted his resignation to the Chamber of Deputies on July 15 and left Mexico City for Puerto Mexico and exile, turning over to Carbajal the problem of dealing with the advancing Constitutionalist armies. The resignation of the president did not, however, satisfy the Zapatistas, especially since federal troops continued to man the outposts around the capital against the forces of the South. The Zapatistas were consistent in their opposition to any government, be it Díaz', Madero's, Huerta's, or his successor's, which did not promise immediate land reforms. Zapata published on July 19 a "rectification" of his Plan of Ayala, declaring that the campaign would continue until all Huertistas were eliminated from public office and until a government "addicted" to the Plan of Ayala was established.[26] On July 18, with

Jesús Carranza's capture of San Luis Potosí, hostilities between the Constitutionalists and the federals were virtually ended, and there were no further major conflicts. Only on the Zapatista front was there any consistent military activity against the revolutionaries.

When word reached Carranza, who was now in Monterrey, of the resignation of Huerta he remained inflexible in his demands on the Huertista government of Carbajal. Silliman and Phillip C. Hanna, the American consul general in Monterrey, were received by Carranza on July 19 and brought further offers from the government of the United States to use its good offices to effect a peace between the revolutionaries and the new president. Carranza expressed his willingness to meet any "duly accredited and fully authorized" representatives of Carbajal, but only on the basis of the unconditional delivery of Mexico City to the Constitutionalists and the unconditional surrender of the federal armies. Carranza suggested to the American mediators that Saltillo might be the appropriate place for a conference and indicated that Carbajal's representatives should come immediately by way of San Luis Potosí, which had, just the previous day, been occupied by the brother of the First Chief. Carranza asked the Americans to relay his offer to Mexico City and promised a "temporary suspension of military hostilities." [27]

President Carbajal preferred that his agents be treated as equals by the Constitutionalists, not as a vanquished enemy, and when the Brazilian minister, Cardoso de Oliveira, brought him Carranza's proposal, he countered with the suggestion that negotiations take place at a neutral point, such as New York. In order to expedite a cease-fire agreement and a settlement as to his successor, Carbajal offered to ratify the credentials of the Huertista delegates still in the United States after the failure of the Niagara Falls conference. In reporting the president's desires to Bryan, Cardoso de Oliveira informed the Secretary of State that conditions were increasingly serious in the capital, with persistent and daily attacks on the outskirts of the city by the Zapatistas. He told Bryan that there were grave apprehensions in the capital

that the federal army might revolt or disband, out of fear of reprisals by the Constitutionalists, leaving the city defenseless
against the men of Zapata.[28]

While Carranza awaited the reply of Carbajal to his demands,
he visited the port of Tampico and was again interviewed by
Silliman, who had followed him from Monterrey. Because of the
dispatch of Cardoso de Oliveira and Carranza's repeated asser-
tions that his government would be military in character, the
American Department of State desired to know his intentions
toward those who surrendered to the Constitutionalists. Carranza
again made it clear that he would countenance only a complete
surrender by Huertistas, but conceded that the victorious revolutionaries might be "magnanimous" toward them. He cautioned,
however, against any hopes that this magnanimity would be
broadly interpreted. Those persons, he said, whether in the army
or the government or as private citizens, who had supported
Huerta's "usurpation" would be regarded as "pernicious" and
would be punished as "enemies of democracy." Carranza promised
that "excesses" would not be permitted, but he warned that the
Huertistas could expect stern treatment and little consideration.
In the course of his conversation with Silliman, the First Chief
made frequent references to the policies of the Union government
of the United States toward the South at the conclusion of the
Civil War.[29]

Forced to make a decision between capitulating to Carranza
on the matter of a meeting place for the peace commissions or
continuing the hostilities against the Constitutionalists, Carbajal
had no choice but to yield. Nevertheless, he was resolved not to
give way on the point of unconditional surrender. On July 26 he
named as his representatives General Lauro Villar, president of
the army's military tribunal, and David Gutiérrez Allende, a
member of the supreme court. They were to be accompanied by
Salvador Urbina, as secretary of the commission. Carbajal decided
to send the delegation by way of Veracruz and Tampico, rather
than overland, as Carranza had suggested, because railroad com-

munications between Mexico City and San Luis Potosí had been interrupted, and the president deemed it too risky for his men to travel through hostile territory.[30]

Since Carranza was in Tampico, Carbajal intended that the conference take place there, though his representatives were given instructions that they might negotiate in the port city "or at any other place . . . in order to save time." [31] Yet, when Carranza heard that the Huertista delegation had left Veracruz, he returned to Saltillo, so that he would not be in Tampico when they arrived. He was insistent that the enemy come to him, suing for peace. Isidro Fabela called Silliman's attention to the distinction between an armistice and a suspension of military operations. The latter had been conceded by the First Chief, he said. But an armistice presupposed a mutual agreement for peace by two equal parties, and this was not even contemplated by the Constitutionalists.[32]

On the last day of July, General Villar, Gutiérrez Allende, and their secretary, Urbina, arrived at Tampico aboard the "México," a steamship of the Ward Line. If they carried any illusions that they were to be accorded the respect due the representatives of Mexico's president, they were soon disabused of these. They were detained on the ship for several hours before the Constitutionalist port authorities would permit them to disembark. Eight newspapers of Mexico City had sent correspondents to cover the projected peace conference, but only the reporter from *El Radical* was allowed to leave the ship. The rest were turned back to Veracruz. Upon landing, Carbajal's representatives were first told that a train would be ready for them at 6:00 P.M., then that it would not be ready until nine, and finally, after their persistent inquiries, the superintendent of railroads in Tampico informed them that he had not heard that a train had been ordered for them at all. At half an hour before midnight, Villar, Gutiérrez Allende, and Urbina were unceremoniously herded aboard a military train bound for Monterrey. By orders of General Luis Caballero, the revolutionary Commander in Tamaulipas, they were permitted to speak to no one during the journey. The delegates had now become aware that they were little more than prisoners of the Constitutionalists.[33]

In the early hours of the morning of August 1, they arrived in Monterrey and were turned loose in the city, without any information as to whether or when they might meet with Carranza. They sought out the American consulate and awakened Hanna, the consul general, to complain of the rude treatment they had received at the hands of the Constitutionalist soldiers. All of them deeply despondent, they had reached the conclusion that their mission would prove fruitless, and they were determined to quit. Hoping to seek asylum in Texas, the three asked Hanna to accompany them to the border in order to afford them diplomatic protection. Concerning his part in the affair, Hanna telegraphed the State Department: "It was only by the strongest appeals to their patriotism and the advantages of peace that this consulate induced them to continue on to the conferences." [34]

Later the same day the delegates of Carbajal made the short train trip up to Saltillo to find again that no preparations had been made for their arrival. They took private lodgings at a hotel. There Silliman found them and offered to help them to gain an interview with Carranza. By chance, Luis Cabrera and Isidro Fabela were both close friends of Urbina, and they arranged to present him informally to the First Chief, so as to secure an early meeting between Carranza and the Huertista delegation.[35]

Although Carranza agreed to see Carbajal's representatives personally, he ordered that they first be brought before Generals Antonio I. Villarreal and Luis Caballero, the governors of Nuevo León and Tamaulipas, to determine if Villar and Gutiérrez Allende were ready to meet him on his own terms, that is, unconditional surrender. In the preliminary conference, which took place on August 2, Villarreal and Caballero examined their credentials and inquired as to the instructions they had brought from Mexico City. It soon became apparent that there was no meeting of minds, for Villar and Gutiérrez Allende presented a program that was thoroughly unacceptable to the Constitutionalists. Where Carranza was willing to concede a cease-fire on the terms of absolute surrender, Carbajal asked for an armistice, to be followed by the reinstallation of the 26th Congress. The Congress would then issue a general amnesty for all political offenders, Huertista or revolutionary, and would elect a successor for Carbajal. None of this was palatable to the Constitutionalists, who had the logic of military victory behind their demands. Since Carbajal's delegates said they had no authority to consider complete surrender, Cabellero and Villarreal decided that it was useless for them to see Carranza.[36]

It was inconceivable that the victorious revolutionaries would have dealt with the government of Carbajal on terms which implied equality. They demanded a Huertista bloodletting and could not be satisfied with a negotiated peace or an amnesty. Carbajal and his representatives and, to some extent, the American State Department, were quite unrealistic in supposing that hostilities could be concluded on the basis of a gentleman's agreement to forget about the crimes of *Huertismo*.

Meanwhile, during the last days of July, Obregón had moved his troops from Guadalajara to Pénjamo and Irapuato, unhindered by any opposition by the federal forces. He arrived at Irapuato on July 31. Like Torreón, this city was an important rail junction. There the line from Guadalajara joined that of the Central Mexicano from Zacatecas, Torreón, and Chihuahua, and the presence of Obregón's forces prevented Villa's passage to the South. While Villa continued to collect arms and supplies, and boasted to newspaper reporters that he would soon be moving toward Mexico City, he could not do so now without risking friction, or perhaps even open warfare, with Obregón and Pablo González. With the capture of San Luis Potosí by Jesús Carranza, the Army Corps of the Northeast continued south and established its headquarters, with Pánfilo Natera's Division of the Center, in Querétaro, sixty-two miles to the east of Irapuato. There was no railroad by which Villa could bypass both Obregón and González to reach the Mexican capital.

On August 1, accompanied by Generals Lucio Blanco and Rafael Buelna, Obregón came to Querétaro for a conference with González to plan for a coordinated movement of their troops on Mexico City. It was a cordial first meeting for these two Carrancista chiefs. While Obregón was in Querétaro news came of the breakdown of direct peace negotiations between Carranza and the representatives of Carbajal. The First Chief ordered Obregón to push on to the capital, taking the city by storm, if nesessary.[37] In his plans for the future, Carranza now ignored both Villa and his powerful Division of the North.

In Mexico City, the foreign colony, as did the government of Carbajal, awaited the impending attack of the Constitutionalist armies with well-founded trepidation. On July 31 members of the diplomatic corps paid a call upon President Carbajal to prevail upon him to establish a neutral zone in the city to be defended by federal forces, thus affording protection for foreigners in the area. Carbajal refused to heed their request, averring that he had complete faith in the loyalty of his troops. He promised to give effective guarantees for the safety of all of the inhabitants of the capital, including foreigners, adding that his government did not intend to resist the Constitutionalists. There would be, he said, no fighting. He felt that to establish a neutral zone would be to give the impression that the rest of the city was not neutral and, consequently, exposed to injury in the event of trouble. But when it became apparent that Carranza was unswervingly determined to treat with the Huertistas solely on the basis of unconditional surrender, and that he would offer no guarantees or concede an amnesty, the concern of the government and the foreign representatives was heightened. It seemed that Mexico City could not escape a siege.[38]

The commanders of the federal forces in the capital conferred on August 4 on whether to defend the city against Obregón or to give it up without a fight. Fearful that an evacuation by the army would leave the capital at the mercy of the Zapatistas and the "rabble," Cardoso de Oliveira brought together Eduardo Iturbide, the Huertista governor of the Federal District, and Alfredo

Robles Domínguez, a Carrancista agent in Mexico City. He asked them to agree that the federal police, commanded by Iturbide, should be considered a neutral force to maintain order during the transfer of authority from Carbajal to Carranza. Iturbide consented to accept the responsibility, while Robles Domínguez promised to refer the matter to Carranza for his approval.[39]

Dissatisfied with Carbajal's rejection of their entreaties, the ministers of Great Britain, Austria-Hungary, Belgium, France, Germany, Italy, Japan, and Russia requested through the British vice-consul at Saltillo that Carranza permit a force of two thousand federal soldiers to remain in the capital to protect foreign interests, pending the arrival of the Constitutionalists. Again the First Chief declined to give any guarantees and demanded that all federal troops evacuate peacefully upon the approach of Obregón. He did grant one concession, acceding to the suggestion of Cardoso de Oliveira that the police be kept under arms until the revolutionaries had entered the city. Carranza promised the ministers that he would soon arrive in the capital and would then take charge of the political situation.[40] At the same time, Carranza threatened Carbajal that if he carried out his intentions (rumors of these having reached Saltillo) of mustering out the federal army to avoid surrendering it to the revolutionaries, he and all the leaders of the army and the government would receive the vigorous application of Juárez' law of 1862.[41]

Carbajal now saw no other course than to accept the terms dictated by the Constitutionalists. He resigned his claim to the presidency, ordered the withdrawal of the federal troops from the capital, and turned over his authority to Eduardo Iturbide. He left by train for Veracruz, in order not to fall into the hands of the revolutionaries, and prudently followed Huerta into exile. J. R. Velasco, Carbajal's Minister of War, assumed charge of the evacuation of the army, telegraphing Carranza that the army would "loyally support" the new government of Mexico. "If you accept the support of the army," said Velasco, "a portion of it will remain to check the entry of the Zapatistas. . . ."[42]

While Velasco's message to Carranza was conciliatory toward the Constitutionalists, it provided a hint for future difficulties within the victorious revolution. Had the federal troops withdrawn completely from the Federal District, even turning over military control of the city to the police of Iturbide, Zapata, rather than Obregón, could have occupied the capital first. The Army of the South was much closer than the troops of Obregón and González, still in Irapuato and Querétaro.

It had been a historical accident that both the Constitutionalists and the Zapatistas happened to be fighting Huerta. From March 1913 to August 1914 there had been not the slightest connection between the two movements. Separated by miles of land and kept apart by the federal troops, it had been impossible, even had the two revolutionary groups desired it, to communicate with each other or to coordinate their efforts in any way. Moreover, for the Constitutionalists, *Zapatismo* bore the stigma of rebellion against the martyred president, Madero, and the continued association with Orozquistas. Thus General Velasco's offer to defend the capital against the Zapatistas until the outlying positions (Cuernavaca, Xochimilco, San Angel, Tlálpam, etc.) could be handed over to the Constitutionalists, fell on receptive ears. But while the acceptance by Carranza of the federal positions intact seemed at the time to have spared the capital a Zapatista sacking, the dragon's teeth of future discord between Carranza and Zapata were thereby sowed. The martial harvest was reaped in the five subsequent years of fighting between their two forces. Until Zapata's assassination in 1919 there was never a moment of peace between the two *caudillos*. It would have taken no perspicacity, even in 1914, to recognize that Zapata would see in Carranza's acceptance of the federal offer exactly what it was —an act of hostility against the men of Morelos.

The vanguard of the Army Corps of the Northwest arrived on August 9 at Teoloyucan, a small station on the rail line from Irapuato, about twenty miles north of Mexico City. Federal troops were encamped at Cuautitlán and Barrientos, less than ten miles away, with their outposts strung along the Central Mexicano almost to Teoloyucan. The moment of decision had come for the transfer of the city. The First Chief had already given Obregón authority to deal with the federal commanders as he saw fit, and from Teoloyucan Obregón sent them a telegram, echoing Carranza's demands for their unconditional surrender. That night members of the diplomatic corps met in the capital, at the invitation of Cardoso de Oliveira, to formulate plans for a peaceful occupation of the city by Obregón.[43] On the following day the Brazilian minister had a telegraphic conference with Carranza, who had come from Saltillo to Dolores Hidalgo, and the First Chief agreed to confer with him personally on these plans at Obregón camp in Teoloyucan. At the same time, Obregón received a communication from Robles Domínguez that the federal chiefs would surrender the capital, and that he and Iturbide would come to Obregón's headquarters to arrange for the delivery of the city and its government.[44]

On August 11, the peace delegation, composed of Iturbide, Robles Domínguez, Cardoso de Oliveira, and the ministers of Great Britain and Guatemala, as well as the French chargé d'affaires, rode through the federal lines to Teoloyucan. Iturbide had taken the precaution of divesting himself of his military rank, for as governor of the Federal District and commander of the federal police, he had been accorded the grade of brigadier. Obregón had threatened to shoot any military man who came as a delegate, under the resuscitated law of Juárez, and the Huertista commander, General Velasco, forbade any member of his army to accompany the party. The delegation reached Obregón's camp before noon to find that the First Chief had still not arrived from Dolores Hidalgo. Obregón, who was capable of both broad and macabre humor, chaffed Iturbide, asking if he was aware that he and all the members of the government were subject to the law of 1862. According to his own account (written, it is true, many years after the event), Iturbide replied that he had not come to Teoloyucan to save his life. If that had been his first intention, he said, he should have gone to Veracruz with Carbajal. Obregón and Iturbide talked for about a half an hour, agreeing, though this was not their province, that Carranza should become provisional president upon his occupying Mexico City.[45]

It was not until nine o'clock that evening that Carranza's train pulled in from Dolores Hidalgo. Although the members of the delegation presented themselves before his headquarters, he testily refused to see them until morning. At 9:00 A.M. the following day, Carranza heard the plans brought from Mexico City, but refused to have any personal dealings with the Huertistas, preferring to leave the matter of the military occupation of the capital to Obregón. In conversation with Iturbide, the First Chief railed against Mexico City as the "cradle of *cuartelazos*," promising that its inhabitants would soon pay for their "crimes." With the issue unresolved, the group of diplomats and Iturbide returned to the capital. Carranza bound Iturbide on his honor to return on the thirteenth with representatives of the federal army to meet with Obregón.[46]

In the capital Velasco designated General Gustavo Salas to accompany Iturbide as far as the federal outposts to take charge of the surrender of his troops. On August 13 Iturbide returned to the Constitutionalist camp to sign with Obregón the fateful Treaty of Teoloyucan. This agreement specified that the federal forces would be withdrawn to a point to be designated later, acceptable to both Velasco and Obregón, whereupon the Constitutionalists would enter the city immediately. At that time Iturbide would deliver the command of the police force and the government of the capital to the occupying authorities. The revolutionary army was to enter the city in perfect order, and the inhabitants of the capital were not to be molested, with Obregón to punish all offenders against the peace.[47] A second treaty was then signed at a position on the highway between Cuautitlán and Teoloyucan by Salas (and Vice Admiral Othón P. Blanco for the navy) providing for the gradual and peaceful disbanding of the federal forces. Salas and Obregón agreed, as had Obregón and Iturbide earlier, that Carranza would become provisional president upon his arrival in the capital.[48] Carranza took no part in any of these dealings with the Huertistas. Obregón accepted the offer of Salas to keep federal garrisons in the towns confronting the Zapatistas, until they could be relieved by Constitutionalist forces. On the fourteenth the accord was ratified by Velasco, and the evacuation of the Federal District was begun at once, with the Huertista troops withdrawing to points along the route to Puebla in groups of not more than five thousand men each.[49]

The Colorado units of Benjamín Argumedo, Higinio Aguilar, and Juan Andrew Almazán, who had retreated south with the Huertistas, refused to participate in the federal surrender to the Constitutionalists. These revolutionary turncoats could expect no mercy from the victorious Carrancistas. Rather than risk reprisals against them and certain death for many, they passed over to Zapata, who had once held their leader, Pablo Orozco, in high esteem. Zapata, in his turn, was pleased to receive reinforcements as he faced a showdown with the revolutionaries of the North. The Southern chief kept them, however, at a safe distance from Morelos, and they operated principally in the states of Puebla and Veracruz.

Obregón's Army Corps of the Northwest, with the troops of Lucio Blanco and Francisco Cosío Robelo in the van, entered Mexico City on August 15. The first official act of the revolutionary commander was to proclaim martial law in the capital, decreeing the death penalty for those who disturbed public order or committed "outrages," robberies, or other crimes. At the same time he banned the sale of alcoholic beverages in the territory under his command. Iturbide, in accordance with their prior agreement, turned over the National Palace to Obregón, offering himself as a prisoner of war. Obregón sent Iturbide home, however, exacting a promise from the former governor that he would not try to escape from the capital. Iturbide was warned that he might be tried later as a Huertista. With the whole area quiet and under military law, the populace of Mexico City, the diplomatic corps, and the army of Obregón awaited the coming of the First Chief, soon—it was expected—to be the provisional president of Mexico.[50]

Venustiano Carranza stood at the threshold of the presidency.

His Constitutionalist armies had toppled the usurper, Victoriano Huerta, and now dominated the larger part of the Republic. Had he been able to achieve the immediate pacification of Mexico, his election and the recognition of his government by the foreign powers would have followed as a matter of course. But the First Chief faced formidable obstacles. Villa, still in control of Chihuahua and Durango, remained hostile and continued to build up his forces. And Zapata stayed in Morelos and showed no inclination to subordinate his movement to that of the Constitutionalists. The future of Carranza—and of Mexico—would be determined by his success in dealing with these two *caudillos*.

3

Summoning the Convention

FOR THREE DAYS MEXICO CITY ENDURED MARTIAL LAW before Venustiano Carranza arrived from Tlalnepantla on August 18 to take charge of the capital and set up Mexico's first national revolutionary administration. He named a cabinet for his provisional regime and formed a civilian government in the Federal District. Carranza made no move, however, to hold elections or to recall the members of Congress who had been dispersed by Huerta in 1913. His government remained pre-constitutional and extralegal. Carranza ignored the foreign diplomatic representatives and was particularly arrogant toward those ministers whose governments had recognized Huerta. He considered expelling the British minister, Sir Lionel Carden, as *persona non grata* to his revolutionary regime, but Cardoso de Oliveira persuaded him that this would be an unnecessary affront to Great Britain. Carden was then permitted to leave the country voluntarily. Within a short time the governments of Spain, Germany, and Guatemala had withdrawn their representatives, leaving in the Mexican capital only the diplomatic agents of Brazil, Belgium, Japan, Italy, Austria, and El Salvador.[1]

Under the Plan of Guadalupe, Carranza should have assumed the office of provisional president upon his occupation of the capital. Most revolutionaries had expected that he would do so, and this course was urged upon him by the various special agents of the United States, as well, as a prelude to American recognition of his regime. The significance of his refusal to declare himself provisional president lay in his determination to become the legally elected president, for in Mexico interim officials could not succeed themselves in permanent office. Moreover, Carranza was determined to punish the "criminals" of the Huerta regime during the informal pre-constitutional period of his First Chieftaincy. One of his first official actions in Mexico City was to halt railroad communications with Veracruz, in order to prevent the flight of suspected Huertistas, who hoped to evade punishment. And on August 19 Carranza closed all the courts in the Republic and suspended legal guarantees of the Constitution, so as to apply the rigors of Juárez' law of 1862, without the hindrances of regular tribunals and due process of law.[2]

With Carranza's occupation of the capital the revolutionaries began to enjoy the fruits of their conquest. The victorious generals, most of them, like the soldiers they commanded, of lower-class origin, threw themselves wholeheartedly into the pleasures of the sybaritic life. They took for themselves the most opulent residences on the fine boulevards and avenues of the capital, while the common soldiers seized their booty where they could find it, despite the complaints of the citizenry. Lucio Blanco, who had been the first revolutionary commander to enter Mexico City with his troops, chose for his headquarters the home of the wealthy Casasús family on the Paseo de la Reforma. Obregón also took a fine home on the Paseo, while the First Chief occupied the house of the Torres Adalid family on nearby Avenida Chapultepec.

The inclinations of the Constitutionalist soldiers to gain compensation for the hardships endured in fighting their way to Mexico City were bridled, however, by the retention of the Huertista police force after the Treaty of Teoloyucan to maintain the peace in the capital. It is not surprising, then, that clashes soon occurred between the armed police and the marauding revolutionaries. On August 27 Canova, now in Mexico City, informed the Secretary of State that hostilities had broken out between the police and the army when two policemen were disarmed and shot by a band of Constitutionalists. When a squadron of police was dispatched to restore order, ten of these were also shot. According to Canova, looting of homes, coaches, and automobiles was widespread, while soldiers protected the depredators by prowling the streets. He told Bryan that a Constitutionalist officer "smilingly remarked to me that they were finishing with their enemies." [3] On the previous night, according to a Red Cross statement, forty-two civilians had been killed and thirty-seven wounded by the revolutionary soldiers.[4]

As a result of continued scrapes between the police and the military, Carranza's government yielded to the revolutionary demands and on August 28 ordered the disarming of two thousand police in the Federal District. At the same time, in order to reduce the provocation for civil disturbances, all the saloons were directed once more to close their doors. Soldiers now replaced the police in patrolling the city, so that sacking, though on a reduced scale, continued. Canova reported that the Constitutionalists "openly state they were promised their loot, and they want it now." [5] Mexico City was beginning to experience what it must now endure for months of revolutionary occupation, alternately by Carrancista or Villista and Zapatista troops; it must pay for being Huerta's capital.

One of the first problems facing Carranza in Mexico City was that of dealing with the Zapatistas. On August 14, while the First Chief was still in Tlalnepantla, he had sent a note to Zapata, inviting him to a conference to be held in the Federal District at some neutral point between the Constitutionalist and Zapatista forward lines.[6] But Zapata in Yautépec was as wary as a badger in his den and refused to be enticed out of the safety of the mountains of Morelos. His suspicions were verified when Obregón took over the federal outposts from the forces of General Velasco. On August 17 a delegation arrived at Tlalnepantla bringing Zapata's answer to Carranza's invitation. He rejected an accord with the Constitutionalists on the basis of submission to the First Chief or acceptance of the Plan of Guadalupe. He declared that plan to be "more worthless" than Madero's Plan of San Luis Potosí. He stipulated as his price for an understanding with the revolutionaries of the North that they sign an "act of adhesion" to his own Plan of Ayala and bind themselves to submit "loyally to all its clauses." Not to do so, said Zapata, would insure that "there shall be no peace in our land." Zapata's emissaries informed Carranza that any meeting with their chief must take place in their own headquarters. Zapata promised, they said, to give full guarantees for the safe passage of Carranza to and from Morelos.[7]

These conditions were thoroughly unacceptable to Carranza, and they were rejected out of hand. It was unlikely that Carranza, who had successfully defied Huerta, Carbajal, and even President Wilson, would now submit himself to the Plan of Ayala. Although the original proclamation of 1911 had twice been modified to take into account the defection of Pablo Orozco to Huerta and then the resignation of Huerta during the previous month, Zapata's plan still designated himself as chief of Mexico's revolution. His attitude, which he maintained with admirable, if unrealistic, tenacity, was that his was the original, hence the only true, revolution, that Carranza must perforce come to him. Yet it had been primarily the Constitutionalist armies which had accomplished the overthrow of Huerta and which now occupied most of the Republic. Though the Zapatistas had been greeted by the fraternizing common soldiers of Carranza with *abrazos* and shouts of "Viva Zapata" and "Viva Carranza," they were considered by the Constitutionalist chiefs to be scarcely more than peon bandits, who had been in rebellion against the legitimate government of Madero. It was this government which the First Chief proposed soon to restore.

Carranza, like Madero, had never favored legislated social reforms or the breaking up of large estates. While he might have swallowed the Plan of Ayala in theory, in order to gain the support of the Liberating Army of the South, he gagged at the

Zapatista rigidity. Even agrarian reforms could have been made more palatable to him if presented in ambiguous terms. But the men of Zapata had learned to their sorrow that the vague promises of reform by Madero were no more than chimeras. They felt that if Mexico was to have land reform it must come by decisive direct action, not through the ephemeral good intentions expressed by middle-class politicians. From Milpa Alta, a Zapatista position in the Federal District, the Army of the South published a declaration to the Mexican people setting forth their case against the half-hearted Constitutionalist revolutionaries. This declaration, written for Zapata by one of his young secretaries, Antonio Díaz Soto y Gama, was a poignantly phrased call for justice for the underprivileged classes of Mexico.[8]

Díaz Soto denied that the Carrancistas were true revolutionaries or had any real concern for the people. The reforms they promised were less than useless, they were inimical to the progress of the rural classes, he insisted. "The country wants something more," said Díaz Soto, "than the vague utterances of Señor Fabela, supported by the silence of Señor Carranza. It wishes to crush feudalism once and for all. . . ." What did the Constitutionalists offer the people, he asked.

Reforms in administration, . . . complete integrity in the handling of public funds, a scrupulous insistence upon official responsibility, freedom of the press for those who cannot read, freedom to vote for those who do not know the candidates, an equitable administration of justice for those who have never had any business with a lawyer. All these beautiful democratic principles, all these grand words, with which our fathers and grandfathers delighted themselves, have today lost their magical allure and meaning for the people. . . .

The people of Mexico, wrote Díaz Soto, had seen that

with elections and without elections, with effective suffrage and without it, with Porfirian dictatorship or with the democracy of Madero, with a muzzled or a libertine press, their portion is bitterness. They continue to suffer poverty and humiliations without end. . . .

What reason was there to think now, he asked, that the new "liberators" would be different from the *caudillos* of yesterday?

For that reason, the men of the South would continue to fight for the cause of the people and would not yield to the false promises of the Constitutionalist leaders. This was to be the program of the Zapatistas for the next five years.[9]

Despite his reluctance to compromise his demands, Carranza was under some pressure to make peace with the Zapatistas. In Washington, Secretary of State Bryan announced that he was sending two special agents to Mexico, H. L. Hall and Paul Fuller, to attempt a reconciliation between the two revolutionary chiefs. Moreover, Carranza was disturbed by the visit of Charles Jenkinson, an American Red Cross representative, to Zapata. Jenkinson had brought back a letter from Zapata to Woodrow Wilson, and Carranza feared that this might lead the United States to grant some form of recognition or aid to the revolutionary movement in the South.[10] Within his own party there were those more radically inclined than their chief, who wanted him to be less unbending in his dealings with the Zapatistas. Acting, therefore, upon a suggestion by the Carrancista periodical, *El Liberal,* and in response to a letter from the Southern general, Genovevo de la O, Carranza agreed to send Luis Cabrera and Antonio I. Villarreal to Morelos as his agents to arrange, if possible, a peace with Zapata. The two Constitutionalists arrived in Cuernavaca on August 21, and two days later Zapata came over from Yautépec to meet them.

Throughout the conference, in which Zapata was advised by Antonio Díaz Soto y Gama, Alfredo Serratos, and Manuel Palafox, the Southern chief maintained the inscrutable silence of an Indian sphinx, permitting his secretary, Palafox, to bear the burden of the discussion. It was, in fact, less a conference than a long harangue on the part of the Zapatistas, who refused to hear any suggestions from Villarreal or Cabrera. Palafox insisted that any meeting between Zapata and Carranza take place in Morelos and refused to consider a neutral place. Cabrera and Villarreal were told that the Southern movement, being the older, must take precedence over the one they represented.

Palafox repeated the demands, made earlier to Carranza, that all revolutionaries must accept the Plan of Ayala, not simply in principle, but in its entirety. And Carranza must abandon his pretense of being the First Chief, since the Plan of Ayala claimed that position, if not the title, for Zapata. Following the lead of the Villistas at Torreón, the Zapatistas now demanded that a revolutionary convention be assembled to name an interim president for Mexico. As a price for conceding to meet with Carranza, they asked the Constitutionalists to surrender to them the town of Xochimilco (which contained the pumping station for most of Mexico City's drinking water).[11]

Cabrera and Villarreal had come to Cuernavaca solely to offer Carranza's terms to Zapata, who now refused to hear them. Since they had no authority to accept the extravagant demands of the Southerners, the one-sided conference came to a halt, without concessions by either party. The Carrancista delegates were detained in Cuernavaca until September 1, not as prisoners, but as hostages to secure the safe transit of representatives of Villa back through Mexico City to the North of the Republic.[12]

Upon his return to the capital Cabrera read a report to J. W. Belt, Silliman's secretary, on the failure of his mission. Both Cabrera and Carranza wished to demonstrate to the American agents the unreasonableness of Zapata. Paul Fuller was expected to arrive in Mexico City within a few days, and the Constitutionalists feared that negotiations between the American government and the Zapatistas might prejudice their own position. Belt assured Cabrera, however, that neither the trip of Jenkinson nor the letter which Wilson received from Zapata had any diplomatic significance.[13] The president did not, in fact, answer or even acknowledge the letter until many months had passed. On September 5, the day Fuller reached the Mexican capital, Carranza gave to the press his reply to Zapata, which was a categorical refutation of the claims of the Zapatistas. He affected a willingness to discuss agrarian reform for Morelos and for the entire Republic and invited the Army of the South to send a delegation for that purpose to the convention of revolutionary chiefs which he was summoning to assemble in Mexico City on October 1.[14]

Despite this invitation, Carranza continued to treat Zapata as a rebellious subordinate and kept the former federal garrisons to the south and west of the capital manned with Constitutionalist soldiers. He seemed unappreciative of, and uninterested in, the proffered good offices of Fuller and Silliman in arranging a settlement with the Zapatistas. In his dealings with the American government Carranza's prime consideration was the evacuation of Veracruz, and he would talk of little else. No further moves of conciliation were made by either the Zapatistas or the Constitutionalists, and Carranza widened the breach by holding incommunicado and without trial two agents of Zapata who were seized in Mexico City, although they bore *salvos conductos* from the Carrancista general Lucio Blanco.

As hostilities between the Constitutionalists and the forces of Zapata smoldered in the South, revolutionary discord erupted again in the North to hinder Carranza's attempts to impose a civilian government upon all of Mexico. In Obregón's Sonora a feud had broken out between José M. Maytorena, the state governor, and Colonel Plutarco Elías Calles, commander of Constitutionalist troops in the Northwest. Although affairs in Sonora were of no real import to Villa, he began to fish in troubled waters by taking the part of Maytorena. During the last part of August he invited Obregón to come with him to Sonora to iron out the difficulties between Maytorena and Calles.[15] Turning over the military command of Mexico City to his subordinate, General Juan G. Cabral, Obregón joined Villa in Chihuahua on August 24.

Villa and Obregón conferred with Maytorena on August 29 at Nogales and reached an agreement that he should be recognized as both the military commander and Constitutionalist governor in the state. All revolutionary groups, including that of Calles, were to be subordinated to his authority. This decision pleased few of the Constitutionalist chiefs in Sonora, and there were so many protests against it that on the following day a new pact was signed by Obregón and Villa (without Maytorena's accord), providing for an armed *status quo* in Sonora. Maytorena would continue as governor and keep the troops then under his command. To placate Maytorena, the troops of Calles would be transferred to General Benjamín Hill. All forces were to remain in the areas they occupied, and there should be no further hostilities between the contending parties. Nogales, the principal entrepôt for the state of Sonora, was left in the control of Maytorena. Before he left for Chihuahua, Obregón gave Hill specific orders to leave Maytorena's troops unmolested.[16]

The second solution pleased no one either and served only to create a situation in which armed conflict seemed inevitable. Once Obregón and Villa had returned to Chihuahua, Obregón changed his mind again, and, as before, Villa deferred to him. On September 3, the two signed a third agreement stipulating that Juan G. Cabral should replace Maytorena both as governor and as military commander in Sonora. The troops of Calles and Hill, which were the occasion of the friction in the first place, were to be withdrawn completely from the state, marching overland to Casas Grandes in Chihuahua, remaining there until Cabral should deem it proper for them to return.[17]

Now convinced that hostilities had been avoided in Sonora, Villa and Obregón turned to the larger problem of revolutionary unity. Obregón hoped that he and Villa could devise a plan to reconcile the differences between the Division of the North and the Constitutionalist chief. Villa's antipathy toward Carranza was of long standing and not easily erased. He and his followers were determined upon the elimination of Carranza as their price for concord. Aside from personal antagonisms, the Villistas' principal complaints against him were that he refused to regularize his anomalous position as First Chief by becoming provisional president, and that he ruled Mexico virtually as a dictator with no courts, no legislature, and no real cabinet. Although he had never wavered in his loyalty to Carranza as his military chief, Obregón, too, in September of 1914, was willing to sanction the removal of Carranza, if this decision could bring peace to Mexico. On September 3, in Chihuahua the two generals agreed to a nine-point program for the revolution by which Carranza would be required to yield either his First Chieftaincy or his chances to become the constitutional president. Although they consented that Carranza should immediately assume the role of provisional president, they stipulated, as had the Pact of Torreón, that no one who held provisional office under the revolution should be eligible to stand for office in the regular elections to follow the pre-constitutional period.[18]

Obregón remained in the North for another five days as he and Villa, in complete harmony, sought to reconcile the differences between Durango's Constitutionalist governor, Pastor Rouaix, and the military commanders in that state, the brothers Arrieta. In the meantime, Carranza had already issued in Mexico City a summons for all revolutionary chiefs to assemble in the capital on the first day of the following month. Therefore, when Obregón returned to Mexico City on September 9 with George Carothers and the Villista representatives, Miguel Silva and Miguel Díaz Lombardo, bearing the document signed in Chihuahua, the First Chief found sufficient grounds for rejecting it. On September 13, Carranza, while accepting in principle the first article, which would designate him provisional president, ruled out the others. He said that such matters "cannot be considered the object of discussion and approbation among three or four persons. . . ." They must be discussed, he said, in the "junta" which would meet within the month in the capital.[19]

This assembly of Constitutionalist chiefs—soon to be the Revolutionary Convention—was Carranza's answer to the critics who accused him of perpetuating a dictatorship and of making agrarian reforms impossible. It is significant, however, that Carranza himself almost invariably referred to the body as a "junta," not a "convention." The former term implied that a group of persons had been called together at the behest of the First Chief to give him advice, which would discuss, not decide. A convention, which was what most revolutionaries were demanding, would presumably be deemed competent to deal with matters of reform, social, political, and economic. These things Carranza would leave to the future, to a regularly elected legislature and government, not a "revolutionary convention."

While Carranza tried to cope with Mexico's internal problems and prepared for the junta's meeting on October 1, his attention was also directed toward foreign affairs, primarily the relations between his government and the United States. Though the United States was principally concerned with finding a stable government in Mexico through a coalition of Carrancistas, Villistas, and Zapatistas, upon which to bestow its diplomatic approval, Carranza hoped to achieve recognition for his own government, regardless of the other factions. When Paul Fuller interviewed Carranza in Mexico City on September 5, the First Chief complained about Jenkinson's visit to Zapata and the letter he had brought back to Wilson. Carranza felt that for the United States to deal directly with Zapata was only more encouragement for his hostile attitude toward the Constitutionalists. Carranza disclaimed any intention of prolonging his interim government or of using it as a prelude for a dictatorial regime, as his enemies had charged. To prove his good faith he informed Fuller that he was summoning the governors and generals to meet soon in the capital.[20]

On September 14, Isidro Fabela called at the Brazilian legation to sound out Cardoso de Oliveira on the matter of American recognition for the Constitutionalist government, though there was no indication that Carranza would call for elections or reconvene the nation's courts. Carranza seemed concerned to gain this recognition during September, perhaps to confront the "junta of chiefs" with a *fait accompli* on October 1. When the Brazilian minister informed the State Department of Fabela's trial balloon, Robert Lansing, the acting Secretary of State, promptly pricked it. He wired Cardoso de Oliveira to "discourage any immediate requests for recognition. You will be advised whenever the president feels the time is ripe for such action." [21]

If the Constitutionalist chief could not gain American recog-

nition it was of more immediate importance that he pry Veracruz from the American army, in the event that hostilities should
break out between his forces and those of Villa or Zapata. The
possession of the port, with its easy access to arms and supplies,
would be his most powerful weapon in dealing with his rivals.
On this matter the American president and his State Department proved more amenable. Fuller had a second interview
with Carranza on September 8, in which the First Chief would
talk of nothing but the evacuation of Veracruz. He told Wilson's
agent that questions about Villa and Zapata and the domestic
pacification of Mexico were not matters which concerned the
American government, and that he was competent to deal with
them. Relative to Veracruz, Carranza complained that the punitive expedition had been directed against a regime which no
longer existed. He asked that it be turned over to his government without delay.[22] On September 16, Mexico's Independence
Day, Cardoso de Oliveira brought Carranza a message from
Bryan requesting him to designate "some responsible officials"
to whom the city and the customs houses might be delivered.[23]
On the following day Carranza ordered Cándido Aguilar, the
Constitutionalist governor of the state of Veracruz, to proceed
to the port city to receive it from the departing Americans.[24]
But the mere act of relinquishing control of the port and turning it over to the Constitutionalists proved more difficult than
either the Americans or the Mexicans had imagined.

President Wilson had intended, in April 1914, that the initial
expedition be of a punitive nature against the customs station
at Veracruz. He hoped to punish the government of Huerta
for flouting American honor and, perhaps even more important,
to halt a large shipment of arms due to arrive upon the Hamburg-
American liner, "Ypiranga." The president did not want to seize
the city and believed he could avoid bloodshed by confining the
attack to the dock area. But the naval authorities under Admiral
F. F. Fletcher soon discovered that it was impossible to re-
strict the occupation to the docks and the customs warehouses.
Contrary to expectations, Mexicans resisted the landings with

small arms fire, and it was necessary to move strong forces into the city in order to protect the American marines and sailors. Once in control of Veracruz the Americans found themselves masters of a complete anarchy. Although the Mexican judges and other public officials were requested to remain in their offices, not one would do so. Under Mexican law an employee of the government who served an invading force was liable to extreme penalties. Little by little, the naval officers, and then army officers, when a brigade under General Frederick Funston was landed, were compelled to take full control of the city government, administering justice, collecting taxes, and caring for the sanitation of the port and its environs.

The occupation forces had been in Veracruz for almost five months when Wilson decided to return it to Mexican control. During that time the city had become a model for efficient, graftless government under a benevolent military dictatorship. It was also a haven for nonrevolutionaries, fleeing the wrath of the successful Constitutionalists. On September 15, Funston received orders from the Secretary of War, Lindley M. Garrison, to prepare his troops for evacuation. In his acknowledgment of this directive, Funston pointed out the difficulties in withdrawing the American forces too precipitously. Many private citizens, who had taken employment with the military government, were now threatened with retaliation by the Constitutionalists. Agents of Carranza circulated openly in the city, he said, compiling lists of persons marked for punishment. Moreover, there was a large number of refugees, including three hundred nuns and priests, who now clamored to leave with the American troops, fearing for their lives if they should fall into the hands of the vengeful revolutionaries. The Constitutionalists threatened monetary, as well as physical, retribution upon the unhappy Veracruzanos. During the military occupation, the American customs officials had collected tolls from goods brought into the port. The army officers in charge of the city government had also collected fees and taxes from the citizens. The Constitutionalists now proposed to collect these taxes, fees, and tolls again after the evacuation. Funston estimated that he could be ready to leave by October 10, but suggested that these difficulties be cleared up with the Constitutionalist government in Mexico City before he handed over the port to Aguilar.[25]

Such palpably unfair acts threatened by the Constitutionalists offended Wilson's sense of decency and fair play. Although a week earlier he had been pleased with the prospect of pulling out of Veracruz, he found by September 21 that he could not do so with honor. After a conference with Garrison, Wilson decided to halt the planned evacuation until he had received assurances from the revolutionary government that there would be no retaliation against the lives or property of those supposedly endangered. On the following day, Cardoso de Oliveira brought a message from Lansing to Carranza requesting such guarantees.[26] Carranza refused to be badgered into giving assurances of any nature, even at a price for so valuable a possession as Mexico's chief port. Unlike Wilson, he saw that the Americans in Veracruz were sheltering many Huertista "criminals" who, by revolutionary standards, deserved to be punished. And the monies paid in customs duties or in the form of taxation had been in Huertista currency, which the Americans proposed to take with them. From the Constitutionalist point of view, the goods would now be imported duty-free, if the demanded guarantees were given. Both Carranza and Wilson were too stiff-necked and self-righteous to concede a point to the other. And so the matter of Veracruz rested, with diplomatic hackles raised on both sides. The American soldiers stayed in the port, with a good part of their equipment stored in the holds of transport ships in the harbor, awaiting the decision of either Washington or Mexico City to back down.

Meanwhile, during the last days of September, the successful, but tortured, Mexican revolution rent itself irrevocably. When the convention of revolutionary chiefs met on October 1 in Mexico City, Villa had severed his last tenuous ties with Carranza and was in open rebellion against him.

The causes for the split were ancient and deeply rooted. They lay in the personal antagonism of Villa and Carranza and in their radically different political philosophies. The immediate occasion was the recrudescence of the Maytorena affair in Sonora and the attempt of Obregón to resolve the situation by means of another personal conference with Villa. The pact of Villa and Obregón in Chihuahua earlier in the month to insure a peace between Maytorena and Calles had had little effect in Sonora. By the second week of September hostilities between the rival revolutionary forces in the state seemed imminent. Moreover, there was a similar revolutionary estrangement in Durango, where Domingo and Mariano Arrieta disputed control of the state with the Villista general, Tomás Urbina.

Obregón left Mexico City for Chihuahua by special train on September 13. Interviewed at the station, he told a reporter for the *Mexican Herald* that he would review the Constitutionalist troops in Villa's state.[27] Since the sixteenth (Independence Day) was a day of celebration, Obregón spoke the truth, though only part of it. Indeed, Villa had prepared a parade in his honor. But Obregón also brought a personal invitation for Villa and his chiefs to attend the convention soon to assemble in the capital. Obregón was accompanied from Mexico City by Cabral, who was en route to the Northwest to replace Maytorena as governor of Sonora; by his chief of staff; and by an American newspaperman from Douglas, Arizona, B. S. Butcher. Their party arrived in Chihuahua on the morning of September 16. In contrast to his cordiality of the previous visit, Villa was now less friendly and more suspicious. By his own account, Villa considered Obregón to be a spy of Carranza.[28] The Division of the North presented an elaborate demonstration of its military strength to impress Obregón, and during the parade Villa stressed to Obregón the quality and quantity of his troops. Afterward he took Obregón to the state capital building to show him the large store of arms and ammunition he had accumulated. Villa's demeanor boded ill for peace in the Mexican revolution.[29]

Leon J. Canova was also in Chihuahua, though not in connection with Obregón's mission. Canova had asked Villa for an appointment on the seventeenth and had been summoned to his office at 4:00 P.M. Upon his arrival, he found that Villa was still in conference with Obregón, and he was asked to take a seat in the patio outside Villa's office. It was soon apparent to him that Obregón and Villa were quarreling. Angry sounds issued from the inner room. Though the walls muffled the words, there was no mistaking the import of the tones. Both strode up and down the room; their military boots punctuating their bitter words. It seemed to Canova as though Villa halted from time to time "to whack the table with his fist." At 4:25 P.M., Canova was startled as Villa's secretary, Luis Aguirre Benavides, bolted past him into the street to summon a "packet" of soldiers. The armed men placed themselves in front of the building to menace the exit. Unfortunately for the historian, Canova left his place of vantage at this point and retired to a coach in the street without, to await, at a safer distance, his appointment with Villa. According to his own explanation to Bryan, Canova did not wish to appear to be "eavesdropping." [30] Because Canova did not try to overhear the altercation, the only accounts have come from Villa and Obregón, whose subsequent recollections may have been tinged by what occurred later between them.

While it may be impossible at a late date to separate legend from fact, it would seem that the meeting between the two chiefs was interrupted by a report from Sonora concerning the renewed hostilities between Hill and Maytorena. As tempers flared on both sides, a telegram from Maytorena was brought into the office, informing Villa that Benjamín Hill's men were advancing from the Estación del Río toward Nogales and that they had burned a railroad bridge near Nogales, which was occupied by Maytorena's troops. Enraged, Villa turned upon Obregón and demanded the withdrawal of Hill's forces to Casas Grandes, as the two chiefs had agreed earlier in the month.[31] Obregón refused to consider such a move until Cabral should arrive in Sonora to relieve Maytorena. Villa, with his customary impetuosity, apprised Obregón that he would be shot if he did not comply. It was at this moment that Aguirre Benavides ran into the street to summon a squad of soldiers for that purpose. But cowardice was not one of Obregón's traits, and he refused to yield to Villa's threat. Villa's lieutenants pacified their chief and persuaded him to relent. His anger subsided abruptly. A few moments later he was clasping Obregón in the characteristic Mexican bear hug, the *abrazo,* and affirming his friendship for Obregón. In order to placate Villa, Obregón then agreed to send a telegram to Hill ordering him to withdraw from the vicinity of Nogales, though later he took the precaution of sending, unbeknownst to Villa, a courier to El Paso to countermand this order.[32]

When Obregón left the office, in seeming rapport with Villa, Canova was invited in for a belated conference. Though Villa did not discuss Obregón, Canova found him very caustic in his comments on Carranza. He told Canova that, though everyone knew that Carranza had a head, since all could see it, no one could understand why he had it. He never seemed to use it to any advantage, said Villa, sarcastically. It might just as well be an empty shell or a solid block for all the good it was to the First Chief. Villa expressed his regret that he had not gone right on to Mexico City after he had taken Torreón. Had he not accommodated Carranza, he said, by capturing Saltillo, he would have arrived in the capital before Obregón and Carranza and obviated the troubles which now beset him.[33]

Villa seemed to take keen pleasure in his animosity toward Carranza, as though he were biting upon an abscessed tooth. His relations with Obregón improved, however. On the evening of September 17, the chiefs of the North and the Northwest went to dinner together. Later the Division of the North prepared a ball to honor Obregón, though Villa, somewhat mysteriously, since he loved dancing, asked to be excused from the revels.[34]

During the next two days Villa and Obregón reached a tentative agreement that the Division of the North should send delegates to the convention (not "junta" as it was denominated by Carranza). Villa refused to come to the capital in person, for he mistrusted Carranza. Before committing himself to be represented in the convention, moreover, Villa demanded that the Zapatistas be assured of representation, as well. On September 19, Villa sent a telegram to that effect, addressed to "Señor General Venustiano Carranza," not to the "First Chief," the customary mode in correspondence with Carranza.[35]

At the same time that Carranza received the demand from Villa he was made aware of the decision inflicted upon Obregón to withdraw Hill's troops from Sonora. Hill had refused to heed the order which had come from Chihuahua and had asked Carranza's advice. Whereupon the First Chief confirmed Hill in refusing to pull out of the conflict with Maytorena. Meanwhile, garbled reports of the affair of the seventeenth were filtering back to Mexico City, and Carranza feared that Obregón was being held a prisoner while the Division of the North was preparing to move on Mexico City. He ordered the suspension of communications with the North of Mexico to prevent an attack by Villa on the capital. On September 21, Carranza directed Pánfilo Natera in Zacatecas to begin tearing up the rail lines between that city and Torreón. But Natera had had no intimations of an attack by Villa, and he refused to heed the order by Carranza, whereupon it was rescinded.[36]

Unaware that Carranza had moved to cut off their communications, Obregón and Villa continued in harmony to work out an agreement for revolutionary peace. Villa's generals desired to present an ultimatum to Carranza, demanding, in addition to an accord with the Zapatistas, that the government of the First Chief redeem the Villista paper money by a new issue to be guaranteed by the sale of federal bonds. These bonds would be paid for through a stamp tax and would be amortized in fifteen years. They demanded, further, that Carranza reopen the courts immediately.[37] On September 21, at the conclusion of their several days of conferences, Obregón and Villa joined to telegraph their protests to Carranza against a convention of generals and governors which did not represent all factions. They accused Carranza of seeking to control the proposed assembly by his authority to designate governors and to confer rank upon the generals. The two chiefs informed him that "the state of affairs of the nation demands the immediate resumption of a government based upon popular will and not on a single revolutionary movement." Villa and Obregón warned that they would not attend the convention until assurances had been given by Carranza that the agrarian problem would be resolved. Obregón and Villa now seemed united in their opposition to Carranza.[38]

Obregón left Chihuahua for the south on the evening of September 21. He and Villa were in good spirits as they parted, and their dispute of the seventeenth was now seemingly forgotten. With Obregón went Eugenio Aguirre Benavides, Severino Ceniceros, José I. Robles, and Roque González Garza, bearing Villa's demands upon Carranza concerning the convention of October 1. The train was already well on its way to Torreón when word reached Villa that Carranza had severed railroad communications between Mexico City and Chihuahua. In a telegram to Carranza dated September 22, Villa termed this an act of hostility toward the Division of the North and requested an explanation. Carranza countered with a demand that Villa account for his conduct toward Obregón. Villa then peppered back a telegram informing the First Chief that Obregón had already left for Mexico City the previous night, but that, in view of the premeditated obstacles Carranza had thrown in front of a satisfactory agreement, he was ordering Obregón's detention at Torreón. And in one of the most decisive actions of the revolution, Villa served notice that he was withdrawing recognition from Carranza as First Chief of the Constitutionalist forces. He said that his division would not be represented at the convocation of generals in Mexico City.[39]

Obregón's train was proceeding without incident toward Torreón on the evening of the twenty-second when a halt was made at Ceballos, a small station north of Gómez Palacios. Here the station master brought Aguirre Benavides a telegram from Villa ordering him to return to Chihuahua with Obregón. No one, least of all Obregón, knew Villa's motives. As the train neared Chihuahua again, Obregón called into his private car the American correspondent, B. S. Butcher. Colonel Serratos, Obregón's chief of staff, opened a safe and gave Butcher thirty thousand pesos in a valise. He was asked to take this money to El Paso and to hold it in safekeeping for Obregón.[40]

In Chihuahua Obregón was confronted by Villa, who brandished the telegrams he had exchanged with Carranza. Villa once again vented his anger against Carranza upon Obregón. According to Butcher and Canova, who witnessed the altercation, Obregón displayed no fear in the face of Villa's tirade. If the printed dispatches of Butcher are correct, Obregón felt secure enough to hurl his own insults at Villa. When Villa accused Obregón of being a Carrancista, he replied: "Like you!" Villa spat out angrily: "I? What do you mean?" And Obregón said: "Read the Plan of Guadalupe over there on that table, my dear general, and you will find that we all agreed to bind ourselves to that plan. And if by chance, Señor Villa, you cannot read Spanish well enough to understand what the plan says, why, one of your secretaries might be able to help you!"[41]

General Tomás Urbina demanded that Obregón be executed at once, but Raúl Madero, Aguirre Benavides, Felipe Angeles, and González Garza prevailed upon Villa to release him. Canova wrote to the Secretary of State concerning Obregón: "He was in a very perilous position that day and the manner in which he bore himself increased my esteem for him."[42] The American agent talked with Obregón later in the evening as he was preparing to leave Chihuahua once more. Obregón told him: "The situation is criminal, Mr. Canova, for everything possible should be done by both sides to avoid another revolution." Villa had insisted that Obregón go to El Paso, but he refused to leave by any way except that by which he had come. It was not until shortly before his train left at 10 P.M. on the twenty-third of September that Obregón was told that he could go south. As he left, he offered to seek to persuade Carranza to call elections immediately, as the Villistas demanded.[43]

It is difficult to assess or to reconstruct the happenings of the following day. Man's fuzzy memory and his natural desire to puff himself up have conspired to make impossible a completely coherent account. More than forty years later it cannot be determined whether Villa intended all along to kill Obregón, or whether the decision to order his execution came as a whim, or perhaps as the result of an unrecorded provocation. It is true that many a revolutionary, since the event, has bestowed upon himself the honor of saving Obregón's life. If Canova's account is correct, the palm must be awarded to the three Parcae.

According to Canova, two hours before Obregón's train was scheduled to leave Chihuahua, another train left without Obregón's knowledge, carrying a guard under the command of General Mateo Almanza. Almanza was said to have received orders to waylay Obregón's party, to remove Obregón from the train, and to shoot him. During the night, however, while Almanza's train was on a siding, Obregón's train passed his, whereupon Almanza informed Villa that their schemes had miscarried. Villa then telegraphed the station agent at Corralitos, further down the line, to detain Obregón's train until Almanza should arrive. On the chance that Obregón might already have passed through Corralitos, the message was sent on to Torreón, as well. Fortuitously, José I. Robles and Eugenio Aguirre Benavides were in the station in Torreón talking to the superintendent of railway traffic when the message arrived. They sent their own orders to the agent in Corralitos to permit Obregón's train to pass. Obregón subsequently confirmed to Canova the accuracy of this relation. He said later in Aguascalientes that his train had been detained at the small station, and that he could see the smoke of Almanza's engine when the telegram from Aguirre Benavides and Robles saved him.[44]

As Obregón recounted his own experience for publication, however, his train had halted at Corralitos and was being hauled back to Chihuahua when he jumped from his car to safety. On the other hand, Butcher, who was again a member of Obregón's party, made no mention of such an incident in his dispatch to *El Paso del Norte,* the Spanish language newspaper of El Paso, Texas. He recorded that Obregón's train stopped at Torreón where "two Villista generals" came aboard to threaten him. According to Butcher, Obregón was not intimidated and the train left Torreón safely for Mexico City.[45] Light is cast upon this incident by Obregón's journal. Robles and Aguirre did meet his train in Torreón. They came aboard, however, not to apprehend him, as Butcher alleged, but to give him a *salvo conducto,* despite the orders of Villa to shoot him.[46] Whatever the truth of the matter, the results are obvious: Obregón survived and probably quite by accident. Had he fallen a victim to Villa's amorality, the course of the revolution must have run altogether differently. In 1915 it was Obregón who defeated Villa to save Carranza. And in 1920 it was Obregón who, as president, was able to bring the Villistas, Zapatistas, and Carrancistas together to make possible the social reforms of the 1920's and 1930's.

Villa was never a man of peace. His entire adult life had been spent in pursuit of the martial arts. In the last week of September 1914, having severed his last ties with the First Chief, he made ready for a seemingly inevitable conflict. According to his own relation, he intended an immediate march on Mexico City, where Carranza was experiencing sufficient difficulties with the Army of the South. He believed later, though his explanation may have been a rationalization, that, had it not been for the defection of his lieutenant, Maclovio Herrera, he would have inflicted a quick defeat upon Carranza.[47] It is true that at that time neither Obregón nor González, and probably not both together, could have matched Villa's strength. A conservative estimate was that his armed forces numbered over forty thousand troops, better weaponed and provisioned than those of González and Obregón. There is no indication that Villa dreaded or regretted the renewal of hostilities. Canova talked with him after he had withdrawn recognition from the First Chief and reported to Bryan that Villa was "a wild, passionate man" who could never be civilized. "I believe," wrote Canova, "he will be disappointed if there should be no clash of arms, but is shrewd enough to affirm his desire for a peaceful solution. When he spoke to me

of a break with Carranza and the preparations he was making
for war against him, his face was illuminated with joy." [48]

To justify their rupture with Carranza, the chiefs of the
Division of the North published on September 30 a "Manifesto
to the Mexican People," setting forth their grievances against
him. He was accused of distorting the Pact of Torreón and of
calling a junta which represented, not the armies, but only himself. The Villistas charged that Carranza refused to accept the
title of provisional president, in defiance of his own Plan of
Guadalupe, and that he had assumed the three governmental
powers, executive, legislative, and judicial, while failing to hold
elections. In conclusion, the men of the North invited all
Mexicans to join Villa in separating Carranza from his command
and in replacing him with a civilian, who would convene general
elections as soon as possible.[49]

As Villa entrained his troops for the march on Mexico City,
he was concerned about the threat to his right flank posed by
Domingo and Mariano Arrieta in Durango. As his division
reached Torreón, it could not pass on to Zacatecas with impunity,
for then these forces in Durango would lie behind him. To assure himself of the friendship of the Arrietas, Villa sent a
telegram on September 23 informing them of his withdrawal of
recognition from Carranza and announcing the determination
of his division to fight against the "personality of Venustiano
Carranza." He called upon the two brothers to follow his example. The next day they replied, terming his action premature.
They invited Villa to eschew war and to cooperate with all the
revolutionary chiefs in the holding of the convention.[50] Villa's
only acknowledgment of this invitation to preserve the peace
was an order to his subordinate, Calixto Contreras, to proceed
to Durango City to drive out the troops of the Arrietas. Contreras
had a large force, superior to that under the Arrietas, only seven
miles from the city. As he broke camp, the two brothers, their
forces greatly outnumbered and not wishing to risk a catastrophe,
withdrew into the hills to the south and west of the state.[51]

There they maintained a precarious independence from Villa for over a year. Contreras occupied Durango without a fight.

Villa moved no further south than Zacatecas, however, for a movement was launched by revolutionaries of all factions to placate Villa, even if it meant the elimination of Venustiano Carranza as First Chief. On September 23 a group of Constitutionalist generals met at the behest of Lucio Blanco to seek means for a peaceful settlement. The meeting was attended by Ignacio L. Pesquiera, Rafael Buelna, Eduardo Hay, and Julián C. Medina, and these, together with Blanco, took the lead in organizing a Permanent Peace Commission. They decided to approach Villa on the possibility of holding the convention at some point other than Mexico City, at a site neutral to both the Villistas and Carrancistas. On September 26 they telegraphed Villa, asking him to suggest some measure by which the differences between his division and Carranza might be reconciled. Villa, undoubtedly influenced by his civilian advisers, replied that Carranza might solve the problem by relinquishing his authority to Fernando Iglesias Calderón. Villa promised that he, himself, would never be a candidate for any political office.[52]

Iglesias Calderón was not a revolutionary, but had won for himself a reputation as an "incorruptible Liberal." He had been a leader of the Liberal Party in Madero's time and had been elected to the Senate. He had not opposed Huerta with any vigor, preferring to leave the country rather than participate in the Constitutionalist revolution. This was the man, known vulgarly in Mexico as "el silencioso Don Fernando," with whom Villa would replace Carranza. When Iglesias Calderón was interviewed in Mexico City by a correspondent for El Liberal, he expressed himself as willing to accept this responsibility, "in order to avoid a civil war." But he would yield, he said, only to the wishes of the Mexican people. He insisted: "I will never accept power by means of an act of pretorianism."[53]

Carranza replied to Villa's suggestion that he eliminate himself with a qualified refusal. "My own desire," he said, "is no other than to relinquish as soon as possible the two high offices which the armed people of the Republic conferred on me. . . ." He refused to yield his authority to any except the "assembled high chiefs of the Constitutionalist forces" to meet soon in Mexico City.[54] It is certain, however, that he did not expect that his resignation would be accepted by the convention. The cards were stacked against Villa and all those who demanded the removal of the First Chief, for most of the delegates being summoned to Mexico City were generals or governors who owed their positions to Carranza.

Alvaro Obregón returned to the capital on September 26 from his adventures and misadventures in the North. He was met at the station of the Central Mexicano by Carranza and Lucio Blanco. After giving his chief a firsthand account of his troubles with Villa, Obregón went with Blanco to the Casasús residence on the Paseo de la Reforma to report to the Permanent Peace Commission. He told the group of generals that all the revolutionary difficulties stemmed from the vicious character of Villa and from the bad influences around him and Carranza. To assure peace, Obregón said, it was necessary to unify the good elements of all the factions and to eliminate the malefactors around Villa and Carranza. (Obregón equated malefactors with civilians.) The commission invited Obregón to join the delegation being sent to Zacatecas to treat with the Villistas concerning the site where the convention would be held. Henceforth it was Obregón, rather than Blanco, who took the lead in striving for revolutionary concord in Mexico.[55]

In Zacatecas Obregón and the other members of his delegation conferred with José I. Robles and Aguirre Benavides, who represented the Division of the North, and Pánfilo Natera, Martín Triana, and Eulalio Gutiérrez, who spoke for other elements of the Center and the North. They agreed that an enlarged convention should meet on October 10 in the neutral city of Aguascalientes. On September 30 Obregón informed Carranza by telegraph of the decision made in Zacatecas. And he told Carranza that if he wished to relinquish his authority as First Chief, it should not be to the exclusively Carrancista junta, but to the "person or persons who are designated in a convention of all the revolutionary chiefs. . . ." Obregón meant an assembly which included Villistas, and perhaps Zapatistas, as well as representatives of Carranza.[56]

In Mexico City the remaining members of the Permanent Peace Commission met on September 30 and agreed to participate in Carranza's junta on the following day. Though all of them were Constitutionalist generals, they decided that they would move immediately to Aguascalientes to meet with the Division of the North. All hostilities were to cease in the Republic for the duration of the Convention, they decreed, and telegrams to that effect were sent to Villa, Hill, Calles, and Maytorena. Lucio Blanco, through the Southern general, Leobardo Galván, invited Zapata to attend the convention, as well.[57] In the last days of September 1914 the hopes of Carranza to continue as First Chief of the Constitutionalist forces and to be elected Mexico's president were dimming. His junta, which met as scheduled on October 1, died a-borning.

4

A Junta of Military Chieftains

AT FIVE MINUTES PAST FOUR ON THE AFTERNOON OF
October 1, 1914, in Mexico City the Revolutionary Convention
was called to order by its presiding officer, Luis Cabrera. There
were in attendance in the salon of the Chamber of Deputies
seventy-nine delegates, all of them Carrancistas or personally
invited by the First Chief. There were no Villistas or Zapatistas,
nor any representatives from Governor Maytorena of Sonora. It
was, from the beginning, a junta intended by the First Chief
to be amenable to his wishes and to the direction of his civilian
advisers. Yet it was a body with no permanence, for the delegates
knew that within five days, whatever the desires of Carranza,
they would recess to meet again at Aguascalientes on the tenth
day of the month. In the sessions in the capital they would be
marking time until the exodus to the more neutral territory to
the north. Only two decisions needed to be made in Mexico City:
Who was to go to Aguascalientes; and what to do about the
"resignation" of the First Chief.

Many of the seventy-nine revolutionaries were in the metropolis for the first time. Though none had come from the Division
of the North or the Liberating Army of the South, all sections
of the Republic were represented, even Oaxaca, which had never

been touched by the revolution against Huerta. As they milled about in good spirits, exchanging ursine embraces or hearty handshakes, they presented a variegated spectacle. Most wore uniforms, for this was a revolutionary assembly. A few of the more affluent wore clothes especially cut for the occasion by the fine tailor shops in the capital. Alvaro Obregón, whose personality was soon to dominate the Convention, was immaculate in a light tan, almost cream-colored, uniform. While Obregón was in the capital he was the cynosure of feminine attention. Eulalio Gutiérrez, soon to be president of the assembly, appeared ill at ease. He reminded one observer of a peddler who traveled from door to door selling bedding on installments. He wore a Panama hat and the rude dress of a countryman, and he was thickly mustachioed "like a Turk." There was a sprinkling of mufti, although the decision had been made at Torreón that the Convention would be military in character. Licenciado Luis Cabrera, who had done a yeoman's job of organizing the junta for Carranza, characteristically had several books tucked under his arm. He was smiling broadly.[1]

Cabrera took immediate charge of the proceedings, bustling about like a biddy clucking motherly advice to her wayward brood. He distributed to the delegates a list of those generals, chiefs, and representatives authorized by Carranza to attend the junta. To those whose names were not on the list, Cabrera suggested that they might come to the Ministry of War on the following morning between eight and twelve to be accredited. He concluded the short opening session by announcing that the delegates should assemble on the next afternoon at three, and advised "absolute punctuality." [2]

The most serious cause for dissension in the ranks of the assembly was the presence of civilians. Although these non-revolutionaries, most of them lawyers, ostensibly represented generals or governors who could not attend in person, they were, by and large, from the group around Carranza. Besides Cabrera, there were Juan Naftalí Amador, José N. Macías, Gerzayn Ugarte, Manuel Villaseñor y Villaseñor, Adolfo de la Huerta,

Eduardo Neri, Onésimo González, Roque Estrada, Emilio Cedillo, and Jesús Urueta. Some of these had been Maderista legislators. Gerzayn Ugarte was an editor of *El Liberal,* while González claimed to represent Guillermo Meixueiro, a Felicista general in Oaxaca and certainly not a revolutionary. This group was subsequently reinforced by José I. Novelo, also a Carrancista editor, and Salvador Martínez Alomía.[3]

In the evening Lucio Blanco entertained the military leaders of the Convention at his great house on the Reforma, where plans were perfected for the shift to Aguascalientes. Those who had not participated in the meetings of the Permanent Peace Commission in September joined in pledging to go to the "Convención Pacifista," and to meet with the Villistas on October 10. Leobardo Galván, of the Liberating Army of the South, observed for the Zapatistas. Once more Blanco requested that Galván invite Zapata to be represented at Aguascalientes.[4] Despite these overtures to the Zapatistas by the Carrancista members of the Convention, Carranza did not cease in his hostile attitude toward the men of the South. The Constitutionalist garrisons around the capital maintained their vigilance, and there were frequent clashes with units of the Liberating Army.

The admonitions of Cabrera for punctuality had fallen on deaf ears, for the second session opened fifty-five minutes late. No important business was negotiated that day, however, and the afternoon was spent—as many mornings, afternoons, and evenings were destined to be spent over the next several months —in interminable wrangling over the acceptance or rejection of a delegate's credentials. The first item to be considered was the proposing of candidates for the *Mesa Directiva,* that is, the presiding officers. Since few besides Cabrera had had any parliamentary experience, he had worked out an agenda and now sought to impose it upon the delegates. He busied himself once more, distributing a list of the prospective candidates for the approbation of the members of the Convention. When some voiced displeasure at Cabrera's presumption in circulating the names of the candidates before they were nominated from the floor, he assured the assembly that this was the "traditional way." He compared this procedure to the menu of a restaurant. On one page, he said, would be displayed five or six "platos del día," while on the facing page there might be another fifty which could be prepared "al gusto del consumidor." A colonel threw his simile back at him and dryly suggested that there would be only two dishes served in this "political restaurant"—reason and justice. Taking control of the Convention themselves, the military members ignored Cabrera's list to elect Eulalio Gutiérrez as president and Generals Francisco Murguía and Francisco de P. Mariel as vice-presidents.[5]

In the evening session of October 3 Venustiano Carranza, as he had promised earlier, came to address the delegates. It was the moment for which all had been waiting. Carranza was now attired in a dark blue civilian suit, rather than the plain brown uniform he had always affected for his role as First Chief. His appearance, according to the correspondent for *Nueva Patria,* was of "solemn serenity." He had worn a blue, visored cap into the salon, and José Ugarte noted, somewhat depreciatingly, that he looked like one of the stewards on a Ward Line steamer. Now Carranza stood uncovered. His mien was that of a patriarch as his ample beard jutted well below his collar, hiding both collar and cravat.[6]

Carranza was not an old man; he was a month short of fifty-five. Yet he was old enough to remember, however vaguely, the last days of Benito Juárez. His adult life virtually coincided with the years of the Díaz dictatorship. Carranza's audience was, in the main, of another generation, of another and more modern mentality. Most were in their late twenties or early thirties. To these youngsters he was of a different age, speaking an alien tongue. He was almost a troglodyte in Mexico's twentieth-century Revolution. Still, despite the willingness of most to go to Aguascalientes against his wishes, they felt genuine respect and admiration and a sense of obligation toward their chief. As he read his address in a low voice to the Convention, he peered alternately at his papers or at his listeners through his spectacles. He stopped frequently, as though overcome by emotion. Carranza's delivery was dull, his expressions platitudinous. Yet he was interrupted many times by applause, and at the conclusion of his speech, as he offered his resignation to the delegates, he was greeted and congratulated with many *abrazos*. A good number, it appeared later, had not heard what he had said at all.[7]

The generally accepted, though thoroughly apocryphal, account of the subsequent proceedings is of an impassioned speech by Luis Cabrera, which led the delegates to reject the resignation of the First Chief by acclamation. Yet an examination of the contemporary records, particularly the Carrancista periodical, *El Pueblo,* fails to substantiate this tale. That Cabrera's declamation was impassioned is not to be denied. That his rhetoric had any influence on the decision of the Convention is problematical. Cabrera, who was throughout the meetings in Mexico City the principal spokesman for the First Chief, initiated the discussion by dramatically casting aside his papers and speaking—for the first time, he said—without notes. He explained this novelty by his surprise at the statement of Carranza. His surprise must have been feigned, for the action of Carranza could scarcely have been unexpected by one of his henchmen. His gesture was most probably that of an experienced orator, seeking to convey to his audience that he was speaking from the heart.

Cabrera recalled the unhappy plight of Mexico caused by the hostile attitudes of Villa and Zapata and the American occupation of Veracruz, asking the Convention if there were anyone but Carranza who could cope with this situation. His concluding exhortation was not a categorial plea for the First Chief: "We should meditate very seriously before making any decision concerning the yielding of authority . . . made in this moment by the Citizen Carranza."

Alvaro Obregón, seconded by Rafael Buelna of the Army Corps of the Northwest, expressed the sentiments of the majority when he counseled against accepting the resignation of Carranza at that time. He reminded the assembly that an agreement had been made with the Villistas to hold a convention in Aguascalientes. "We have bound ourselves to respect whatever decision the majority might make at that convention," he said. "Therefore I consider the resignation of Señor Carranza to be inopportune. . . ." Buelna added that, since the assembly lacked representation from Villa and Zapata, "the question of his renunciation can be dealt with only in Aguascalientes."

Cabrera, sensing the apathy with which Obregón and Buelna supported the First Chief, rose again to the rostrum to gibe at them. He insinuated that they were afraid to assume the terrible duty thrust upon them by Carranza. He recited once more the vicissitudes of the revolution and was harshly critical of the role of Obregón in the occupation of Mexico City. He compared Obregón's conduct in signing the Treaty of Teoloyucan with that of a maiden who will sacrifice the entire country in order to preserve her own virginity. Cabrera concluded his peroration by daring the Convention to have the courage to name a new chief. After Obregón had defended himself against the charges of Cabrera and several delegates spoke for or against Carranza's renunciation of authority, Obregón introduced a resolution that it be refused "until the Convention should meet in Aguascalientes." This proposal was accepted by an overwhelming majority.[8]

Carranza was absent during the debate and was probably unaware of the true import of the decision. He returned to the salon amidst a tumultuous ovation to be told that his resignation had been rejected. He made a short address accepting the Convention's judgment: "Gentlemen, I appreciate profoundly this further proof of the confidence placed in me. I shall endeavor, wherever my services are needed, to contribute to the securing of peace in the Republic." [9]

Whatever the interpretation of Carranza or of historians of the Mexican Revolution of the decision of the Convention, it was not a victory for the First Chief. His tenure in office was secured by the fragile thread of the will of the Convention in

Aguascalientes where Villistas and Zapatistas, his avowed enemies, would join the delegates from Mexico City in passing
judgment on him. At that point most revolutionists, Constitutionalist or otherwise, were willing to disburden themselves of
Carranza, if by so doing they could prevent war.

The proceedings of the next day would have been anticlimactic
were it not for the raucous bickering between the civilians and
the military delegates concerning the right of the former to
go with the Convention to Aguascalientes. As the session of
October 4 opened, the atmosphere was calm enough. The secretary noted that there had been, on the previous night, no vote
on the second part of Obregón's resolution, which provided that
the delegates should reassemble in Aguascalientes as a military
convention to consider a new form for the government of the
nation. General Hay asked that that part of the resolution be
withdrawn and replaced by another now proposed by Blanco,
Pesquiera, Medina, Buelna, and Obregón, inviting all the members to sign a pledge to go to Aguascalientes. Hay thought that
a discussion was unnecessary, but Colonel Samuel de los Santos
disagreed, insisting that he needed to know more about the
Convention at Aguascalientes before he would sign such a statement.

Obregón strode quickly to the rostrum to reassure the delegates. The Convention of Aguascalientes would be, he said, "more
or less" the same as this body. "Thus we should consider that
Convention as a continuation of this one." Colonel David
Berlanga, by profession an educator and a newspaper correspondent, by nature a tactless pepperpot, and at that time a representative in the Convention of Antonio I. Villarreal's forces, rose to
ask for a "clarification" of the resolution. He wondered who
among them would be allowed to go to Aguascalientes. Hay
replied that that was a matter to be decided by a commission
after all the delegates had signed the pledge. Blanco added that
there could be no question of signing or not signing since the
majority of the generals and chiefs present had already agreed
at his house to go with the Convention to Aguascalientes. If

there were any "almas pueriles," however, who feared to meet with the Villistas, these could withdraw their signatures, he said.

Berlanga and de los Santos, not satisfied with the explanations of Hay and Blanco, persisted in their queries as to who was going and who was not. Obregón, exasperated by the quibbling, interjected that the generals would go to Aguascalientes. Blanco amended Obregón's statement, saying that the representatives of generals and governors would also be there. A voice rang out in the salon demanding to know who would "arrange" the Convention. An unknown delegate responded: "Obregón and Villa." Blanco insisted, however, that neither Obregón nor Villa had made the decision to go to Aguascalientes. Instead the idea had come to a group of generals independently at his house. He read to the assembly the documents pertaining to the Permanent Peace Commission to satisfy the delegates that the move was not a Villista plot.

Cabrera entered the fray as the champion of *civilismo,* expressing misgivings over the vagueness of the invitation to go to Aguascalientes. He wanted assurances, he said, as to the time, place, and the matters to be dealt with. Especially he wished to know whether the invitation included civilians. "This should be made clear," he insisted. Obregón interrupted: "It is clear." But Cabrera retorted: "No, it isn't." Obregón replied that the "paper says so." To which Cabrera said; "The paper does not speak clearly. And the reason it does not speak clearly is that we do not even know who are generals and who are not. No one can say for certain who is a general, a colonel, or a major." This assertion by Cabrera elicited an objection from Francisco Coss, a general in the forces of Pablo González. He told the assembly that he had fought for many months in Coahuila and Nuevo León for the Constitutionalists, and that the First Chief had granted him his grade. Cabrera assured the delegates that he did not mean to offend the "valiant General Coss," but he knew that some chiefs, such as Felipe Angeles, held their ranks from Huerta and were by that token not genuine revolutionaries.

Weary of parliamentary prattling, Obregón rose to his feet to tell Cabrera that "in the North we signed a pact of honor with Villa and his generals, and in virtue of that pact the civilians will not go to Aguascalientes. Do you know why, Licenciado Cabrera? Say it!" Cabrera refused to be goaded by Obregón and kept his peace. Obregón changed his tone: "I don't command you. I ask you." Cabrera then asked: "To change the form of government?" Instead of answering, Obregón took a different tack: "I may commit errors, but they will be the errors of a patriotic man who wears the sign of his patriotism." He indicated his uniform. "Because," he said, "we knew how to be patriotic, not like some others. . . ." He was interrupted by Juan Neftalí Amador, like Cabrera a lawyer, who objected to Obregón's implications concerning the civilians. "We too are honorable," he said. Obregón continued as though he had not heard Amador: ". . . and whether you like it or not, I am going to Aguascalientes, come rain or thunder," and he concluded with a magnificently illogical boast, "even though they hang me from a tree in Chapultepec."

When Obregón had concluded his tirade against the civilians, Cabrera mounted the platform to lament that "the battle has now begun between the new militarism and the constant *civilismo*. . . . I insist that the military must not go alone to Aguascalientes. The generals hold that only the 150,000 armed soldiers . . . should be represented, while I believe that the fifteen million Mexicans should have a voice there as well." Recognizing, however, that the sentiment of the majority of the delegates was against him and that he was waging a losing fight, Cabrera advised his civilian companions to withdraw voluntarily. He would insist, nevertheless, that Obregón erred in denying to these civilians the right to be at Aguascalientes. Villa would be represented, he said, by a North American Jew, Felix Sommerfeld. Sommerfeld, said Cabrera, was an agent of the Guggenheims and Standard Oil. He added that Zapata, too, would send Manuel Palafox to the Convention. Despite his simulated military rank, Palafox was, he thought, as much a civilian as Cabrera and others now in the assembly.

Eduardo Hay replaced Cabrera in the rostrum to suggest that the matter be put over until the next day so that a committee could work out the details of the transfer. But David Berlanga refused to be silenced and demanded once more that the civilians be allowed to go with the Convention, even though Obregón said they could not and Francisco Coss menaced them. Coss bounded up to say that he had never asked the advice of a civilian in battle, and he would not permit them to sit in the military assembly. Berlanga rebutted: "General Coss, we are not dealing here with attacks, marches, and strategy. We are dealing with the future of the nation, and that is not a matter for the military alone to discuss." After various delegates had expressed themselves for or against the proposal, the session was concluded without a vote on the matter.[10]

On October 5 the final session of the Convention was held in Mexico City. As a gesture of reconciliation to all the revolutionary factions the delegates voted to ask Villa, Maytorena, and Carranza to free all of the political prisoners each held. Although the resolution was broadly conceived, it applied almost exclusively to the First Chief. Francisco Villa had not bothered to imprison his enemies when they came into his grasp. Carranza, on the other hand, continued to hold several Zapatista agents incommunicado in Mexico City, as well as some purported Villistas who were seized by the Constitutionalist authorities in the capital. Among these were Enrique C. Llorente, Martín Luis Guzmán, José Vasconcelos, and Luis G. Malváez.[11]

The Convention then voted to uphold Obregón's contention that only the soldiers should be permitted to go to Aguascalientes. But the debate was marred again by bitter and acrimonious recriminations between Cabrera and Obregón. Obregón again expressed his contempt for those who failed to take up arms to redress their wrongs and the wrongs of Mexico. When Madero was murdered by Huerta, he said, the civilians stayed comfortably at home. "They pleaded: 'I'm neutral.' 'I have too many children.' Or 'It would hurt my business.' We, on the other hand, have restored, or tried to restore, their liberties. Now we are going to represent them again. The people are behind us." On this note the junta of chiefs terminated its business in Mexico City. In the face of the hostility manifested against them by the generals the civilians had no choice but to leave the assembly. When the Convention met in Aguascalientes there was no one to represent the civilian viewpoint of Venustiano Carranza.[12]

Confirmed by the Convention, however temporarily, in his position as First Chief, Carranza continued to exercise the executive power in those areas of Mexico dominated by the Constitutionalist armies. Zapata in Morelos and Villa in Chihuahua and Durango controlled virtually independent satrapies, paying no attention to his pretensions of governing all the Republic. But they maintained an armed truce until the Convention should meet in Aguascalientes. If Carranza realized that the extension of his authority and the rejection of his resignation had been a temporary expedient, he did not indicate it by any debility in his government. He designated interim Constitutionalist governors in all states. He decreed the attachment of Quintana Roo to the State of Yucatán, ending its status as a federal territory. To stabilize Mexico's chaotic monetary situation, he decreed the sale of government bonds to the extent of 130 million pesos. In this way he hoped to issue a new national currency to replace the plethora of revolutionary bills. And in international matters, Carranza continued to negotiate with the United States to effect an unconditional withdrawal of the American troops from Mexican territory.

During the first two weeks of October, Carranza and the American State Department sparred politely but firmly on the question of the military occupation of Veracruz. On October 1 Bryan asked Cardoso de Oliveira to take up once more the matter of the guarantees demanded by the government of the United States. He said that his department was "anxiously awaiting" a reply to its message of September 22, requiring such guarantees as a price for American evacuation. And on the following day, Woodrow Wilson wrote to Bryan expressing his concern that the occupation be quickly terminated. He told the Secretary of

State: "I am clear in the judgment that we ought not linger in our departure. It would make a very bad impression not only in Mexico but in Latin America generally, and I sincerely hope that the department's correspondence with the temporary authorities at Mexico City has resulted in something definite which we can use as a basis for handing over the civil authority on our departure. My wish is to get out at the very earliest possible date." [13]

Despite the urgency felt in Washington to turn Veracruz back to the Mexicans, the unyielding demands of the State Department placed Mexico's Constitutionalist government in an embarrassing position. Carranza was asked to give guarantees concerning relations with Mexican citizens in order to secure the release of the port when, from the Mexican viewpoint, the United States had no right to be there in the first place. The rectitude of Carranza's case only stiffened him in what was already a pronounced predilection to be stubborn in his dealings with foreign powers. On October 5 Fabela tardily answered the several requests of the United States. He informed the State Department that Cándido Aguilar had received full instructions from the First Chief to take over the port from the Americans. Fabela made no guarantees; indeed, they were not even mentioned in his note. He asked Washington to fix a date for the departure of Funston's troops.[14]

On October 7 Bryan replied that Fabela's note was not "sufficiently explicit." He repeated the earlier demands for a "clear, explicit, and public" statement from Carranza that in cases where customs duties had been paid to the occupational authorities, no new duties would be collected by the Constitutionalists. And he requested once more that the guarantees of immunity be made to all the citizens of Veracruz, except those guilty of crimes. Bryan stipulated, however, that the acceptance of employment under the military government should not be construed as a criminal act.[15] Isidro Fabela assured Silliman privately that no one would be molested, nor any back duties collected, but he said no such public guarantees could be conceded by his government.[16] Carranza gave his final answer to Bryan on October 27. It was, though framed in diplomatic language, a flat refusal. Fabela informed Cardoso de Oliveira that "Carranza cannot make any statement or issue any manifesto to comply with the requests of the American government, as the affairs to which such requests have reference ought to be of the exclusive initiative of the Mexican authorities. . . ."[17]

The unfortunate American troops in Veracruz were cast between the nether stone of Carranza's obstinacy and the upper stone of Wilson's sense of fair play and decency. They had spent the summer in an unsalubrious, hot climate, many of them troubled with dysentery or malarial attacks. Now the short fall of the year was quickly giving way to the threat of winter storms. Since September 26 the army transports in the harbor had been loaded with the soldiers' gear. They had taken up temporary quarters in tents in the day-to-day expectation of immediate departure. On October 30 Funston cabled the War Department that his troops had "already suffered no inconsiderable hardship." He asked for a quick decision in Washington as to whether the troops must stay or go. If the occupational force was to remain in Veracruz, he said, he must soon begin to build sturdy, permanent barracks. Funston reported that it was the "unanimous opinion" in Veracruz that no canvas tent could withstand the "northers"—the violent winter windstorms from the Texan gulf. There had already been three "mild" storms in which the gusts had "reached only sixty miles per hour," and many of the tents in the encampment had been torn to shreds. Funston warned that the "strong ones" would begin "any time now."[18]

There seemed to be, as the month of November began, no way out of the diplomatic dilemma for either Carranza or Wilson, no way, that is, to escape with honor. Although capricious nature seemed to favor Carranza by conjuring up tempests to drive out the American troops, in the end it was the Mexican who was forced to retreat. An eruption of Mexico's internal difficulties brought back the war which the Convention had hoped to avoid, and Carranza was to need Veracruz as a refuge from the armies of Villa. The First Chief's failure to control the Frankenstein's monster he had created by summoning the Convention led to the renewal of hostilities throughout the Republic.

5

The Revolutionary Convention of Aguascalientes

SO LONG AS MEXICO'S REVOLUTIONARIES HAD A COMMON enemy in Victoriano Huerta their mutual hatreds and jealousies were kept within reasonable bounds. But in the late summer of 1914 relations among the various *caudillos* degenerated. There were no open hostilities (except on a small scale between the Constitutionalists and the Zapatistas), but there seemed no way to achieve permanent peace without a drastic change in the leadership of the revolution. This was the aim of the members of the Convention as they assembled on October 10 in Aguascalientes' Morelos Theater.

They moved quickly to assert their independence from Carranza, voting that they were a sovereign body and not a consultative junta of chiefs. Antonio I. Villarreal, a Carrancista, but a known radical, was chosen as president to replace Eulalio Gutiérrez, while Generals José Isabel Robles and Pánfilo Natera, both of the North, became the Convention's vice-presidents to form the *Mesa Directiva*. After the installation of Villarreal each delegate came forward to swear an oath of allegiance to the Convention and to place his signature on the Mexican flag displayed on the stage of the theater. Villistas and Carrancistas embraced in an impressive demonstration of revolutionary solidarity.[1]

It is a moot point as to whether or not the group in Aguascalientes was the same body which had met in the capital ten days earlier. Most of the delegates at Mexico City did go to Aguascalientes; but some, notably the civilians, did not. Many more came who had not attended the junta, most of these Villistas. The bases for assembling the two groups were diametrically opposed, however. In the capital it had been the First Chief who had conferred credentials upon those he chose. In Aguascalientes the delegates sat in the Convention by a right inherent in their military rank, regardless of any invitation by one chief or a group of chiefs. It was generally accepted by the members themselves, nevertheless, that this was a continuation of the Convention of Mexico City, and the decisions made there were held to be still in effect. Though the assembly returned to Mexico City in January 1915 and subsequently moved to Cuernavaca, and even to Toluca, it was always known thereafter as the Revolutionary Convention of Aguascalientes.

Several sessions were expended in the consideration of credentials. At the insistence of the Villistas, the Convention agreed that an aspirant to membership must demonstrate that he commanded a least one thousand troops and that he had joined the revolution before the battle of Zacatecas.[2] No Johnny-come-lately revolutionaries would be welcomed by the men of the North. This was the formula for admission to the Convention which had been laid down at Torreón by the pact between the Division of the North and Pablo González' Army Corps of the Northeast. In all, fifty-seven generals or governors and ninety-five representatives of other chiefs were in attendance.[3]

Carranza did not appear, nor did he send a representative. For the most part he remained aloof from the proceedings of the Convention or ignored it completely. When Villarreal optimistically informed him of the action of the assembly in declaring its sovereignty, asking him to "display the colors over every public building in the Republic," Carranza demanded to know by what right the Convention took this action.[4] Villa, too, abstained from attending, but he appointed his friend, Colonel Roque González Garza, as his personal agent in the assembly. Villa remained as skeptical as ever about the possibilities of peace with Carranza. He was disgruntled by the failure of the Convention in Mexico City to accept the resignation of the First Chief. He was evidently unaware that the resolution had been merely to postpone the decision until the arrival of the Villistas in Aguascalientes. On October 12, Villa wrote to his agent in the United States, Felix A. Sommerfeld, that any hopes he had held that a conflict could be avoided had now vanished completely. He said that he would not permit Carranza to remain in power, that this would be "detrimental to the country and obnoxious to the interest of the revolution." Villa anticipated that hostilities would soon occur, in which case "we are ready to defend once more the interests of the people." [5]

Day by day, the Convention continued to mark time, pending the arrival of the Zapatistas, and there was much wonderment concerning the size of Zapata's expected delegation. The number of the Southern forces was not known in Aguascalientes. All of Zapatista Mexico was, in fact, shrouded with mystery, and Zapata, himself, was already a legend. As session succeeded barren session, it seemed that Zapata was rebuffing or ignoring the Convention. It is true that Carranza's threat to arrest any Zapatistas encountered in the capital, and the maintenance of Constitutionalist garrisons around Mexico City, made it difficult for a delegation to leave Morelos, even had Zapata so desired. But *Zapatismo* was too egocentric and xenophobic to respond to a general call for representation from all factions. Unable to attract Zapata to Aguascalientes, the Convention determined to go to his mountains. On October 16, the delegates voted to send a direct invitation by General Felipe Angeles, one of the most personable members of the Convention.[6]

Meanwhile, Francisco Villa made his headquarters at Guadalupe, a railroad station one hundred miles north of Aguascalientes and a short distance from Zacatecas. The neutrality of Aguascalientes and the Convention was assured by the troops of Pánfilo Natera, who policed the town. On October 17, Villa came down to render his oath of allegiance to the Convention, and he too added his signature to the banner in the Morelos Theater. He made a short address to the assembly disavowing any desire for self-aggrandizement. As he left the theater to return to Guadalupe, he and Obregón exchanged *abrazos* of apparent amity.[7] Villa's earlier threats against Obregón in Chihuahua seemed to have been forgotten. Back at his headquarters, Villa informed Carothers that he would support any provisional president the Convention might designate, "except Carranza." He promised that, while that body was in Aguascalientes, he would remain in Guadalupe "free of politics." [8]

Because Villa had visited the Convention and was represented there by González Garza, the delegates voted at a secret session to extend the same courtesies to Venustiano Carranza, who continued to ignore the earlier invitation to come to Aguascalientes. A delegation was dispatched to Mexico City to make the invitation a personal one. But Carranza, his civilian advisers, and his newspapers were becoming daily more hostile to the Convention and its claims of sovereignty. It was maintained in Mexico City that the Convention was still no more than an advisory "junta," without competence to make political decisions.

Heriberto Barrón's *El Liberal* and Ciro B. Ceballos' *El Pueblo* took the lead in ridiculing the sovereignty of the Convention. On October 17 *El Liberal* carried a viciously sarcastic editorial by Barrón, "Desconozcamos a Don Venustiano." In words purporting to come from Aguascalientes, he wrote: "Let us refuse to recognize Don Venustiano. But why not more? To finish the job let us hang him from a tree in the Plaza de Armas, crying with the voice of Stentor: Long live Huerta! Death to Don Venustiano!" [9]

The editorial elicited from Obregón a vigorous letter of protest. And even General Eduardo Hay, an ardent Carrancista, wrote to Barrón that he considered the attack on the Convention to be "unpatriotic." [10] The newspapers in the capital carried almost daily reports alleging that the lives of the members of the assembly were endangered in Aguascalientes. An editorial in *El Pueblo* on October 20, "A new coup d'état?," stated that forces of Villa were but an hour's journey from the site of the Convention. "Is it possible," wrote the editor, "that under such conditions the Conventionists can have the freedom to speak and to work as their consciences dictate?" *El Pueblo* advocated that the delegates move to another, more neutral city, lest Villa disperse them, as Huerta had dissolved the Federal Congress in 1913.[11]

It is true that assaults on members of the Convention or upon their retinues were not infrequent. Marcelino Murrieta complained in the Convention on October 19 that he and other delegates had been accosted by drunken soldiers and at pistol point had been forced to shout "Viva Villa!" And later the same day, for the first time, the officers of the Convention found need to place a guard before the doors of the Morelos Theater, because of rumors of attempts to disrupt the meetings and force the assembly to move to another city. These rumors soon proved to be baseless, however.

The charges that Villa dominated Aguascalientes and thereby the Convention, first made in the the Constitutionalist newspapers in Mexico City, can in no way be substantiated, however. A careful analysis of the recorded debates shows no such pressure on the delegates. The instances when members of the Convention were molested or forced to shout "Vivas" for Francisco Villa were not overly numerous, under the circumstances. These occurrences were isolated acts of irresponsible, ignorant soldiers on drunken sprees. Although the forces of Natera patrolled the city to "neutralize" it, most chiefs in attendance at the Convention had brought at least a small contingent of soldiers with them. There was never any attempt, however, to force the Convention to bend its will to that of Villa or of any other revolutionary leader. The members were free to debate and vote as they pleased. During the sessions of October 21 and 22 there were heated protests against such allegations in the press of the capital. The delegates particularly took as an insult Barrón's rude editorial on the recognition of the First Chief. They voted to invite Barrón to come to Aguascalientes in person to see the true conditions for himself. In the following sessions a motion of censure, supported by most of the Carrancistas, was adopted by the Convention against both Barrón and Ceballos.[12]

Whatever motives might be ascribed to the delegates to explain the subsequent decisions of the Convention, fear of Villa was not one of them. Villa scrupulously kept his promise to remain in Guadalupe with his troops until the rupture between Carranza and the Convention had become complete. The majority of the delegates, including the non-Villistas, were as willing as Villa to deprive Carranza of his First Chieftaincy. By the end of the second week of sessions in Aguascalientes the real import of the decision in Mexico City to refuse Carranza's resignation was clear. Carranza could not reasonably expect to remain in office long. As the Convention awaited the arrival of the illusive Zapatista delegation, Villarreal and Eduardo Hay were openly canvassing for votes in the expected election of a successor for Carranza. The Villistas had as yet no candidate of their own, but indicated that, like their chief, they would support anyone except Carranza.[13]

Francisco Villa was not idle in Guadalupe, however. He planned for—perhaps even hoped for—a renewal of conflict. He assured Carothers that though he was "using no pressure whatsoever" upon the Convention in Aguascalientes, he was prepared for any hostile act by Carranza. He seemed, according to Carothers, to find great pleasure in contemplating war against the First Chief.[14] It was the aim of the Convention to prevent hostilities by eliminating Carranza and replacing him with a provisional executive acceptable to all factions.

Felipe Angeles passed through Mexico City and arrived in Cuernavaca on October 22. Zapata was in Tlaltizapán, but he consented to come over to Cuernavaca with his staff to receive the emissaries from the Convention. Angeles later described the attitude of Zapata as that of "courtesy and cordiality," which contrasted strongly with the reception accorded Villarreal and Cabrera by the men of the South. When Angeles explained the nature of his mission Zapata expressed his willingness to be represented in the Convention. He regretted, however, that, because of the extent of his lines and the difficulty in consulting all of his chiefs, he could send but twenty-six representatives at that time. The Southern leader stated his wish that this interim delegation be given "voice and vote" in the proceedings of the assembly until the full number should arrive.[15]

When reports reached the Convention that the Zapatista train had cleared Mexico City unmolested by the Constitutionalist authorities, the members expected that their vigil of two weeks would end on October 24 or on the following morning at the latest. But the train arrived in Aguascalientes and continued through to the North without stopping. The Southern delegation had expressed the wish to go first to Guadalupe in order to "exchange impressions with Villa." [16] For most of the Zapatistas it was a journey to the utter antipodes, for they had never before been this far from home. During the entire train ride they maintained an attitude of almost feral vigilance, born of the years of revolution against Díaz, Madero, Huerta, and Carranza. It was a picturesque group; most wore the accouterments of Morelos and of Zapatista Mexico—the huge, wide-brimmed sombrero, the skin-tight breeches with a peasant blouse. Even Antonio Díaz Soto y Gama, an intellectual and a lawyer from San Luis Potosí, had affected the peasant garb of Morelos. Among the twenty-six, in addition to Díaz Soto y Gama, were Gildardo Magaña, Otilio E. Montaño, to whom Zapata had dictated the Plan of Ayala, and Paulino Martínez, a Zapatista journalist. Five bore the rank of general, sixteen were colonels, while the rest were of lower grade. None, ostensibly, was a civilian.

On the morning of October 26, the party entered the Morelos Theater. They passed over the threshold, according to Vito Alessio Robles, who was a recording secretary of the Convention, with the same precautions taken by a troop of soldiers crossing a dangerous defile. Some of the Carrancista delegates noted with pleasure that Zapata had sent only twenty-six representatives. Since Villa had but thirty-seven, a coalition of these two parties could still be outvoted by the rest of the assembly. No business was conducted during that session, the time being spent in polite formalities. Most were meeting the Zapatistas for the first time. With pride, the men of the South were shown the flag upon which all the delegates of the Convention had placed their signatures.[17]

The following day saw a wonderful metamorphosis among the Zapatistas. No longer did they act as though hunted. Their wariness was gone and they were now full of self-assurance. They began to press the Convention for concessions to the South as their price for cooperation in the assembly. As the session opened on the morning of October 27, Paulino Martínez was led to the rostrum, amid clamorous applause, to speak for the Zapatistas. He reviewed for the Convention the history of the revolution, the revolution, that is, of the South. He was scornful of the Liberal notions that magic words like "effective suffrage" and "no re-election" could heal all of Mexico's ills. The real needs of the people, he said, were for "bread and justice." These ideals could be achieved only by Villa and Zapata, "Indians, both of them," not by the Constitutionalists, and only under the banner of the Plan of Ayala.

"Land and Liberty! Land and Justice! With these the Plan of Ayala will bring economic liberty to the Mexican people." The Army of the South, he said, did not fight for special privileges or for riches, nor was it ambitious for the presidential chair. Rather it fought for "a home for every family and a piece of bread for all those who have been deprived of their heritage. . . ." "Farms, . . . lands for all"—the Plan of Guadalupe could guarantee none of these. Therefore, said Martínez, the Zapatistas would continue to reject that plan and could never accept Carranza as the chief of the revolution. He concluded by inviting all the delegates to embrace the Zapatista Plan of Ayala as the sole standard for the Convention. Martínez' speech was a welcome exhortation to the Villistas, for an alliance between the men of the North and the South was a natural result of their mutual antagonism toward Carranza.[18]

The mood of revolutionary amity and camaraderie received a rude jolt when Paulino Martínez was succeeded in the rostrum by Antonio Díaz Soto y Gama. At the age of thirty, Díaz Soto was already an accomplished revolutionary. He had been a Flores Magonista, a founder, with Rafael Pérez Taylor, of a Mexican Socialist Party, and was now a colonel and one of Zapata's secretaries. He knew nothing of the battlefield; his forte was the quintain of parliamentary oratory. Díaz Soto had a propensity for inciting dislike. He talked too much, heaping abuse and scorn upon his listeners as unfeelingly as though he were unloading garbage in the public dump. His subsequent rationalization was that he was an "anarchist," though this is scarcely an explanation for his bizarre behavior, and certainly not an exculpation. Perhaps all that can be said is that he was the complete revolutionary, in the intellectual, if not the physical, sense of the word. By his speech on that day, he made the session of October 27, 1914, one of the most memorable in the history of the Convention.

Díaz Soto began disarmingly enough, assuring the delegates that he had not come before them to make attacks, but rather to arouse patriotism and honor. He challenged them to have the courage to defy both Carranza and Villa and to speak within the Convention whatever was in their hearts. He spoke of the integrity of the Convention and affirmed that the delegates' word of honor was more important than a few names scribbled upon the flag. As he spoke, he seized the banner, which was draped beside him on the stage, crumpling it in his fist and shaking it at his audience. This rag, he said, disdainfully, was but the symbol for the triumph of clerical reaction, "headed by Iturbide."

As Díaz Soto profaned the colors of the Republic, the Conventionists stirred uneasily in their seats and murmured at his lack of patriotism. There were cries of "No! No!" Oblivious or unheeding of the magma of anger which was seething beneath him, he continued to belabor his theme: "I, gentlemen, will never sign this banner. We are making a great revolution today to destroy the lies of history, and we are going to expose the lie of history that is in this flag. That which we have been wont to call our independence was no independence for the native race, but for the creoles alone. And if the heirs of the conquerors, who have infamously continued to cheat the oppressed ones and the indigenous. . . ." By now his voice had disappeared in the rumblings of protest. As he still held the crushed banner in his hand, hisses and shouts of rage rained upon him. Eulalio Gutiérrez, the stolid countryman, was moved to cry: "More respect for the flag! You are a traitor!" [19]

It is fortunate that Leon J. Canova was present during the tumult. In one of his colorful and lengthy dispatches to Bryan he has left a fine account of it:

The members of the Convention rose to their feet, their faces livid with indignation, trembling, and shaking their fists at the speaker, who stood calmly in the tribune above them, awaiting the passing of the storm. The beautiful flag, which was affixed on the left side of the stage, was snatched away and borne to the center, while on the floor pandemonium was rampant. The delegates screamed at one another, with left hands pounding their chests, and their right hands on their pistols, for all were mad. The chairman was pounding the bell for order, but the sound of the bell could not be heard. Hay, González Garza, and others were in all parts of the house at once, endeavoring to calm the uproar. From the crowded boxes and galleries of the theater, humanity was tumbling over itself in a mad effort to escape imminent danger. Obregón, Hay, and other prominent delegates mounted to the stage or stood by the flag. Presently, out of the hubbub, quiet reigned as suddenly as the tumult had begun.

Throughout the disorder the Zapatista orator remained motionless in the rostrum. He seemed unaware of the threats made against him or of the cocked pistols leveled at his breast. It was a courageous, if foolhardy, act. When the storm of anger had subsided and Díaz Soto was finally permitted to continue, he protested that he had been misunderstood. He made no apologies to the Convention but assured the delegates that he meant no disrespect for the colors. He concluded by echoing Martínez' eulogy of the Plan of Ayala: "For that banner . . . we men of the South have come to do battle!" [20]

As Díaz Soto dismounted from the platform Carrancista Eduardo Hay took his place. Before he made a reply to the previous speakers, he ostentatiously pressed the Mexican colors to his lips, as though to emphasize the lack of patriotism of the Zapatistas. This gesture brought heavy applause from the delegates and the public galleries. Hay noted that Díaz Soto had disclaimed any personalist motives. Yet it seemed to him, he said, that the Southerners were in truth personalists. The Constitutionalists were willing to reject the Plan of Guadalupe if it pleased them to do so, he insisted. Hay warned, however, that they were not willing to accept the Plan of Ayala in its entirety, if they did not like parts of it. Directing himself to Díaz Soto, he declared that the Convention would admit only those delegates who were "genuine representatives of the people." He continued: "And you, Sr. Soto y Gama, if you want, you may come here to preach socialism. We have socialists here, but not those who simply talk. . . . Our socialists are those who can act without preaching about it. We know that our people will not be ready to listen to socialistic doctrines until they get bread and peace. Without these, socialism would turn into anarchism." [21] Díaz Soto's reputation as an anarchist had preceded him to Aguascalientes, and his political predilections were to make him the butt of many a jest by his enemies for the duration of the Convention.

Colonel Alfredo Serratos, coatless, wearing khaki trousers, a brown shirt, leggings, and a black neckerchief, came forward to defend Díaz Soto against the attack by Hay. Pointing at the colors, he said that the Zapatistas did not carry that flag while fighting against their brothers. Rather, they went into battle with courage in their hearts and their rifles in their hands. He assured the Convention that if the time should ever come when Mexico was at war with a foreign enemy, then the Southern army would follow the Mexican colors to a man. When he had finished he took his seat with the greatest outburst of applause of the entire session.[22]

While many delegates clamored to be recognized, Roque González Garza spoke up from the floor for the Villistas to support the men from the South. "I am in accord," he said, "with absolutely everything that Sr. Soto y Gama has said here. . . . I announce in the name of [Villa] that the principles of the Plan of Ayala are those of the Division of the North." Alvaro Obregón, "visibly agitated and with his voice filled with doubt and choler," challenged the Northern delegates to say whether González Garza represented the opinion of them all. Angeles replied that while González Garza could speak only for Villa, "if there are any doubts about the matter, I should like to declare personally that I adhere to the principles of the Plan of Ayala." To satisfy Obregón as to the sentiments of the other members of the Division of the North, González Garza asked all the Villistas who would not accept the principles of the plan to remain seated. All rose to their feet with alacrity. When they had resumed their seats, González Garza asked those who opposed the plan to rise. Every delegate from the North sat fast. It was an impressive demonstration of unity among the men of Villa and Zapata.[23]

González Garza then asked the representatives of the Army of the South if they were disposed to accept the invitation to become members of the Convention. Instead of answering González Garza directly, Paulino Martínez equivocated: "When this honorable assembly has adhered to the principles of the revolution, we of the South will not find it inconvenient to collaborate with it. . . ." Díaz Soto placed a price upon cooperation by the Zapatistas. They made two demands, he said: That the Plan of Ayala be accepted by the Convention unconditionally; and that Carranza be removed as First Chief of the Constitutionalist revolution.[24] As the arrogance of the Zapatistas was revealed to the Convention, their Plan of Ayala began to appear more and more like the bed of an Indian Procrustes.

As the session of October 25 opened, Villarreal announced that the credentials of each of the Zapatistas would be considered individually, since that had been the procedure with the other delegates to the Convention. This statement brought a buzz of angry protests from the Southerners, who by now had made themselves thoroughly and rudely at home in the Morelos Theater. Antonio Díaz Soto y Gama, Zapata's personal representative and the chief Southern spokesman during the life of the Convention, explained that the twenty-six had come to Aguascalientes as a commission, seeking the adherence of the Convention to their program. They were not, he said, delegates asking admission. If a program of reform was adopted that was to their satisfaction—that is, if the Plan of Ayala were accepted in its entirety—then they would ask all of the chiefs of the South to send their delegates.

For the first time, the Carrancistas and Villistas were made aware that the Zapatistas intended to send more than twenty-six delegates to the Convention. This news was unsettling to the Carrancistas, who had complacently seen the representatives of Villa and Zapata as a permanent minority. Although the Southern "commissioners" refused to submit credentials or become members of the Convention at that time, they quite illogically demanded the rights of "voice and vote" in the proceedings of that body. They were granted the first, but were not accorded voting rights until they should bring their credentials before the assembly.[25]

During the discussion of the number of Zapatista delegates to be expected, Díaz Soto asserted that the Army of the South counted sixty thousand well-armed troops. If this estimate was correct, the Southerners might well claim sixty seats in the Convention. Obregón interrupted to say sardonically that, while they all respected Zapata and his men for continuing their revolution with few soldiers and poor arms, he doubted whether the Army of the South had as many troops as Díaz Soto claimed. If there had really been sixty thousand well-armed men in Morelos, asked Obregón, why had they not taken Mexico City, when he and the Constitutionalists had accomplished this task with only twenty-six thousand men.

Obregón had driven his barb deep in a festering wound, for the Zapatistas could not forget the means by which Obregón had been given the capital, while they themselves had been fended away by both the Federals and the Constitutionalists. Paulino Martínez retorted to Obregón that if he had entered Mexico City before the Army of the South, it was only because of the "deal" made at Teoloyucan with Carbajal and Velasco. In any event, said Martínez, the Zapatistas had no political ambitions and had never desired to take the capital. He charged that the hostilities begun by the Constitutionalists against the forces of the South had never ceased to the present moment. Within the past few hours, he related, the Zapatistas had "driven back the Carrancistas from Tizapán and from Matamoros Izúcar."

Despite the truculent attitude of the Zapatistas and the angry words between Obregón and Martínez, the Convention was in a mood to conciliate the men of the South. When Martínez had concluded, the members voted to accept the Plan of Ayala "in principle," while reserving the right to reject those articles which were not consonant with the ideals of the Convention.[26] It was not, however, a clear-cut victory for Zapata, for the words "in principle" could cover a multitude of hedging and evasive actions on the part of the assembly. The Carrancistas were still in the majority in the Convention. Their disposition to see the First Chief replaced did not turn them willy-nilly into ardent bedfellows of the more radical Villistas and Zapatistas.

In its dealings with Carranza, the Convention had become increasingly unmindful of his asserted prerogatives, and the invitation to him to come in person or to send a representative to Aguascalientes did not alter the estrangement. As First Chief, he could do neither. To have become a delegate would have put him on equal footing with a hundred others, his vote having no more weight than that of a captain or a major. And even to have sent a representative, as Villa had done, would have been a tacit admission on his part that he recognized the sovereignty of the Convention, that it was more than a "junta" of advisers with no legal status. Further, Carranza could see the political winds blowing against him as the Convention moved to elect his successor as First Chief. He determined, therefore, upon a spectacular gesture to force the hands of his enemies. He composed and sent to Obregón, on October 23, a reply to the invitation of the Convention, though the contents of the letter were kept secret until after the arrival of the Zapatistas.

On October 29 Obregón dramatically opened the sealed envelope to read to the assembly the message of the First Chief. Taking cognizance of the opposition of some members of the Convention, Carranza termed these delegates "reactionary." The real reason these persons wanted to separate him from his power, he said, was that he was "too radical" for them. If the Convention should decide, however, that he was an obstacle to revolutionary unity, wrote Carranza, he was "disposed to retire" as First Chief. But the price for his resignation, he insisted, must be the simultaneous retirement of Villa and Zapata. If the Convention should find "patriotic means" to solve the present difficulties, he would "march in accord" with it. But if the delegates should fail, he warned, to display the same self-abnegation as he, and if, as a result, the salvation of the country should devolve upon him, then he would summon all the Constitutionalist forces to rally around him once more to fight against the "enemies of the liberty of the Mexican people." [27]

The letter's final note of hostility vexed many of the delegates, and the Zapatistas were especially outraged by the gratuitous demand of Carranza for the demission of their own leader. The men of Villa were no less caustic in their comments on the message of the First Chief. Despite his loud pleas for order and pounding upon the bell, Villarreal lost control of the assembly, and the session broke down into hoots, catcalls, insults, and personal attacks among the members of the various delegations.[28] If Carranza had hoped to sow seeds of discord in the Convention, he had succeeded eminently. In the last days of October, the bickering and wrangling between the factions threatened to rend the Convention.

With Obregón as the chief peacemaker, a group of delegates, including Aguirre Benavides, Gutiérrez, Chao, Martín Espinosa, Guillermo García Aragón, Raúl Madero, and Miguel M. Peralta, sought to find a formula satisfactory to all. On October 30, they presented for the approval of the Convention a letter to Carranza. The resignation of Carranza would now be accepted in the best interests of the country, but glowing tribute would be paid him for his patriotic labors for the revolution. The Zapatistas could not see peace restored so easily, however. When Obregón had finished presenting his resolution, they immediately demanded the right to vote upon, as well as discuss, the dismissal of Carranza. Díaz Soto proposed the formation of a triumvirate to lead the revolution, one of the three to be a representative of the Army of the South. Obregón thereupon accused the Zapatistas of extorting concessions from the Convention, though they were unwilling to make any themselves. Because the representatives of Zapata still refused to present credentials, insisting they were only "commissioners," their request to vote on Carranza's dismissal was denied.[29]

In the afternoon, the Constitutionalist delegates proposed that Carranza's letter be discussed in a secret session in order to avoid public scandal. But the Zapatistas, notably Díaz Soto, contended that matters of such transcendent importance for Mexico must be debated in public. As Díaz Soto poured vials of hatred upon the name of Carranza, accusing him and his lieutenants, Luis Cabrera and Rafael Zubarán Capmany, of intrigues against the Convention, Obregón broke into his diatribe on a point of order. "I shall not permit you to interrupt me, sir," cried Zapata's representative. "I have the floor!" Obregón shouted in return: "I protest!" But he could not dam the flow of angry words by Díaz Soto.

When Díaz Soto concluded his attack upon the Carrancistas, Eduardo Hay attempted to conciliate the dissentious delegates. He supported the Constitutionalist demands for a secret session, but stressed the heavy responsibilities for peace placed on all the members of the Convention, "those of us who have signed our names on this banner." As he gestured respectfully at the signatures on the flag, he added in the rude language of the soldier: ". . . los que serán tachados más bien con mierda que con oro!" This unwonted obscenity in the midst of a parliamentary debate elicited hisses of censure from the floor of the assembly, and Hay quickly apologized for "esta palabra." [30]

Over the protests of the Zapatistas, the assembly then voted to recess and to continue the discussion of Carranza's letter with the public excluded from the galleries. In the secret session the delegates agreed on the elimination of both Villa and Carranza from their commands. No decision was made on Carranza's demand for the resignation of Emiliano Zapata. By an overwhelming vote, the "resignations" of Carranza and Villa were accepted by the Convention, though at that time the Carrancistas possessed an absolute majority and could easily have overridden the wishes of the Villistas to keep Carranza in his post. Only twenty delegates supported Carranza's continued tenure in office.[31]

The assembly failed to observe, or deliberately overlooked, Carranza's hedging statement that he was only "disposed to resign." Villa expressed his willingness to abide by the decision of the Convention, but his reply to the resolution contained the hidden threat of a booby trap. In writing to the delegates he showed clearly that he anticipated trouble with Carranza. He said that he was prepared to place himself and his troops "at the disposal of the Convention." He did not seem to take at all seriously Carranza's "resignation." [32]

In the first days of November, the Convention moved to complete the transfer of power from Carranza to a provisional president to be selected from among the members of that body. The delegates gave no consideration to an extension of the First Chieftaincy. As various generals cast straws to the political winds, the leading candidates were Antonio I. Villarreal and José I. Robles. Villarreal, the radical Carrancista, appeared to have the support of the majority in the Convention. The Zapatistas, remembering Villarreal as an emissary from Carranza to Zapata in August and September, proved to be unalterably opposed to his candidacy, however. And since the representatives from the South had been denied the right to vote upon a provisional president, they insisted that the person designated by the Convention serve for only fifteen days, or until November 20, when the full Zapatista delegation would presumably be in Aguascalientes to "ratify or reject" the choice of the assembly.

Because the Constitutionalists refused to support a Villista while the Zapatistas extended their opposition to Villarreal to include any Carrancista, the Convention reached a stalemate. Obregón then took the initiative in calling for a recess and prevailed upon the dissident groups to accept Eulalio Gutiérrez as a compromise candidate. When Díaz Soto indicated that the Southerners would approve the election of Gutiérrez, his name was proposed to the assembly and quickly accepted.[33]

Eulalio Gutiérrez was not a leading revolutionary figure and was a man of limited capabilities. He was, nonetheless, completely honorable and well-meaning. As a general who had done little to incur the animosity of any man, he was the perfect compromise candidate. Gutiérrez was a native of the state of Coahuila, but he had lived during the Porfirian regime in Concepción del Oro, Zacatecas. He had served the revolution under Madero as a member of the staff of Rafael Cepeda, governor of San Luis Potosí. Before the coup of Huerta he had returned to Concepción del Oro, where he found employment with the Mazapil Copper Company as a mining foreman. In the spring of 1913, Gutiérrez "pronounced" against Huerta and led forces in the triangle between Saltillo, San Luis Potosí, and Concepción del Oro. He had gained some fame in the revolution, since he had few troops and little armament, in blasting railroad bridges and trains. At the time of his unexpected designation as Mexico's provisional president, Gutiérrez was the military governor of San Luis Potosí.[34]

Although Gutiérrez' elevation to the presidency had been chiefly due to Obregón's endeavors in the Convention, many Constitutionalists rallied to the support of Carranza. Villa gave credence to the doubts as to the authenticity of his "resignation" by shifting several thousand troops from Zacatecas into the northern part of the state of Aguascalientes. For the first time

a threat loomed to the neutrality of the Convention. Learning
of these Villista troop movements, Pablo González telegraphed
the assembly from Querétaro that Villa's actions infringed upon
the freedom of the assembly to act independently, that he would
refuse to accept any decision of that body until it complied with
all of Carranza's stipulations. Francisco Coss, the Carrancista
military commander in Puebla, was even more bellicose. He
ordered his representative at Aguascalientes, Rafael de la Torre,
to withdraw from the Convention. And he informed the members of the assembly that he would continue to recognize only
Carranza as First Chief.[35]

Gutiérrez was now faced with the superhuman task of organizing a stable government out of the congeries of revolutionary
hostilities and jealousies. He had to placate the Constitutionalists and woo them from the First Chief, without alienating the
Villistas and Zapatistas. Hoping to gain the support of the Army
of the South, he offered Paulino Martínez a post in his government. Martínez was pleased with the choice of Gutiérrez as
"presidente accidental." He wrote to Zapata soon after the election that the new president was a "radical." As governor of San
Luis Potosí, said Martínez, he had always demonstrated his concern for the rural classes of the state. Gutiérrez had "shot many
of the old caciques and made prisoners of the rest." Martínez
refused Gutiérrez' offer of a cabinet position, but he insisted,
as the most prominent Zapatista at the Convention, that the posts
of Commerce and Agriculture belonged to the South.[36]

The Convention voted on November 3 to send a commission
to Mexico City to deliver to Carranza in person the notification
that his "resignation" had been accepted and that Gutiérrez
had been named in his stead. The message, carried by Obregón,
Aguirre Benavides, and Eduardo Ruiz, informed Carranza that
the Convention had voted him the rank of general of division to
honor his services to the revolution. At the same time, by the
orders of the Convention, all revolutionary armies and divisions
were to be broken up into units no larger than brigades and
placed under the command of Gutiérrez' Secretary of War.[37] In

this way, the delegates hoped to avoid hostilities between Villa and Carranza. When the commission arrived in the capital, however, Carranza had already left the city.

In the crisis between the First Chief and the truculent Convention, Carranza was plagued by the difficulties of the civilian leader surrounded and protected by troops of dubious loyalty. Whether as a matter of policy on the part of Carranza or quite by chance, the troops used by Obregón in capturing Mexico City had been dissipated while Obregón was in Aguascalientes. In the capital, only Lucio Blanco, with his strong force of cavalry, remained to ward off the Zapatistas. But Blanco had been a prime mover in the agreement to shift the Convention to Aguascalientes, and his actions in late October and through November indicated that he fancied for himself a larger role in the revolution than he had occupied heretofore. Taking cognizance of rumors of the impending defection of Blanco and concerned for his own safety, Carranza determined to forsake the capital to seek refuge with Coss in the safer terrain to the East. On Sunday, November 1, even before the election of Gutiérrez, Carranza entrained for San Juan Teotihuacán, ostensibly on a sightseeing tour among the pyramids. Though he could not have known it at the time, he was not to return to Mexico City for more than a year. Safely away from the capital, Carranza went by rail to Apizaco and thence to Tlaxcala. Here in the ancient Nahua citadel, the First Chief awaited the decision of the Convention.[38]

The exodus of Carranza's government began on November 3 as members of his cabinet left the capital on a special train, taking with them the Constitutionalist archives. Although Isidro Fabela informed the foreign diplomatic representatives that the cabinet would return within a day or two, it was apparent that Carranza intended to forsake Mexico City permanently. Assured of the fidelity of Francisco Coss, Carranza moved his headquarters from Tlaxcala to Puebla, where he was joined by his cabinet.[39]

On November 4 Carranza received a message from Obregón, who had gone to Querétaro to confer with Pablo González, that the commission he headed was bringing a message from the Convention. Carranza replied that it was useless to come to Puebla, for he, himself, would shortly be in Querétaro. It is highly improbable that the First Chief intended to forsake his sanctuary to venture as far north as Querétaro. At this juncture he had grave misgivings about the loyalty of Obregón and feared even to let him come to Puebla. The demeanor of Obregón at Aguascalientes in leading the movement in the Convention to replace Carranza with Gutiérrez was reason enough for the alarm of the First Chief. As he rebuffed Obregón in one message, Carranza sent another to the Convention directing the delegates' attention to his three conditions for his withdrawal. He warned the recalcitrant members of the "junta" that he was receiving assurances of loyalty from many generals and governors. All of these, he said, disapproved of, or rejected, the decisions made in Aguascalientes.[40]

The members of the Convention reacted sharply to the strong note of hostility in Carranza's message. On November 5 they voted that, unless he delivered the executive power to Gutiérrez by 6 P.M. on November 10, he would be considered to be in rebellion against the Convention. And on the following day, in open defiance of Carranza's authority as First Chief, the Convention formally installed Gutiérrez as Mexico's provisional president. By now all of Villa's troops had moved into the state of Aguascalientes to await the Convention's declaration of war should Carranza persist in his defiance. Villa still gave no sign that he intended to relinquish his command of the Division of the North.[41]

Undeterred by Carranza's refusal to see the commission, Obregón went from Querétaro through Mexico City to Puebla, only to find that Carranza had moved on to Córdoba in the state of Veracruz. Despite the unquestioned loyalty of Coss, Carranza was not entirely safe in Puebla. It was uncomfortably close to Mexico City, a few hours' train ride away. And the troops of Zapata's Army of the South, notably ex-Federals under Juan Andrew Almazán, ranged at will through the countryside, menacing even the city of Puebla. Carranza found it prudent, therefore, to take the route of Juárez during the War of the Reform, to retire to the state of Veracruz. Soon, he hoped, the United States would turn over the port city to Cándido Aguilar, and he could move the seat of his government there.

From Córdoba the First Chief published on November 8 an answer to the ultimatum of the Convention. He was in no mood to capitulate, even when confronted by the overwhelming might of Villa. As before, he scorned the pretensions of authority by the Convention: "Until this day I have never for a single moment recognized the sovereignty of that junta." He denied that the military officers in Aguascalientes could give him, their chief, orders of any kind. As for the deadline set by the assembly for compliance with its demands, Carranza ordered all the members there under his command to withdraw before the evening of the tenth.[42] In that moment there seemed little likelihood of a peaceful solution.

Obregón arrived in Córdoba on November 9 to meet with the First Chief. As Villa moved his troops toward Mexico City, Obregón had begun to have misgivings about having foisted Gutiérrez upon the Convention. His assurances of loyalty to Carranza at this time helped strengthen the latter's hand in his dealings with the Villistas. In public Obregón continued to maintain a façade of optimism for peace. Privately, however, he vowed to fight Villa "to the death" if the Division of the North continued to menace the Constitutionalist forces.[43] On the same day, Carranza telegraphed the Convention to acknowledge the arrival of its commission. But he reminded the assembly that his letter of October 23 was in no way a resignation. It contained, he said, only the conditions under which he was "disposed to resign" his office. Carranza informed the Convention that he was unable to recognize the authority of Gutiérrez, since that general did not possess the qualifications for high office. Gutiérrez had been designated to the executive power, Carranza said, without his having relinquished it. He ridiculed the claims of the Convention that Villa had been retired from his command.

Villa continued to exercise military and civil control of the area north of Aguascalientes, said Carranza, and even administered the customs houses on the frontier.[44]

When the term set by the Convention had passed with no act of compliance by Carranza, the remaining members declared him in rebellion. Nevertheless, Gutiérrez continued to express optimism at achieving a reconciliation. And in a last-minute effort to stave off civil war, he telegraphed Carranza on November 10 to plead with the deposed First Chief to carry out the intention to resign he had revealed when the Convention first met in Mexico City. "If you recognized that Convention," said Gutiérrez, "there is greater reason for recognizing that of Aguascalientes, for in the latter are represented all the factions of the Revolution." He concluded by exhorting Carranza to order all his followers to accept the government of the Convention. Carranza retorted telegraphically from Córdoba that he considered Gutiérrez' appointment illegal, "because you have been named president by a junta which cannot name presidents. . . . There is no law which authorized that junta to designate a president of the Republic, nor plan, nor document, nor treaty." Directing himself to the Convention, Carranza said: "You were called together purely as a consultative body. You think that because you call yourselves sovereign that fact gives you the right to do as you please, even to name a president. To conclude, I tell you that I am not disposed to hand over my power. . . ." [45]

In the city of Silao, several leading Constitutionalist generals, including Obregón, Blanco, González, Villarreal, and Hay, met to decide what course they might pursue in the critical situation. Because of reports from Aguascalientes which showed that Villa's "retirement" had been a fiction, they united in a demand upon the Convention that Villa disassociate himself immediately from all connection with the political and military affairs in his area. When this was done, they said, they would pledge their support to the Convention and its provisional president, Gutiérrez. If Villa should resist the orders of the Convention, however, they promised to fight against him. The Constitutionalist generals suggested that the Convention could give Villa a mission which would take him out of the country. If Villa were willing to exile himself for the good of Mexico, they would, in turn, secure Carranza's retirement and exile.[46]

Gutiérrez responded that he had restored Villa to his old post only after the Convention had declared Carranza a rebel. If Carranza would now retire voluntarily from power, promised Gutiérrez, then Villa's forces would again be taken from him. He added, rather optimistically in view of his subsequent debility before Villa, that he would remain personally responsible for Villa's retirement.[47] The absurdity of the revolutionary predicament was now revealed by the mutually exclusive demands. Carranza was "disposed" to resign if Villa did so first. Villa would be retired by Gutiérrez if Carranza made the first move. In the middle of November 1914 Carranza and Gutiérrez played Alphonse and Gaston, while Mexico drifted into chaos.

The next few days saw a welter of charges and counter-charges, offers and counter-offers in which Pablo González, Lucio Blanco, and Eulalio Gutiérrez tried vainly to find a peaceful way out of the impasse. As a last resort, Blanco assembled a group of Liberal civilians in the capital to propose to Carranza, once more, that he yield his authority to Fernando Iglesias Calderón. But this scheme failed to move either Carranza or the Convention.[48] Carranza did agree, however, after consultations with González, to make one ultimate concession to the Convention. On November 15 he offered to relinquish his authority to a person of his entire confidence, such as González. In turn, Villa should be required to turn over the territory under his domination to Gutiérrez. The two chiefs, Villa and Carranza, would leave the country, both to arrive at Havana by November 25. If this could be accomplished, said Carranza, the Convention could return to Mexico City to elect a provisional president for the entire pre-constitutional period, and Gutiérrez and González would relinquish their forces and authority to him. If the Convention could not secure the election of a president within thirty days, however, and the country was not completely pacified, Carranza served notice that he would return to Mexico to re-assume his First Chieftaincy.[49]

It is interesting to note that Zapata was neither considered nor consulted during the entire affair. It was, at any rate, too late for concessions of any character from Carranza, for it was now Villa, not Carranza, who was the insuperable obstacle to peace. He had shifted his troops from Aguascalientes south to Lagos and showed no signs of halting short of Mexico City. He paid no heed to either Gutiérrez or the Convention.

As war became certain the center of political gravity in Mexico shifted from the Convention to the military camps, and the proceedings of the assembly came to a temporary halt. By the time the last session was held on November 13, most of the Carrancistas had withdrawn from the Convention in accordance with the orders of their chief, and the body consisted of a rump of Villistas, the representatives of some non-Villista northern forces, and the twenty-six Zapatistas. A majority of the delegates had deserted the Convention to follow Carranza into rebellion. To provide for the holding of future sessions, Díaz Soto proposed that a quorum be considered to be half of the delegates, plus one, "who shall remain loyal to the Convention." The decimated assembly accepted this formula without a discussion, the terminology being conveniently vague so as to cover any conceivable situation in which the number of delegates should dwindle to a mere handful. In terminating the sessions in Aguascalientes, the Convention voted to proceed to Mexico City after Villa's occupation of the capital. A Permanent Commission of twenty-one members, headed by Colonel Roque González Garza, was designated to act for the Convention until the sessions were resumed. Since Gutiérrez had been elected only until November 20, the delegates, in view of the uncertain future, voted to extend his term of office "until the Convention is able to hold elections in conformity with Article 12 of the Plan of Ayala." For the time being, Gutiérrez transferred his headquarters to San Luis Potosí, and the Permanent Commission followed him there until the members could move on to Mexico City.[50]

Of the commission sent by the Convention to inform Carranza of his demission, only Aguirre Benavides, the Villista, returned to Aguascalientes. The others preferred to entrust their fate to Carranza. Obregón's decision to forsake the Convention and remain with the Constitutionalist leader was one of the most decisive acts of the revolution. It is improbable that, without Obregón, Carranza could have prevailed against Villa and Zapata. It must have been a difficult choice for Obregón. He had never been wedded to the idea of keeping Carranza in the First Chieftaincy, for two months earlier he had agreed with Villa at Chihuahua on Carranza's elimination. Obregón's actions in the Convention demonstrated his desire to preserve the peace among the revolutionary factions, and Gutiérrez had been his own personal choice to replace Carranza. But Obregón wanted to curb the authority of Villa as well, and he now saw Gutiérrez relying on Villa to uphold the sovereignty of the Convention and his own position as provisional president. In the last analysis, Obregón found the Villista, hence Conventionist, camp unsavory. When the die of hostilities was cast, he could not side with Villa.

On November 16 Obregón relieved General Salvador Alvarado of the military command of Mexico City, assuming that post himself. As Villa's Division of the North continued to move beyond Lagos and Silao, Obregón prepared to evacuate the capital. On the following day, he was interviewed by a correspondent for *El Sol*. Obregón scored the Villistas for blocking a settlement when an agreement had been reached in Aguascalientes that both Villa and Carranza should resign. He charged that Aguascalientes had been dominated by Villa's troops and was not a neutral city, seemingly unmindful that in the Convention he had denied the same accusations by the Carrancista press of the capital. Obregón told the correspondent that he now considered all attempts to deal with the Convention "useless unless they are made with weapons in our hands. . . . Fortunately, and to my own pride, the Army Corps of the Northwest . . . is, as always, ready to go to battle once more in defense of the principles for which the Mexican people have been fighting for three years. . . ." [51]

Yet this was a vain boast by Obregón, for the once powerful army corps was only a shell. Some generals, including Juan G. Cabral and Rafael Buelna, had defected to the Convention, while Lucio Blanco was too ambitious to be relied upon. By November 18 the Division of the North had reached Irapuato. Obregón had no means now of resisting Villa and must inevitably fall back upon Puebla, where Coss was having his own troubles with the Zapatistas. On November 19 Obregón announced to the press in Mexico City a formal declaration of war against Villa. The revolution of the Constitutionalists from the North, which had successfully overthrown and expelled the sanguinary "usurper," Victoriano Huerta, now turned on itself and began to devour its own vitals.

As the Division of the North (now designated an Army of the North by Villa, though by no one else) moved ominously nearer the capital, the exodus of the Constitutionalists continued. By November 20, except for the Ministry of War, all governmental offices had been shifted to Córdoba. Communications were kept open between Mexico City and Córdoba by way of Puebla, and trains ran all the way to Veracruz, which was still in American hands. But Zapatista bands had penetrated Constitutionalist territory as far as Apizaco, and their sporadic raids on the trains of the Mexican Railroad threatened to isolate the capital.[52]

In view of the impending evacuation of the capital by the forces of Obregón, Isidro Fabela requested those members of the diplomatic corps still in Mexico City to transfer their residence to Córdoba and then, when the American forces were withdrawn, to Veracruz, where Carranza intended to establish his government. The foreign ministers unanimously rejected Fabela's offer of sanctuary, however, holding that to follow Carranza to Veracruz would be tantamount to recognizing his regime, and none of their countries had done so as yet. Rebuffed, Carranza then made it clear that the Constitutionalists could not be held responsible for the safety of the foreign nationals still in the capital. As a result, Acting Secretary of State Robert Lansing asked Cardoso de Oliveira to undertake negotiations with Villa, as he had done four months earlier with Obregón, to secure the protection of foreigners while the Division of the North occupied the city.[53]

As Obregón's troops withdrew from Mexico City they took with them what they could. Horses and automobiles were commandeered to facilitate their departure, and trains and railroad equipment were taken out as well. Obregón placed Lucio Blanco in charge of the rear guard. His troops were to occupy the Constitutionalist outposts to hold back the Zapatistas until the Army Corps of the Northwest, or what was left of it, was safely out of the capital.

Fearful that the city would be sacked by the irresponsible Zapatistas, Silliman and Cardoso de Oliveira conferred with Blanco, hoping to prevail upon him to remain after the departure of Obregón to protect the citizenry until the arrival of Villa. Whether the intervention of the diplomatic representatives was decisive, or whether it was his own intent to boost himself to power is not clear. But the result was that Lucio Blanco, over the strenuous objections of Obregón, decided to stay in the capital. Although Obregón, as his superior officer, commanded him to leave with the rest of the Constitutionalist troops, Blanco disobeyed this direct order, preferring to take his chances with Villa. His defection, in this critical moment, was a severe blow to the Constitutionalists.[54]

On November 22 Blanco assumed full military control of the Federal District, forming his own government, appointing a provisional governor of the district, an inspector of police, and other minor officials. In the end, however, he was unable to face up to the prospect of a meeting with Villa and Zapata. On November 23 Xochimilco and San Angel fell to the Liberating Army of the South, and on the following day, after holding the capital for only two days, Lucio Blanco pulled out. There was only one safe exit for him now and that was to the west. He withdrew his cavalry to Toluca and from there, by way of El Oro de Hidalgo, to the state of Michoacán, which was still neutral territory. On the same day, an advance guard of Zapatistas under General Antonio Barona entered Mexico City. To the North of the capital all resistance to Villa disappeared with the complete collapse of Carranza's armies.[55]

As the Division of the North approached Mexico City during the last two weeks of November, Villa's train stopped for one or two days at the major cities on the rail line of the Mexicano: Lagos, León, Silao, Irapuato, Celaya, and Querétaro. In each city Villa replaced the Carrancista officials, most of whom prudently fled before his arrival, with men sympathetic to the Division of the North. He did not consult Gutiérrez or attempt to communicate with him concerning these appointments. He was enlarging his own private bailiwick to include most of the territory north of Mexico City. On December 1 Villa arrived at Tacuba, five miles from the capital, where he halted and established his headquarters. He carefully refrained from committing the errors of Obregón, which had incurred the wrath of the Zapatistas. He remained in Tacuba, making no further move toward Mexico City, until an accord could be reached with Zapata for the joint occupation of the capital by the Liberating Army of the South and his own Division of the North.[56]

Through the first three weeks of November, while Carranza and the Convention drifted into war, the diplomatic representatives of the United States and Carranza's Constitutionalist regime negotiated on the evacuation of Veracruz. The passage of time served to heighten the desire of both parties to secure a quick settlement, the Americans because of the imminence of the "northers," the Mexicans because Carranza had no place else to go. Wilson continued to insist, however, that the Constitutionalists first make the gesture of publishing the required guarantees. The plight of the Constitutionalists since leaving Mexico City forced Carranza to yield. On November 10, Fabela informed the State Department that the Chamber of Commerce in Veracruz, the property owners there, and the civilian employees of the American occupational authorities had all indicated their satisfaction with the treatment they expected from the Mexican government. In view of these opinions, Fabela said, Cándido Aguilar and Carranza now felt that they could issue the guarantees. Fabela stressed that a general amnesty had been decreed by his government on November 9, covering all Mexicans who had served the American military regime.[57]

Although William Canada, the American consul, warned his department that the petition of the Chamber of Commerce, which Carranza alleged was spontaneous, was in reality circulated by a colonel in Aguilar's forces, the American government considered the matter closed to its satisfaction. On November 13 Bryan and Wilson ordered that the evacuation of American troops be effected on the twenty-third. By November 20 it was apparent that war between the Convention and Carranza was approaching, and Henry Breckenridge, the Acting Secretary of War, ordered General Funston to withdraw his forces without committing the United States to recognize one or another of the revolutionary factions.[58]

Three days later the American army transports steamed out of the harbor of Veracruz. The military forces of the United States had occupied the port for two days more than seven months. The benevolently dictatorial rule of the military authorities provided the city with a government such as it had never seen before or since. Graft and corruption were ended both in the administration of the city government and in the dispensation of justice. The effective sanitation measures taken in order to protect the health of the American troops reduced the death rate in the city to an all-time low. Markets were cleansed and screened. Garbage and refuse were collected frequently and destroyed in order to combat fly-borne dysentery. Mosquitoes were reduced by drainage ditches and the copious use of oil. Stringent prophylactic measures and enforced hospitalization and treatment for diseased prostitutes reduced the venereal incidence markedly. Veracruz was infinitely better off when the American troops left than when they had come.

As the soldiers of Funston withdrew from their outposts and embarked for Galveston, the troops of Cándido Aguilar entered the city without friction. In the last week of November the fugitive government of Venustiano Carranza had a home as well as a base of operations for the impending hostilities with Villa and Zapata. It was not friendship with Carranza which prompted the Americans to leave the port open for his occupation. He was simply closer to Veracruz than were the Conventionists. Yet in this fortuitous proximity lay Carranza's ultimate salvation. Without the possession of the port facilities he would have been immediately and decisively defeated by the combined armies of Villa and Zapata. There must have been times in the months to come when Woodrow Wilson and the American Department of State regretted their decision, for Carranza proved to be the most irritating canker in the Mexican policy of the United States.

6

A Meeting of Titans

THE ENTRY OF THE ZAPATISTAS INTO MEXICO CITY was more an infiltration than a storming, for Lucio Blanco had already evacuated all his troops, leaving the capital undefended. To the surprise of the populace, the men of the South were un-expectedly un-Hunlike in their demeanor. Some carried banners imprinted with the image of the Virgin of Guadalupe. There was a little looting, as was to be expected. But the Zapatistas were few in numbers, so that their impact upon Mexico City was less than had been anticipated and considerably less than that of the larger Constitutionalist force in August. Martial law was decreed by Barona, who assumed military command in the name of Zapata. He ordered the death penalty for robbery or other public disturbances "which dishonored the cause of the Liberating Army." He reopened the Foreign Office, which had been closed by Isidro Fabela, and placed his own official in charge. As a temporary expedient, Barona decreed that all revolu-tionary bills would be legal tender until a new currency could be issued.[1]

Late in the evening of November 26 Emiliano Zapata arrived in the capital on a train of the Interoceanic Railroad, a narrow-gauge line which connected Cuernavaca to Mexico City. His coming was even more quiet and unobtrusive than that of his advance guard. Never concerned with the flimflammery of politics, Zapata refused to go to the National Palace to be accorded the traditional conqueror's accolade. Instead, he lodged at a modest hotel, the San Lázaro, near the suburban railroad station of the same name. On the following day he was interviewed by a correspondent for *El Sol* and proved uncommunicative and singularly monosyllabic in his responses. Beyond an occasional "yes" or "no," he had little to say.[2] Zapata was too shy and reticent, too unlettered, too much the Indian peasant, ever to become accustomed to the ways of the metropolis.

He remained in the capital for but three days. On November 28 Felipe Angeles, with the advance guard of Villa's Division of the North, arrived in Tacuba. Although the Villistas made no move to enter Mexico City, preferring to await their chief, the news that strangers were in the vicinity sent Zapata scurrying back to the hill country. He and Villa had a natural affinity, both being enemies of Carranza, but the bitter past experiences of Zapata with outlanders had filled him with distrust. On the morning of November 29, Zapata entrained for Amecameca with his staff, leaving Antonio Barona behind to police the capital with his troops.[3]

Despite the fears of Zapata, Villa had no intention of entering Mexico City until he had reached an agreement with the Army of the South. Upon his arrival in Tacuba he prepared a letter to Zapata attesting to the mutual friendship of the forces of the North and the South. Villa expressed the wish that he might soon meet with Zapata to give him "a mighty *abrazo*." [4] On the afternoon of December 2 a delegation left Tacuba for Cuernavaca entrusted with Villa's letter. In the group were Roque González Garza, to represent Villa, and two men of the South, Juan C. Banderas and Alfredo Serratos, who had come with Villa from Aguascalientes. Serratos was an ancient revolutionary with Zapata in Morelos, but General Banderas had originally been the Maderista governor of the state of Sinaloa. During Madero's regime he had been accused of killing in cold blood a federal prisoner, Colonel Luis G. Morelos, and had been imprisoned in Mexico City. He escaped, however, and, embittered by his treatment at the hands of the president, he joined the nearest revolt against Madero's government, thus passing over to the Zapatista cause. Banderas, Serratos, and González Garza were accompanied to Cuernavaca by George C. Carothers, who had also travelled to Tacuba on Villa's train.

In contrast to the treatment accorded Villarreal and Cabrera in August and September, González Garza was cordially received by Zapata. Of all the revolutionaries in the field, said Zapata, only Villa had his trust and could draw him out of his mountains for a meeting. Yet the faith he expressed in Villa did not completely overcome his native caution, for Zapata agreed to come on December 4 only as far as Xochimilco, now in Zapatista hands. He required Villa to meet him on his own grounds.[5]

Eulalio Gutiérrez, meanwhile, had come down by train from San Luis Potosí. Passing through Tacuba into the capital without fanfare, he arrived unostentatiously at the National Palace on the afternoon of December 3. Villa escorted Gutiérrez and the members of his government from Tacuba as far as Mexico City's Plaza de Armas (Zócalo) with fifty Dorado cavalry. But Villa scrupulously maintained his resolve to occupy the capital only with the Zapatistas. He returned immediately to his camp in Tacuba to await the reply to his message to Zapata. As Mexico's executive, Gutiérrez assumed control of the government of the Federal District, appointing Villistas Manuel Chao governor of the Federal District, Vito Alessio Robles inspector of police, and Mateo Almanza military commander of the capital.[6] The Zapatistas in the city took no notice, however, of Gutiérrez, of his government, or of his public proclamations. Gutiérrez was as yet provisional president only in name.

On the morning of December 4, the day Villa and Zapata were to meet in Xochimilco, Canova and Carothers, who had taken quarters in the capital, obtained an automobile and rode out to the site of the floating gardens, arriving at the Zapatista stronghold at 8:30. Finding no signs of an impending meeting between the two commanders—it was, after all, much too early in the day for any official function in Mexico—the two American agents returned to Mexico City. As they drove into the capital, however, by the Calzada de San Antonio Abad, they passed Villa and a small cavalry escort leisurely jogging south. So Carothers and Canova turned back once more to be in Xochimilco to witness the historic encounter of the two revolutionary chiefs.[7]

It was just at midday that Villa rode into Xochimilco, and a warm winter sun shone down on the narrow, dusty, cobbled streets. The usually quiet town wore an air of festive expectancy. As the band of Norteños headed into the center of the town, they were greeted by Otilio Montaño. After a short speech of welcome by Montaño and a hearty *abrazo,* Villa was led down the street to be introduced to Emiliano Zapata. In this, their first meeting, was symbolized the union of North and South. Zapata said little, but his sharp hawk's eyes missed nothing. He seemed deeply appreciative of Villa's trust in coming to see him in his own territory with only a small escort. He was now convinced that Villa, first of all the revolutionary leaders, was willing to give him the recognition he felt he deserved.

After the customary *abrazos* and a few more noncommittal words of courtesy, the two locked arms, and Zapata drew Villa into the municipal school building for their conference. On the second floor in a spacious classroom they took seats at a large oval table. There were few chairs in the room, but it was filled immediately as Zapatistas and Villistas crowded about the table. It is fortunate that two observers have left detailed accounts of the proceedings: Canova, whose journalistic eye caught the color of this gathering; and Gonzalo Atayde, the private secretary of González Garza, who took stenographic notes of the conversation.[8]

In Canova's account of the proceedings Villa and Zapata were a study in contrasts. Villa was tall and robust, weighing at least 180 pounds, and with a florid complexion. He wore a tropical helmet after the English style. Though he had given up the nondescript garb he had affected before the battle of Torreón, he still seemed oblivious of the demands high fashion made upon successful revolutionaries. He was clad in a heavy, brown woolen sweater, which was loosely woven, with a large roll collar and buttons down the front, khaki military trousers, army leggings, and heavy riding boots. Zapata, in his physiognomy, was much more the Indian of the two. His skin was very dark, and, in comparison with Villa's, his face was thin with high cheek bones. He wore an immense sombrero, which at times hid his eyes. These, said Canova, were dark, penetrating, and enigmatic. He was much shorter than Villa and slighter. He weighed about 130 pounds. Where Villa was attired in rough, field clothing, Zapata's dress was gaudier and more fastidious. He wore a black coat, a large light blue silk neckerchief, a lavender shirt, and the tight *charro* trousers of the Mexican rural dandy, black with silver buttons down the outer seam of each pant-leg. While Villa had no jewelry or ornaments of any kind, Zapata wore two gold rings.

The conference began haltingly as the two chiefs comported themselves like bashful swains. Both were men of action and verbal intercourse left them uneasy. For about half an hour they talked aimlessly about the letter from Villa which González Garza had brought to Zapata in Cuernavaca. But then the conversation touched on Venustiano Carranza and suddenly, like tinder, burst aflame. They poured out in a torrent of volubility their mutual hatred for the First Chief, and their dialogue was animated for more than an hour. "Carranza," said Villa, "is a man who is very—well, very insolent. . . ." Zapata agreed: "I have always said that . . . that Carranza is a scoundrel."

Villa pronounced his opinion of the middle-class revolutionaries who followed Carranza: "Those are men who have always slept on soft pillows. How could they ever be friends of the people, who have spent their whole lives in nothing but suffering." Zapata concurred: "On the contrary, they have always been the scourge of the people." Villa continued: "With those people we shall never have progress, or prosperity, or division of lands. Only a tyranny in the land. . . . Carranza is a person who has come from God knows where, to turn the Republic into an anarchy."

Manuel Palafox leaned across the table to interject an opinion about the Constitutionalist troops: "What they did in Mexico City was without precedent. If barbarians had come in they would have behaved better than those people did." Villa nodded: "It's a barbarity!" Zapata said: "In every town they passed through . . ." His voice trailed off, and Villa picked up the thread: "Yes, they do nothing but massacre and destroy. . . . Those men have no patriotic sentiments." Palafox echoed: "None. No kind of feelings whatever."

Villa complained of his military difficulties with Carranza, asserting that his Division of the North was the only force to fight against Huerta. Pablo González had promised him, he said, in the Division's attack on Saltillo, to prevent the passage toward Saltillo of federal troops. But, "he let eleven trains get by!" said Villa. "Luck was running our way, however, and we took care of them and finally took Saltillo and other points." Amid laughter and jests at González' reputed cowardice, Villa added that "if he hadn't been careful, we'd have taken him too!" Villa relished the prospects of his impending war with González, Obregón, and Carranza. His eyes bright with anticipation, he promised to deal with them as the "bulls of Tepehuanes handle the horses up there!"

From the war, the two passed to a matter dear to Zapata: the partition of lands. With the Carrancistas there could be no real agrarian reforms, they were agreed. "But now," said Villa, "they will see that it is the people who give orders and that the people will know who their enemies are. . . . Our people have never known justice or liberty. All of the best lands belong to the rich, while the poor naked peasant works from sunup to sundown. I think, however, that hereafter things will be different. And if not, we won't lay down these maussers [sic]. I have here close by the capital forty thousand *mausseritos* and some seventy-seven cannons and some. . . ." Zapata was amazed at this catalog of military affluence and he broke in: "Very good!" Villa continued: ". . . sixteen million cartridges and plenty of equipment. When I saw that that man [Carranza] was a bandit, I began to buy ammunition . . . ."

The reference to Carranza brought an outburst from Zapata, who was, now that the ice had been broken, less reserved and much more garrulous. He reviled the Constitutionalists: "Those *cabrones!* As soon as they see a little chance, well, they want to take advantage of it and line their own pockets! Well, to hell with them! I'd have 'broken' all of those *cabrones*. I never could put up with them. In a minute they've changed and off they go, first with Carranza, and then with some other fellow. They're all a bunch of bastards. I wish I could get my hands on them some other time!"

Villa was increasingly pleased with Zapata. He said: "I am a man who doesn't like to fawn on anybody, but you surely know that I have been thinking about you for a long time." Zapata replied: "And we, too. Those who have gone up north, of the many who have gone—those fellows Magaña and the other people who have come to see you—they have told me that things looked hopeful for me up there. He is, I said to myself, the only one I can count on. And so let the war go on. I am not going to make deals with anybody. I shall continue to fight, even though they kill me and all of those who follow me."

Zapata then called for someone to bring a bottle of cognac to the table, but Villa asked for a glass of water instead. Partaking of strong liquors was not among his vices. Zapata refused to take Villa seriously and poured two large tumblers full of cognac. Proposing a toast to the fraternal union of the two factions, he thrust the glass at Villa. With all eyes upon him, Villa reluctantly and hestitatingly reached for the cognac. Unable to do otherwise under the circumstances, he grasped the tumbler and gulped down the contents as though it were, in reality, the glass of water. As the spirituous liquor reached his gullet he nearly strangled. His face turned livid and his features became contorted. But he drank the cognac. As he finished the glass, his eyes were swimming and tears ran down his cheeks. In a husky voice Villa called for his glass of water.

When he had recovered his composure, Villa expressed to Zapata his pleasure in knowing the men of the South. "Well, *hombre*," he said, "I have finally met some fellows who are really men of the people." Zapata returned the compliment: "And I give thanks that I have at last met a man who really knows how to fight." "Do you know how long I have been fighting?" asked Villa. "Nearly twenty-two years." And Zapata replied: "I, too, began to fight at the age of eighteen. . . ." They continued to chat, their conversation leaping from hats to the *cientificos,* to the Orozcos, father and son. Outside a military band struck up a tune and, finding further discourse impracticable, Zapata and Villa left the room, arm in arm.

As Villa and Zapata ended their public conference they passed to a private room where they discussed the immediate problems facing their two armies. Among these was the disposition of personal enemies still within the revolution. With the increasing success of the revolution, many Mexicans, who had originally supported Huerta, passed over to one or another of the revolutionary factions. Where he could, Villa ruthlessly eliminated these. Zapata, too, was completely amoral and relentless in dealing with enemies who had haplessly fallen into his hands. Thus he had in 1913 ordered the execution of the elder Pascual Orozco.

As calmly as though they were drawing jackstraws, the two chiefs selected human victims. Zapata requested that Villa turn over to him for execution an ex-Zapatista, Guillermo García Aragón. Villa agreed to this, though García Aragón was a member of the Permanent Commission of the Convention and had just been appointed governor of the National Palace by President Gutiérrez. He, too, bore a grudge against García Aragón, who had been outspoken in his criticism of Villa while the Convention was in Aguascalientes.

In his turn, Villa asked for the sacrifice of three Orozquistas, Benjamín Argumedo (the "Lion of the Laguna"), Lázaro Alaniz, and Juan Andrew Almazán. These three had served Huerta and, after the Treaty of Teoloyucan, had made common cause with Zapata, rather than surrender to Obregón. In this instance, however, Zapata denied Villa's request, though he had no compunctions about offering other victims in their stead. He maintained that he had given Argumedo, Alaniz, and Almazán his hospitality, and he would not break his word to them. He pointed out to Villa that all three were in places where he could watch them (between Puebla and the federal capital), and he did not think that their presence in the Liberating Army constituted a danger to the revolution.[9] Had Zapata acceded to Villa's pleasure, Mexico's subsequent history would have been considerably different, for Juan Andrew Almazán, with his second name Mexicanized, was a strong and almost successful candidate for the presidency in 1940.

The most important question to be settled before the two chiefs parted company was the military campaign against the Constitutionalists. Both relished the prospects of war, and neither felt that there would be any difficulty in finishing off Carranza. Obregón's forces had been shredded by defections, while Francisco Coss was completely unreliable. Pablo González, following the break between Carranza and the Convention, had scurried northeast across the mountainous Huasteca, rather than risk a conflict with Villa. In Xochimilco Villa and Zapata decided to split their attack. The Army of the South was to drive on Puebla, while Villa's Division of the North moved on Veracruz by way of Apizaco. Zapata complained, however, that he had heretofore been hindered by a lack of weapons and ammunition. His shortage of heavy artillery was critical, he said. Villa, in an expansive mood, promised to supply the needs of the Zapatistas. The conference of December 4, 1914, was concluded in an atmosphere of enthusiasm and sanguine expectations. The two chiefs agreed that their armies should be passed in review in a joint occupation of the capital on the following Sunday, December 6.[10]

On December 7 Villa and Zapata came to the National Palace to confer with Gutiérrez on the campaign against the Constitutionalists. It is probable that the conference was no more than a perfunctory courtesy toward the provisional president, since neither Zapata nor Villa recognized a military (or political) superior in Gutiérrez' government. The generals of North and South had already completed their battle plans at their meeting in Xochimilco. Gutiérrez designated Juan G. Cabral, the onetime Obregonista, as chief of operations on the West Coast for the projected campaign against Jalisco, Sinaloa, Colima, and Sonora. Full of confidence Villa and Zapata parted company. They never met again.[11]

Zapata left Mexico City on December 9 with troop reinforcements and several cannons, given him by Villa, to support the attack already begun on the City of the Angels by Juan Andrew Almazán and Higinio Aguilar. By December 16 the Zapatistas had occupied most of the towns and villages around Puebla and had choked off water and food supplies from the city. Coss was forced to evacuate Puebla and to fall back toward Veracruz. Zapata's Army of the South had gained the greatest victory of its long revolutionary career.[12]

Yet the campaign, which had begun so full of promise a week earlier and which was now consummated by the seizure of Puebla, bogged down immediately. The Zapatistas got no further. They had no real concern for capturing Veracruz or even for defeating the First Chief. To the men of Zapata their country was not Mexico, the Republic, but the *patria chica* of Morelos. Grandiose campaign schemes, which delighted Villa, were alien to their mentality. They had taken up arms to defend their ideas of "land and liberty," and the paved streets of great cities and the highways between them were hard and strange to their sandaled feet. The feel and smell of the freshly tilled soil in the plots so hardly won in their revolution against the *hacendados* of Morelos were a siren call they could not resist. Like the soldiers of Alexander at the Hyphasis, they would not go on. They had reached the end of their earth and now clamored to return to their lands and families. They had already won what they wanted and for them the revolution was over. From the moment his army began to disintegrate at Puebla, Zapata was no longer an important military force in Mexico. Upon Villa alone fell the onus of defeating Carranza and Obregón. The role of Zapata thereafter was purely negative. He could only prevent actions by the enemy; he could not, or would not, compel them.

Nor could Villa carry out his part of the bargain made at Xochimilco, and the aims of the mighty coalition (perhaps as many as sixty thousand troops) were thereby doubly frustrated. There seems little doubt that, had he acted with resolution, Villa could have captured Carranza, or else driven him into the sea and exile. Yet he hesitated, and the opportunity was lost. Although many of the Constitutionalists had gone over to the Convention, the salvation of Carranza and the ultimate military success of Obregón stemmed from the fidelity of sufficient forces in various parts of Mexico to make Villa fearful of risking an attack on Veracruz.

Francisco Murguía, who had served with Pablo González before the schism in the Convention, was by chance in Toluca, capital of the state of Mexico, when Villa thrust his division into Mexico City to cut off Murguía from both Obregón and González. Rather than join the Conventionist forces, he moved his troops westward into Michoacán, to link his fortunes with those of Manuel Diéguez, who controlled Jalisco for the First Chief. Murguía negotiated a temporary truce with Gertrudis Sánchez, the revolutionary *caudillo* in Michoacán, whereby Sánchez agreed to withhold support from the Convention while at the same time not recognizing Carranza as First Chief. This *modus vivendi* in Michoacán (Murguía, himself, was from Zacatecas) permitted the Constitutionalists free rein in the state to threaten Villa's communications. Had Murguía or Diéguez captured Acámbaro, Celaya, or Irapuato, they would have cut off Villa completely from his base of operations in Torreón and Chihuahua.

Another threat to Villa was posed by the independent movement of the Constitutionalist troops of Maclovio Herrera and Antonio I. Villarreal from Nuevo León and Coahuila in the direction of Torreón. The coming together of Diéguez, Murguía, Herrera, and Villarreal in the center of the Republic would not only have bottled up Villa in the South, but would have wrested from him his two principal sources of dollar revenues: the cotton of the Laguna and the cattle of Chihuahua. It is conceivable, even probable, that he had time to fall upon Obregón in December, inflicting a quick defeat upon the unprepared Constitutionalists, then to wheel north to head off the threatened attack on Torreón. But to Villa, as to the Zapatistas, the most important part of Mexico was his own countryside.

On December 10, less than a week after the pact between Villa and Zapata, the Division of the North entrained from Mexico City for Irapuato and Jalisco. *La Opinión* announced that a new plan of battle had been formed.[13] Leaving but a token force near the capital under Generals Manuel Madinaveitia and Agustín Estrada, Villa operated thereafter north and west of Irapuato. He left the Federal District in the hands of the Zapatistas and the few troops that Gutiérrez could call upon to support his government. Though Villa still held the upper hand, Carranza had been granted the precious gifts of time and space to reorganize the shattered Constitutionalist armies and to supply them through the port of Veracruz. A quick victory was now impossible for Villa.

While the generals were preparing for the most important revolutionary business, that of winning battles, the government of the Convention was being organized in Mexico City. On December 5, President Gutiérrez announced the names of his cabinet members. José Vasconcelos, the young philosopher-revolutionist, was named Minister of Public Instruction, while the post of Commerce went to Valentín Gama. Felícitos Villarreal became Minister of the Treasury and Eugenio Aguirre Benavides, the Sub-secretary of War. Heeding the demands of the Zapatistas, Gutiérrez awarded the newly created post of Minister of Agriculture to Manuel Palafox. Antonio Díaz Soto y Gama was offered the position of Minister of Justice, but declined, preferring to labor for the revolution from the rostrum of the Convention. The post then went to another Zapatista, Rodrigo Gómez. In staking out these two offices for themselves, the Southerners indicated that their principal aims in the revolution were to effect agrarian reform and to punish their enemies. The cabinet was completed when Lucio Blanco, upon his return to Mexico City, became Minister of *Gobernación*.[14]

Until December 6 the deportment of the occupying forces in the capital had been fairly good; that is, the number of the troops was not large enough to create an insoluble problem for the government. But with the entry of several thousand soldiers of the North and the South the capital experienced a repetition of the sacking by the Constitutionalists in August and September. Robbery, rapes, murders, and assaults by the motley soldiery of the Convention increased despite the protests of Gutiérrez to the commanders of troops stationed in the capital.[15] In personal conduct, Villa and his generals, as well as the Zapatista leaders, set the standard for licentiousness and brutishness, as the rude, simple countrymen explored the fleshpots of Babylon. Villa, though abstemious in matters of alcoholic beverages, was completely self-indulgent in other vices, gaming and visiting the cockpits, and, above all, in his amorous proclivities. As long as Villa remained in Mexico City, there could be no orderly government. But even more indicative of the inability of Gutiérrez to deal with the generals nominally under his command were a number of cold-blooded assassinations of leading revolutionaries and the summary execution of an untold number of alleged "enemies of the revolution." When Gutiérrez was apprised that García Aragón had been arrested by the order of Villa he protested and ordered his release. But Villa turned a deaf ear to Gutiérrez' complaint and delivered the unfortunate García Aragón to Zapata to be shot without a trial.[16]

More serious than this *quid pro quo* of two revolutionary chiefs were the wanton murders of two members of the Convention, David Berlanga and Paulino Martínez, by Villa's savage henchman, Rodolfo Fierro. Berlanga had been publicly critical of Villa, both in Aguascalientes and in the capital. He had called Villa a bandit and had, on occasion, alluded to him as a despot and a dictator. The sole determinable reason for the slaying of

Martínez was the publication in his periodical in Cuernavaca, *La Voz de Juárez*, of an attack upon Madero. Villa idolized the dead president, and one of his first acts upon arriving in the capital had been to place a wreath upon the tomb of Madero.[17]

Gutiérrez had a police force; he was sworn to keep the peace. Yet he dared not touch Fierro, a double assassin. The president had no means of compelling Villistas or Zapatistas to preserve decorum, public or private. He had been elected by the Carrancista majority of the Convention to a post he did not seek, only to be abandoned by them to the Villistas and Zapatistas. He was caught in a trap not of his own making, and it was only a question of time until he recognized the futility of continuing to hold an empty office. So long as Villa had as counselors men such as Aguirre Benavides, Robles, or González Garza, there was some check upon his irresponsibility. But these were no longer at his side, for they were either in the government of Gutiérrez or in the Convention. It was Fierro who had his ear, and Villa's temper was completely unrestrained. During the time he was in the capital, Villa performed no constructive act to further the cause of the revolution. On December 14 Canova estimated in a dispatch to the State Department that 150 persons had lost their lives for "alleged political crimes" since the Villistas and Zapatistas had come to Mexico City.[18] Alarmed by the reports of his agents in Mexico City, who relayed accounts of disorders and frequent executions, Bryan asked John Silliman to make representations to Gutiérrez. The president maintained, however, that no one had been executed by his order. He told Silliman he hoped to end this lawlessness by decreeing the prohibition of summary executions and by providing for a full court martial for anyone accused of antirevolutionary acts.[19]

By the middle of December rumors were current in Mexico City that Gutiérrez was plotting to leave the capital to establish his government in San Luis Potosí.[20] These rumors were based upon fact, for the provisional president had come to see that to rely upon Villa and Zapata for support was to build his regime on sand. He aspired to construct a new and more powerful coalition in San Luis Potosí by eliminating both Villa and Zapata, and Carranza, as well. On December 19 *El Monitor,* which reflected the views of his government, asked editorially for an end to the "fratricidal war" between the Convention and the Constitutionalists by bringing all factions once more under the banner of the Convention. And on December 22 *El Monitor* announced that the government of Gutiérrez was "inclined to listen to all rebel chiefs . . . who are convinced of their errors and desire to acknowledge again the sovereignty of the Convention and the legitimacy of its government." [21]

Obregón in Veracruz published an open letter to Gutiérrez, calculated to sow discord among the adherents to the Convention. He called upon the president to admit whether or not he had said on repeated occasions in Aguascalientes that Villa was a bandit and a murderer. "General Gutiérrez," wrote Obregón, "it is never too late to amend a wrong. Retire from that atmosphere which has neutralized your energies and honesty and return to the field of struggle with your brothers. . . ." [22] Gutiérrez saw, however, that for him to join Carranza would bring no peace, but would rather perpetuate the factional schism. Instead he began to make overtures to the various Constitutionalist generals, seeking to woo them away from their First Chief. He felt that Obregón and González and their kind were closer to him than they were to Carranza. He made no attempt to conceal his designs, for he was too honest and stolid to be devious. The newspapers of the capital carried reports of his open negotiations with Villarreal in Nuevo León and Luis Caballero in Tamaulipas to win those Constitutionalist generals to the support of his government.[23]

Having given up for the time being any plans for attacking Obregón and Carranza, Villa was now in Guadalajara organizing a campaign against the Constitutionalists in the state of Jalisco. There reports reached him almost daily from Mexico City of the activities of the provisional president. Alarmed by the evidence of Gutiérrez' contumacy, Villa left Guadalajara in the hands of his lieutenant, General Julián C. Medina, and returned to the capital. He brought a large force as far as Tula, far enough away so they could not be trapped by any treasonable action by Gutiérrez with Obregón, yet close enough to be used as necessity dictated. Though he arrived in Mexico City during the night of December 21, he did not act immediately. Instead Gutiérrez was kept under surveillance. By Christmas Day Villa was convinced that Gutiérrez was in correspondence with Obregón in Veracruz and might at any moment bolt to the enemy. He could contain himself no longer. On December 26 Villa ordered that rail communications to the north of the capital be cut, so no one could leave in that direction.[24]

On the following morning he summoned the members of the Convention's Permanent Commission, who had come to Mexico City from San Luis Potosí, to a meeting in the Green Room of the Chamber of Deputies. There he harangued the Conventionists about Gutiérrez' perfidy, accusing the provisional president of planning to desert to Obregón and Carranza. So ferocious was Villa's attack upon Gutiérrez that several members, who remembered the fate of David Berlanga, thought it prudent to leave the capital by whatever means they could. Led by their president, Martín Espinosa, they returned to San Luis Potosí, anticipating that they would soon be joined by Gutiérrez. To the later chagrin of the Convention, they took with them the Convention's banner, the flag upon which all of the original members had placed their signatures.[25]

As the members of the Permanent Commission dispersed, Villa led a group of his henchmen, including Rodolfo Fierro, to the palatial home of Oscar Braniff on the Calle de la Fragua, which Gutiérrez had made his official residence. Though Villa threw into his face the reports of treason with the enemy, Gutierrez did not quail. Nor did he bother to equivocate or deny Villa's charge that he planned to leave Mexico City. Why should he remain, he demanded, when no one respected or obeyed his orders as the president of the Convention? Villa asked Gutiérrez sarcastically where he intended to go, and Gutiérrez replied that if it was necessary he would go "to the top of a mountain." Reminded by Villa that all train traffic outside Mexico City had been halted, Gutiérrez retorted that in that case he would ride out on a burro. Villa informed Gutiérrez that Mexico could not afford to be without a president and that he must remain in the capital, even against his will. Villa ordered Fierro to throw a guard around the house so as to prevent an attempted escape.

General José I. Robles, Gutiérrez' Minister of War, conciliated Villa, who withdrew his order to Fierro and agreed to place himself once more under the president. Gutiérrez then demanded to know why Villa had ordered the execution of David Berlanga, and why he had threatened José Vasconcelos, the Minister of Education. Villa scorned to deny his part in Berlanga's death. "Look!" he said. "I ordered Berlanga killed because he was a lapdog who was always yapping at me. I got tired of so much noise and I finally took care of him. . . ." As for Vasconcelos, Villa told Gutiérrez that he only wished to protect him from General Banderas, who nursed an old grudge against Vasconcelos. He felt that Vasconcelos had rendered him poor service as a lawyer when he had been jailed for the murder of Morelos. Villa warned Vasconcelos that if he valued his life he would leave the capital before Banderas encountered him. As Gutiérrez and Villa parted they exchanged *abrazos,* but their reconciliation was more apparent than real.[26]

Later the same day Gutiérrez assembled a group of close friends in his home to plan for the future of his government. Vasconcelos, now thoroughly antagonistic toward Villa and concerned for his own safety, proposed that Gutiérrez leave Mexico City at once, to seek the support of Lucio Blanco, Maytorena, Villarreal, and Obregón in a new war on Villa and Zapata. Vito Alessio Robles, who was Angeles' representative in the Convention as well as Gutiérrez' inspector of police, advised the president to pay no heed to Vasconcelos. Although Gutiérrez at first accused Alessio Robles of being "more Villista than Villa," he ultimately agreed to attempt a concord with Villa and Zapata.[27] Unable to dissuade Gutiérrez from remaining, Vasconcelos left for Pachuca, to remain away as long as Villa was in Mexico City.

Gutiérrez did not cease, however, to seek means of bringing all the factions together again. When a reporter for *La Opinión* queried him concerning rumors of his "imminent retirement," he denied on the last day of the year that he had resigned or that he intended to do so. He informed *La Opinión* that he hoped his position as provisional president would be "regularized" when the Convention met on the following day, that either his right to office would be confirmed or another man would be elected in his place. He did not deny that he planned to transfer his government to San Luis Potosí.[28]

As the year ended and the Convention prepared to assemble once more in the capital, Gutiérrez' tenuous hold on the presidential office was guaranteed only by the caprice of the unpredictable Villa. So long as Villa remained in the capital there could be no law but that of the Division of the North. And outside Mexico City the authority of Gutiérrez was defied or ignored by the chiefs of North and South, who exercised all the functions of a government within their own areas. In the territory dominated by the Liberating Army, Zapata controlled the postal and telegraphic offices, despite contrary orders by Gutiérrez. To the North Villa rejected Gutiérrez' choice for director of telegraphs and kept them under tight military control. He named governors and other officials, without considering the president, and controlled, as did Zapata in Morelos, the railroads. Ignoring the protests of Gutiérrez, Villa issued fiat money without regard for the financial repercussions to the entire Republic of a large amount of paper money, unredeemable in gold. Even in matters of diplomatic relations with the United States, Villa superseded Gutiérrez' efforts to get the American State Department to deal directly with him.[29]

It is not strange that Gutiérrez dreamed of a new coalition in San Luis Potosí of all those revolutionaries who could not abide Villa, Carranza, or Zapata, or that he continued into the New Year, despite the threats of Villa, his dangerous correspondence with Obregón, Villarreal, González, and other Constitutionalist and Villista chiefs. It was too late, however, for peaceful overtures, for there could be no revolutionary conciliation without a try at arms. There was no way that Mexico could be spared another bloodletting.

7

The Defection of Eulalio Gutiérrez

As the new year began the forces loyal to the Convention seemed to have the upper hand in Mexico. They controlled the largest and most important part and had the most formidable armies. A neutral observer in January 1915 would have conceded scant hope for the ultimate success of the First Chief. Only the peripheries of Mexico were held by the Constitutionalists: Veracruz, Tampico, Matamoros, Nuevo Laredo, and part of the West Coast. The issue was contested in Jalisco with the Villistas holding a temporary advantage. In Sonora Maytorena was struggling with Calles and Hill, who supported Carranza. But a solid block of territory down the center of the Republic was controlled by the Division of the North, its ancillary troops, or the Zapatistas. From Chihuahua, Coahuila and Nuevo León through Durango, Zacatecas, and Guanajuato to the states of Mexico, Puebla, Morelos, and Guerrero, Villa and Zapata maintained interior supply lines which could shuttle troops much more effectively than could the Constitutionalists on the extremities. The rest of the Republic, Oaxaca, the southern coast of Guerrero, and the tropical states of Tabasco and Chiapas were of no military importance and thus played almost no part in the outcome of the war.

Still, the resources of the Constitutionalists were not meager. Tampico furnished oil for export and a source for revenue in dollars with which to buy arms. Pablo González, who had regrouped his Army Corps of the Northeast, was ordered to defend Tampico from the Villistas at all cost. Yucatán produced sisal fibers which could be marketed in the United States. Above all, the possession of Veracruz gave Carranza an uninterrupted flow of arms and supplies. Although the outbreak of hostilities in Europe had sent soaring the prices of armaments in the United States, the Constitutionalists could compete favorably with the agents of the Conventionist armies in buying war goods. And it was vastly easier to bring in goods by ship than for Villa to haul them by rail the length of the Republic. In a sense the paucity of territory held by the Constitutionalists was an advantage since their lines of communication were thereby shortened. Obregón, who was to spearhead the Constitutionalist attack against Villa and Zapata, was always close enough to Veracruz to be supplied rapidly and efficiently.

Carranza was determined to leave no stone unturned in an effort to win support throughout Mexico, even to the extent of prostituting his own political principles. As a Liberal, he had always opposed legislated labor reforms and, in particular, direct action through land seizures. But during December and early January he and his civilian advisers hammered out a program of social reform which seemed much in advance of the simple formula provided in the Plan of Guadalupe. It provided for the development of small properties, the equalization of tax loads, improvement in the conditions of the peasants and urban workers, municipal liberty, electoral reforms, an independent judiciary, revision of the laws of matrimony, reform of the legal procedures, and the destruction of monopolies. Under these additions to the Plan of Guadalupe, Carranza would continue as First Chief and was to issue decrees to implement this program. The job of filling in the details was given to Luis Manuel Rojas and José Natividad Macías, both Liberals and former Maderista legislators. Just before Christmas they sent to the First Chief their projected agrarian reforms. They proposed that Carranza void all confiscations of *ejidos* and that he decree the formation of new pueblos from the expropriated lands, granting five hectares of land to each Constitutionalist soldier at the end of the war.[1]

The first tangible result of the proposed program was the publication by Carranza on January 6, 1915, of the famous Veracruz decrees. Though these decrees have subsequently been called the basis for the land reforms sanctioned under Article 27 of the Constitution of 1917, they were in reality mere window-dressing. They offered little more than had Madero's Plan of San Luis Potosí. Carranza declared that all lands taken by the *jefes políticos* in contravention of the Ley Lerdo would be returned to their rightful owners. But it would have been difficult for villages or peasants to establish that land had been taken illegally, for the law of 1856 specifically banned the holding of land by corporations such as the pueblos. If the burden of proof were put on the claimant—as it was later—no large turnover of land could be expected as a result of these decrees. Provision was made for expropriation of land to provide *ejidos* in case of need, but the main emphasis was the formation of small plots from all *ejidos* eventually.[2]

The decrees, whatever their merit, were issued *in extremis,* with the First Chief penned up in Veracruz and with the enemy in control of most of the Republic. Never thereafter did Carranza make any real effort to put them into effect. Other enactments by Carranza were, in his eyes, more important and more permanent. These were Liberal, not radical, in nature. He decreed municipal independence, a divorce law—the first in Mexico—was promulgated, and the control of education was taken from the federal government and put into the hands of the towns and villages. The judiciary was freed from the domination of the executive power, thus effecting a balance of authority among the three branches. It was the intent of Carranza to bring about these reforms in the pre-constitutional period of his First Chieftaincy so they would already be the law of Mexico when the revolution was terminated and the constitutional regime could be restored. At the same time, his advisers, notably the engineer, Félix F. Palavicini, began to call for a new constitution to replace the now outmoded charter of 1857.[3]

In Mexico City the Revolutionary Convention was approaching the nation's social and economic problems in a different manner. There was no authoritarian First Chief to bring about reforms by executive fiat. Only by the dint of hard work and acrimonious debate could its program be shaped. The Convention reconvened on the first day of January, 1915, in the building of the Chamber of Deputies. The first few sessions were spent in the examination of the credentials of delegates who had not been at Aguascalientes. There were now few Carrancistas, for most had left the assembly when ordered to do so by the First Chief. Their place was taken by a large group of Zapatistas, who came to Mexico City as delegates and no longer as commissioners. From the recorded proceedings in the sessions down to January 16 two facts emerge. A cleavage developed between the delegates of the North and South; and this cleavage followed, in general, an ideological divergence. The South was more radical, more concerned with social reforms by direct action. The Division of the North stood for more continuity with the past and for more gradual reform. But all were agreed that the social revolution could not be carried forward under the banner of the Constitutionalists.

In part, the disunion within the Convention was attributable to an abrasion of personalities. Antonio Díaz Soto y Gama cared not a whit for the niceties of parliamentary procedures. He had the tongue of an adder and the spirit of a Danton. Yet his adversaries, with the exception of Federico Cervantes, the representative of Felipe Angeles, tolerated his onslaughts because the Villistas were always in the majority. As long as the Convention remained in Mexico City—and it was compelled by untoward circumstances to move to Cuernavaca before the end of the month —the difficulties did not prove insurmountable. The delegates began in adequate harmony to construct the program of reform which was to guide what they hoped would be their successful revolution. These hopes rested squarely on the military achievements of Villa and Zapata.

The new year saw a resurgence of the waning fortunes of the Constitutionalists, however. During November and December Carranza in Veracruz had reformed the shattered armies still loyal to him, putting together a new Army of Operations under the command of Alvaro Obregón. It contained the remnants of Obregón's Army Corps of the Northwest, a cavalry division of Cesáreo Castro, and a Division of the East, commanded by Cándido Aguilar, the military governor of Veracruz. On December 31 Obregón began a drive calculated to retake Puebla from the Army of the South. In Puebla, eighty-four miles to the southeast of Mexico City, a garrison under Juan Andrew Almazán protected the Convention in the capital. But what had been won with difficulty in December by the Army of the South was now taken too much for granted. Zapata had withdrawn most of his troops to the mountains of Morelos, leaving in Puebla an inadequate force which was largely Orozquista. And since the Zapatistas had penetrated but little beyond Puebla, while the Villistas had withdrawn to the north of the capital, Obregón was free to move his troops on the two railway lines connecting Mexico City with Veracruz, the Interoceanic and the Mexicano del Sur, dangerously close to the valley of Mexico.[4]

Obregón's main thrust was made along the broad gauge line from Tepeaca through Amozoc, and by the evening of January 4 his troops had reached the outskirts of Puebla. On the following day, after more than twenty-four hours of bloody fighting, they succeeded in forcing Almazán, who was short of supplies, especially artillery, to evacuate the city. No attempt was made by the Constitutionalists to run him down, as the capture of Puebla was Obregón's immediate objective. A second prong of Obregón's army, under Generals Francisco Coss and Agustín Millán, was simultaneously driven beyond Atlixco, and it succeeded in reaching Guadalupe, a small station of the Mexicano, less than sixty miles from the capital.[5]

On January 11 Carranza telegraphed Obregón from Veracruz

to suggest an attack upon the capital. But Obregón demurred, for there still remained in the Federal District the troops of Blanco, Gutiérrez, and Robles, and these, with the Zapatistas, could provide formidable opposition for the approximately twelve thousand men under his command. Moreover, Obregón hoped to win his way to Mexico City by means more subtle than a costly military assault. Instead he began to apply pressure on Gutiérrez to pry him away from the Conventionist forces. On January 7 Gutiérrez sent a message to Obregón asking him to suspend his expected advance upon the capital so that they could work out together a plan for eliminating Villa. He referred to such an accord which he had already made with the Constitutionalists in Tamaulipas, Nuevo León, and San Luis Potosí. In reply Obregón refused to commit himself to halt his attack and suggested that Gutiérrez cease his vacillating and make a public declaration against Villa. Unfortunately for Gutiérrez, this exchange of telegrams was relayed by Obregón to the First Chief, and the contents were released to the press in Veracruz. The reports were carried by the wire services to the United States and published in El Paso, revealing to Villa, who had gone north to discuss border problems with General Hugh Scott, the continued traitorous activity of the provisional president.[6]

Gutiérrez summoned John R. Silliman to the National Palace on January 9 for a conference. Although the president did not specifically betray his intentions, he indicated to Silliman that he could no longer tolerate the conduct of Villa and Zapata. He said that "something very important" would happen "in a very few days." As a result of his conversation with Gutiérrez, Silliman telegraphed Bryan that he was convinced that the president was seeking an accord with Obregón which would eliminate both Villa and Carranza and permit Obregón to reoccupy Mexico City. For public consumption Gutiérrez disavowed any intention of resigning his office, and both he and his Minister of War, Robles, emphatically denied rumors that an attack on the capital by Obregón was imminent. The president conferred with Silliman again on January 13 and confirmed Silliman's suspicions that he was bargaining with Obregón. And although he was in a sense the creature of the Convention, he now informed Silliman that it had no authority, that "agencies were at work" to aid him in building "a strong, independent provisional government." He accused Villa of moral and financial peculation and complained to the American agent that Villa was still issuing paper money in the North without any authority from Gutiérrez' government.[7]

On the same day Gutiérrez, with the help of Vasconcelos, who had returned to the capital after the departure of Villa, prepared a "Manifesto to the Mexican People." In it the president reviewed his grievances against Villa and concluded by relieving both Villa and Zapata of their commands, calling upon all revolutionaries to join in eliminating Carranza as well. Although Gutiérrez had never hidden his desire to gain a concord among the revolutionary factions and *El Monitor* had supported his stand editorially, on this occasion he had the perspicacity to withhold the manifesto until he was safely out of Villa's grasp. Yet it was clear from all signs, public and private, that a showdown was near.[8]

Gutiérrez' troubles were increased by growing friction with the radical members of the Convention. In Aguascalientes the assembly had voted to give Gutiérrez indefinite tenure in office beyond the original twenty-day term demanded by the Zapatistas. Prodded by Gutiérrez, who demanded a confirmation or rejection of his election, the delegates began on January 12 and 13 to consider his status as provisional president. In a report concurred in by González Garza, a committee of Zapatistas presented a plan for parliamentary government. It was proposed that the provisional president, presumably Eulalio Gutiérrez, should remain in office until the end of 1915, when a constitutionally elected president would take his place. The Convention, meeting as a grand jury (*Gran Jurado*) might remove the provisional president by a vote of two thirds of the delegates present, if he should violate or fail to comply with any of the decisions of the Convention, including the principles of the Plan of Ayala; if he should leave his office without the permission of the Convention or its Permanent Commission; or if he should make important decisions without prior agreement with his council of ministers. The president's ministers were to be made responsible to the Convention for any official action and would be named by the Convention from a list of three candidates for each office (*terna*) prepared by the president. The executive was forbidden to remove any minister without the consent of the assembly, while the Convention, itself, might depose a minister, or the entire cabinet, by a vote of a simple majority at any session.[9]

Debate on the proposal began on January 13 after the Convention had voted to invite Gutiérrez (though he refused the invitation) to attend the proceedings and to give his opinions on parliamentary government. After Díaz Soto had eulogized this type of polity and alleged that it would be the salvation of Mexico, Cervantes took the floor to oppose the Southern plan. He said that the proponents of this scheme would end the tyranny of one only to substitute the tyranny of the many. He recalled that the terrors of the French Revolution had been due to such a regime. Díaz Soto retorted that the representative of Angeles was a "reactionary and a conservative." He expressed a desire for a few Dantons, Robespierres, and Marats in the Convention to destroy "the enemies of the Nation." The Constitution of 1857, which Cervantes was wont to invoke, had only served to sanctify the rights of the *conquistadores* and their descendants, he said. Cervantes interjected a defense of the Liberal concepts of the rights of man imbedded in "that Magna Carta," but Díaz Soto replied that they had benefited only the rich and powerful landowners, men such as the Terrazas. The rights of man, he said, had "consented to the exploitation and despoiling of the Indians . . . [and] sanctioned the slavery of the proletariat. . . ."

After Pérez Taylor and Otilio Montaño had supported parliamentary government Manuel Zepeda denounced the attacks from the South on the Constitution of 1857. "Let us educate the people!" he cried. "That is the essential thing. . . ." The system proposed by Díaz Soto, said Zepeda, would institute a government subjected to the passions of the public. Genaro Palacios Moreno, a Zapatista delegate, responded to Zepeda, characterizing him as a reactionary and a Porfirista. Though Cervantes was a conservative, he said, in upholding the Constitution, he was an idealist. "A stupid idealist, if you please, but an idealist!" Zepeda, on the other hand, had no faith in the revolution, Palacios Moreno charged, but was a mouthpiece for the political ideas of Jorge Vera Estañol (a member of Huerta's cabinet). On this bitter note the debate was ended, and the Convention voted to accept the report and to begin in the following days to consider the plan article by article. Although no recorded comment by Gutiérrez on this proposal is extant, it is inconceivable that he could have been sanguine in the middle of January 1915 about the prospects of being an emasculated president in the parliamentary regime envisaged by the Zapatistas.[10]

While the Convention debated a new form of government for Mexico, Villa had become embroiled in a diplomatic problem of more immediate concern to the success of the revolution. Repeated violations of the American frontier by revolutionary troops threatened to bring about the intervention of the United States to protect its nationals and American property in towns along the border. The principal point of contention was Naco, a dusty, sleepy settlement which straddled the frontier between Sonora and Arizona. The instance of the trouble was the rivalry between Maytorena and the Constitutionalist generals, Calles and Hill, for the control of Mexico's northwest. It had been this same rivalry which had caused Villa to abuse Obregón in Chihuahua City, and which had helped precipitate the final rupture between Carranza and Villa at the end of September. Though Obregón and Villa had ultimately agreed that Juan G. Cabral should replace both Maytorena and the Constitutionalist commanders, this transfer of power had never taken place. Cabral, deserting Obregón for the Convention, remained in Mexico City to take charge of the planned campaign of the Conventionist armies through Jalisco and up Mexico's west coast.

Hill and Calles had refused to withdraw their troops to Casas Grandes, and instead took up a position in Naco. Dug in with their backs against the American border, they defied Maytorena to root them out. The forces of Maytorena, in the main Yaqui Indians, began the attack on Naco on October 14, throwing wave after wave of assaulting infantrymen against the implaced machine guns and trenches which semi-circled the portion of the town south of the border. In the first rush a few Yaquis penetrated the defenses, but they were thrust back, and the Constitutionalists continued to hold their positions against periodic attacks for over a month. Soon the Mexican half of Naco was a town no longer. Instead it was a system of fortifications by which fifteen hundred Constitutionalists warded off perhaps two thousand Maytorenistas.

Given the intensity of the fighting and the duration of the campaign, it was not surprising that the American authorities in Naco and in Washington began to be alarmed by the damage and casualties suffered in the American half of the town. The proximity of the combatants to Naco, Arizona, caused many projectiles, principally those of Maytorena, to fall on American soil, and a number of Americans were killed or wounded by the Mexican gunfire. On December 10, the Department of State brought the issue to the attention of Gutiérrez in Mexico City, demanding through Silliman an end to the hostilities at Naco. Gutiérrez telegraphed Maytorena, asking him to prevent bullets from passing into American territory, or, if necessary, to suspend the attack entirely, "in order to prevent difficulties with the United States." But Maytorena did not even deign to answer the provisional president. A similar demand was served upon Carranza in Veracruz with a notification that the United States would take "positive measures" to assure that these depredations should be halted.[11]

In his reply of December 12 to the note of the American government, Carranza categorically rejected any interference in Mexican affairs upon whatever pretext. He denied that the Constitutionalist troops of Hill and Calles had violated American territory or were responsible for loss of American lives, since the border lay behind them. Any damage must have been caused by the Villistas, he insisted. He questioned, moreover, whether the

accidents had "occurred through the carelessness of the contending forces or the imprudent curiosity of the American citizens."
He remembered, he said, "that in 1911 during the attack of the
Maderista forces on Ciudad Juárez, most of the accidents were
due to the imprudence of the residents of El Paso, who occupied
all elevations trying to see the battle just as if it were a festivity."

Carranza informed Bryan that the use of force by the government of the United States to settle the matter at Naco "would
have to be considered by this government as an act of hostility
and as an attack against the sovereignty of Mexico, independent
of the pacific or well disposed intentions that might cover the
employment of force. . . . I should like to find words sufficiently
expressive, to state to you that the Department of State does not
appreciate to the fullest extent the seriousness which the use of
force on Mexican territory . . . would entail. . . ." Carranza
called upon the American government to "strive that under no
circumstances should acts of force be employed against us." [12]

Although it was true, as Carranza pointed out, that the danger
to American nationals came from the Maytorenistas, not the
Constitutionalists, the United States could not permit the First
Chief to block a settlement at Naco. Therefore George C. Carothers, who had come from Mexico City to Villa's headquarters
in Torreón, was sent by Bryan to Sonora to confer with Maytorena
personally about a cessation of hostilities on the border. Meeting
Maytorena near Naco on December 18, Carothers found him
"anxious to avoid a clash with our troops," and willing to pull
back his forces from the border if necessary. But Maytorena
protested against any arrangement which would leave Hill in
full control of the port of Naco, able to import arms, ammunition, and provisions freely. He suggested that the American government close the frontier and halt shipments to the Constitutionalists. Then the Maytorenistas could withdraw with the
assurance that Hill would be compelled to fight his way out of
Naco or else surrender. Carothers commended this course to
Bryan. But the American government had already decided to
send General Hugh Scott to Naco in an effort to bring the con-

tending revolutionary leaders together and to achieve a peaceful
solution satisfactory to both factions. In the meantime, prepared
for any eventuality, the United States Army stationed five thousand troops along the Arizona border and, in addition, a large
amount of heavy artillery was moved from Fort Sill, Oklahoma,
to Naco.[13]

In sending General Scott, Wilson hoped that the bluff soldier
could achieve what was impossible through regular diplomatic
channels. Since November 17 Scott had been the chief of staff and
before that had commanded the Southern Department of the
army for five years. He knew the borderlands, had great prestige
among the revolutionaries, and was already a warm friend and
admirer of Pancho Villa.

Scott arrived at Naco on December 20 to find that the battle had
simmered down to a few desultory rifle shots without much apparent effect on either side. An inspection of the customshouse
at the border showed the pockmarks or perforations of over two
hundred balls or shells—"with our flag flying over it," reported
Scott. In all, fifty-three persons were killed or wounded on the
American side of the border before hostilities were ended.

Scott asked Hill and Maytorena to meet him in Naco, Arizona,
and wired Roberto V. Pesquiera, now an agent for Carranza in
the United States, requesting him to represent the First Chief in
the negotiations. Meanwhile, Tasker H. Bliss, who had succeeded
Scott as commanding general in the South, had come to Naco as
well, and he and Scott drew up a proposed cease-fire agreement
to be presented to Hill and Maytorena. Although Hill, Calles,
and Pesquiera arrived in Naco and signed the agreement for the
Constitutionalists on December 23, Maytorena requested a post-
ponement of the conference, alleging that he was ill. And several
days of torrential rains had turned the dirt roads of northern Sonora into mud sloughs and fords into swirling rapids,
so that Maytorena could not get to Naco before the twenty-
fourth.[14]

When he saw the agreement prepared by Scott and Bliss, Maytorena balked and refused to sign it until he should receive au-

thorization from the government of the Convention in Mexico City. Scott sent Felix Sommerfeld to obtain Villa's assent to the agreement, but Maytorena remained adamant, insisting that he needed the permission of Gutiérrez before consenting to withdraw his troops from the investment of Naco. In the interim an uneasy truce prevailed, punctuated by sporadic raids or occasional rifle shots. More shells fell across the border.

Sommerfeld brought information to Scott that Villa was now determined to settle the matter quickly by military action. He was sending eight thousand troops under Juan G. Cabral, who would be in Casas Grandes, Chihuahua, by January 4. From there they would march overland to Naco to drive out the Carrancistas. Villa told Sommerfeld: "If Scott will give us eight hours of battle, we can take Naco." Bliss and Scott urgently requested the American government to make attempts in Mexico City to halt this projected campaign, which could only increase the likelihood of American casualties and subsequent intervention. As a result, Bryan requested Villa to confer with Scott in El Paso to make a definitive settlement of all border problems, including the situation at Naco.[15]

Pleased with the prospect of meeting Scott again, Villa left Mexico City on January 4, arriving in Ciudad Juárez on the eighth. Scott had already come to El Paso on the previous day with Carothers, who was to serve as his interpreter, and the two generals met at the center of the international bridge which spanned the Rio Grande between El Paso and Ciudad Juárez. After a "very friendly meeting," they arranged for a conference in El Paso on the morrow. Wilson preferred that Scott not go into Mexican territory, if at all possible.

On January 9 Villa came to the Texan side of the border to meet Scott and, according to the American chief of staff, they "were locked for two hours like bulls with their horns crossed, but we finally came to an agreement." Villa again proposed that he send Cabral with eight thousand men to Naco. Within eight hours, he said, he would have cleaned out the Constitutionalists and have settled the matter. When Scott refused to consider this proposal, Villa seemed to think his stand unreasonable. Scott wrote later to his friend, Leonard Wood, that Villa "said that after having our people killed and wounded for two months and a half he could not see why I would not agree to having them fight there for eight hours, and end the whole business. I told him that they could not fight for eight minutes, and we arrived at an understanding on that basis. . . ." At the conclusion of the conference, Villa told Scott that no situation could arise on the border that could not be settled between them, and that "he would come up from the City of Mexico to the border any time I asked him." Villa sent a telegram from Ciudad Juárez to Maytorena, informing him of the agreement "after mature discussions" with Scott, and requesting him to sign the accord with the Constitutionalists.[16]

When Scott came back to Naco, he found that Benjamín Hill had been replaced by Plutarco Elías Calles as commander of the Constitutionalist forces in Sonora. Carranza had ordered Hill to proceed by way of American territory to Veracruz, in order to join Obregón's Army of Operations. On January 11 Scott brought Calles and Maytorena together, and the agreement to end hostilities at Naco was signed by both. Under the terms of the treaty, Calles was to evacuate Naco, while Maytorena was to withdraw his troops westward to Nogales or to Cananea. Neither could occupy Naco, which was to remain neutralized and closed to military traffic. Calles would take his troops east to Agua Prieta, and neither Agua Prieta nor Nogales was to be attacked, so as not to endanger American territory. A plan was afoot, however, to undo the settlement achieved by Scott and Villa.[17]

As Scott returned to El Paso aboard the Santa Fe's Golden State Limited, he was met by the American consular agent from Nogales, W. D. Cartwright, who had taken the same train in order to present a scheme to Scott for the complete end to hostilities in Sonora. According to General Bliss, who was approached first by Cartwright, he was "connected with the Consolidated National Bank of Tucson." He proposed to Bliss and to Scott that his bank would put up thirty thousand dollars "to buy up the weak-kneed members of the Agua Prieta garrison," thus permitting the passage of Maytorena's troops through the Constitutionalist lines into the town. Cartwright told Scott that Maytorena was willing, but would not go through with the venture unless the War Department of the United States would give its consent. Scott replied that he had no authority to commit his department, but that he would report their conversation to the Secretary of War when he arrived in Washington.[18]

Bliss told Scott that the scheme was no more than a "speculative venture," in which the bank would receive for its investment a lien on the customs receipts at Agua Prieta until it was "reimbursed for the original thirty thousand dollars, plus a considerable bonus." The plan seemed so "rank" to him that he thought neither Scott nor Henry Breckinridge, the Acting Secretary of War, should "touch it with a ten foot pole." On January 29 Scott received a telegram in Washington from Cartwright, informing him that the plans were ready to put into effect within two hours "if you think [it] feasible." But when Scott showed the telegram to Breckinridge, he directed Scott to inform Cartwright that the War Department "disapproves of the whole matter and will have nothing to do with it." The plan was thereupon abandoned and Maytorena was left to his own devices to deal with the Constitutionalists.[19]

In the meantime, Cabral had arrived in the state of Sonora to assume command of the troops of the governor, Maytorena. He brought to Cananea a large shipment of military clothing, shoes, blankets, and other supplies to outfit a force to fight against the Carrancistas in the Northwest. The truce imposed at Naco had no effect in the rest of the state. From Agua Prieta, Calles began to prepare for a showdown with the Villistas, importing supplies and ammunition from the United States. In the South, General Ramón F. Iturbe, Constitutionalist commander in Sinaloa, threatened the borders of Sonora and was rumored to be as far north as Alamos and Navajoa. While he awaited a force of eighteen hundred men promised him by Villa, Cabral went to Nogales to see Maytorena, but the governor refused to turn over his troops to Cabral. He was reported to be jealous of Cabral, who had brought a large store of money and had much equipment, while his own troops were ill equipped and unpaid.

The troops from the Division of the North never arrived in Sonora, however. They had been recalled to Casas Grandes by Villa when word reached him that Gutiérrez and Blanco had left Mexico City. Cabral and Blanco had been close friends, and Villa feared that Cabral would now turn against him in Sonora. When the news was bruited about Nogales that Maytorena, evidently acting in accord with Villa, intended to arrest him, Cabral crossed the border into American territory to seek safety in Douglas, Arizona. As Villa's attention was directed elsewhere in the Republic, he was forced to write off Sonora from his campaign plans. After many months of fighting, Calles was ultimately to drive out Maytorena and claim the entire state for the Constitutionalists.[20]

While Villa was in Ciudad Juárez and El Paso for his conference with General Scott, he was made increasingly suspicious of Eulalio Gutiérrez. Border newspapers, especially the Carrancista *El Paso del Norte,* featured dispatches from Veracruz of Gutiérrez' alleged invitation to Obregón to join him in rebellion against both Villa and Carranza. And upon his return to Chihuahua Villa received further confirmation of the president's dealings with the enemy when Felipe Angeles telegraphed him from Monterrey that he had captured documents giving graphic proof of Gutiérrez' inconstancy. In December Angeles had been sent by Villa from Torreón toward the East to blunt the threatened attack of Villarreal and the other Constitutionalists in Nuevo León, Coahuila, and Tamaulipas against the Villa-controlled Comarca Lagunera. On January 5, the same day that Puebla fell to Obregón, Villa's "grey lieutenant" retrieved some of the prestige lost by the forces of the Convention by soundly defeating Villarreal and Maclovio Herrera at Ramos Arizpe. In his precipitous flight Villarreal abandoned his archives, including correspondence with Gutiérrez and other Constitutionalists and Conventionists in that area. When Villa came to Monterrey, which Angeles had occupied as Villarreal fell back to Nuevo Laredo, he was shown the incriminating letters of Gutiérrez.[21]

In a towering rage, Villa dispatched a coded telegram on the evening of January 15 to José Isabel Robles in Mexico City, ordering the immediate execution of the provisional president. Villa had, of course, no trust in Lucio Blanco or others close to the government of Gutiérrez. But he hoped that Robles' old loyalty to him as a general in the Division of the North, would prove stronger than his attachment, as Minister of War, to Gutiérrez. Villa left Monterrey immediately for the South to assume control of the capital. But he had misjudged Robles and this error in judgment proved the salvation of Gutiérrez.[22]

Electing to cast his lot with the provisional president, Robles divulged to him the contents of Villa's telegram. The time for vacillation had passed for Gutiérrez. In anticipation of this moment, José Vasconcelos had already made arrangements with Daniel Cerecedo, the revolutionary chief in the state of Hidalgo, for the safe passage of the government of Gutiérrez through the Huasteca. Gutiérrez' hopes for an agreement with Obregón were by now almost gone, for a commission, sent by him to Puebla, had been arrested by Obregón and handed over to Carranza for confinement in Veracruz. And earlier on the fifteenth the Convention—or at least a large portion of it—had manifested its hostility to him in adopting the first article of the program for parliamentary government. Soon or late, Gutiérrez would fly from his distasteful predicament. The telegram from Villa forced his hand.

During the night of January 15 and the early morning hours of the sixteenth, Gutiérrez gathered his meager forces and assembled those members of his government in whom he had implicit trust. Neither Palafox nor Gómez, the two Zapatistas in his cabinet, were informed of his plans. Lucio Blanco, never certain of the right course to pursue, at first sent his troops from the capital. In the end, however, he decided to trust his fate to Gutiérrez. The choice for Blanco was not a happy one: to follow the ignominious Gutiérrez, to await the wrathful Villa, or to fly to Obregón, whose orders he had defied in November and whom he had deserted for the Convention. At 2:00 A.M. Gutiérrez sent three officials to the treasury to order Julio Poulat, the Convention's treasurer, to turn over thirteen million pesos in gold and in bills, of the twenty-three million pesos then on hand. Although the Convention subsequently branded him a thief, Gutiérrez was doubtless honest in assuming that he, as president—and he did not relinquish his office in his flight—was justified in taking the treasury with him. But the loss of the larger part of the funds belonging to the national government in Mexico City was later to prove embarrassing to the Convention.[23]

Although most of the revolutionary chiefs in Mexico City had ensconced themselves in palatial residences, Roque González Garza, the Convention's president, had taken modest rooms in the Hotel Lascuráin fronting on the Alameda. At about three in the morning of the sixteenth he was awakened by the clattering of hooves on the cobbles beneath his window. Though it was still dark he could recognize the troops of Gutiérrez and Robles. As the agent of Villa in the Convention he was aware of Villa's prohibition against Gutiérrez' leaving his post, but he had insufficient forces of his own to halt the flight of the president. Acting with dispatch, González Garza went to the National Palace to assume control of the Convention's government. He decreed martial law in the capital, ordering that "anyone, who for whatever reason, disturbs public order, commits any crime, bears arms, or attacks property, shall be shot." All public meetings or assemblies were forbidden. Meanwhile, unaware that they had been seen, the small band continued out of the city on the road to Pachuca.[24]

Because Villa controlled the railroads leading from Mexico City, Gutiérrez, was, perforce, limited to horse or automobile transportation, or to marching afoot. There was really only one way he could go. To the south were the Zapatistas, to the east, Obregón, while Villa's troops lay in wait to the north and the west. His sole chance was to get to Pachuca and, guarded by

Cerecedo, cut through the mountains of Hidalgo to his own territory of San Luis Potosí. Forlornly he still dreamed of eliminating Villa, Zapata, and Carranza and erecting a new government, independent of, and superior to, all factions. In Pachuca Gutiérrez released the manifesto he and Vasconcelos had composed three days before in the capital. And he sent a telegram to Villa, notifying him that he had been relieved of his command of the Division of the North. Gutiérrez said: "If you continue to lead your troops, despite these orders, you will be considered a rebel against this government." He asked Villa to proceed to Ciudad Juárez "to await new orders." [25]

This message and a similar telegram to the municipal president of Mexico City were intercepted by González Garza, who was thus apprised of the direction taken by the fugitives. He established telegraphic contact with Villa and informed him of the contretemps within the government of the Convention. He relayed to Villa the contents of Gutiérrez' telegrams and, while stressing that he was in complete control of Mexico City, informed his chief that he must come immediately "to save the situation." Villa's reply to González Garza was short, but noncommittal. He had by now decided to come no further south than Querétaro, for it appeared to him that Gutiérrez might be on his way to join Obregón in Puebla. [26]

The news of Gutiérrez' flight caused the Zapatista garrison to bolt from the capital, and many members of the Convention, in momentary bewilderment, took to their heels as well. But in the morning the clear January sun banished the phantasms of the hours of darkness, and most returned, reassured by González Garza's competent handling of the crisis. In the evening of January 16 the Convention assembled to hear González Garza's report on the defection of Gutiérrez. On this momentous occasion the galleries were crowded with spectators as he mounted the rostrum. He accused Gutiérrez of "committing the grave crime of not informing the Convention" of his plans to leave the presidency. Concerning Gutiérrez and his associates, González Garza said: "They were never on our side . . . General Zapata, with whom I spoke recently, said the same thing and that he was disposed to come to Mexico City to remove Gutiérrez from his office!" Díaz Soto followed González Garza to heap scorn on the departed president: "All of us who truly love our fatherland should be proud because for the first time the revolution has triumphed over the reactionaries. . . . Now the reign of personalities is terminated, and from this day on we shall look forward to the complete triumph of the revolution!" He called the president the "last of the Carrancistas" and "the traitor Gutiérrez," concluding his tirade by asking the Convention, itself, to "manage the destinies of the nation."

When all the speeches were concluded, Otilio E. Montaño, Santiago Orozco, Díaz Soto, and other representatives of the Army of the South introduced a resolution that the Convention assume all of the powers of the government, including those of the executive, and that the assembly then delegate its executive functions to its president, Roque González Garza. There was no opposition to González Garza's assuming the office of Gutiérrez, but a heated discussion ensued as to whether he should continue, at the same time, to serve as president of the Convention. Federico Cervantes felt that the two offices should be separated, while Díaz Soto held out for the union of the two positions in the person of González Garza. Cervantes stood for the traditional Liberal view of the separation of powers. Díaz Soto and those who supported him, on the other hand, saw a rare opportunity to achieve at once their aim of a parliamentary government for Mexico, and in this instance the Zapatistas prevailed.

Although contemporary newspaper accounts held that González Garza had been designated provisional president and correspondence was frequently addressed to him by that title, in reality he was not. The delegates simply yielded to him, as their presiding officer, the executive authority, and until his resignation in June 1915 he remained president of the Convention, "in charge of the executive power." In this way, the assembly kept the reins of government in its own hands, and González Garza not only had no power beyond that grudgingly conceded by the

Convention, but was completely subjected to a majority decision of the delegates. This hamstringing of the executive office did not appear so damaging at the time, for González Garza, as the personal representative of General Villa, had great prestige and the support of the Villista majority. When the Convention moved to Cuernavaca at the end of January and the Northern delegation was reduced to a minority, the position of a man so vigorous and independent of mind as González Garza became untenable. But on January 16 no one could foresee that eventuality, and the alarms raised by Cervantes went unheeded. Only three delegates opposed the Zapatista plan for a union of the offices, while seventy-nine supported it.[27]

With characteristic vigor González Garza began to reorganize the shattered government of the Convention. On January 19 he named his cabinet and sent his nominations before the assembly for its approval. Three members of Gutiérrez' cabinet were kept in their posts: the two Zapatistas, Manuel Palafox and Rodrigo Gómez, and Agustín Gama, subsecretary in charge of Commerce. Reflecting the Villista preponderance in the Convention, most of the members of González Garza's government were from the North. At the same time the new executive reinforced his earlier decrees of martial rule in the Federal District. With the consent of the Convention he ordered the death penalty for robbery, looting, murder, for the counterfeiting of stamps, money or bonds, or the falsification of telegraphic dispatches, and for the "circulation of false rumors" or "abuse of authority." [28]

One of the most serious problems facing the new government was that of currency circulation. Many types of money had been broadcast throughout the Republic, from the official issue of the government of Huerta, now outlawed by all revolutionary factions, to the shoddy bills printed by a group of revolutionaries in the state of Guerrero. The Villistas had brought with them banknotes printed for Villa at Monclova in April 1913. These bills were known popularly, if derisively, as "sábanas" (bedsheets). Other Villista bills, printed by the state government of Chihuahua, were termed "dos caras" or "dos caritas" because they bore the portraits of the two martyred idols of Villa, Madero and Abraham González. The Constitutionalists, of course, had used their own paper money in the capital between August and November 1914. After his assumption of power in Mexico City Gutiérrez had permitted the various currencies to circulate indiscriminately. The plethora of revolutionary banknotes in the capital not only drove from circulation the gold and silver coins minted by pre-revolutionary governments, but it presented an unhappy and perhaps insoluble problem for the merchants and businessmen for the next half year.

Because rival factions alternated in control of Mexico City until August 1915, the merchants could never be certain that money received at any one time would be legal tender at a later date. Each government, Conventionist or Constitutionalist, demanded that its own currency be circulated to the exclusion of all others. Those detected using or holding enemy bills were liable to a quick military trial and possible hanging as a *falsificador*. In periods of fluidity, therefore, when one faction seemed about to replace another, many prudent tradesmen preferred to close their shops or else to refuse to accept the prevailing currency. Since these actions threatened economic anarchy, they could not be tolerated, and the government would decree the forced acceptance of its own banknotes and demand that all closed shops be reopened for business. The problem remained unsolved until the final occupation of Mexico City by Pablo González in August 1915.

The Convention, taking into account the precarious monetary situation, voted on January 19 to urge the governor of the Federal District to use stringent measures against those merchants who refused to accept the Villista paper money. And on January 23, González Garza decreed the nullification of all Carrancista currency in circulation in the area dominated by the armies of the Convention. At the same time, in order to make the "sábanas" more palatable to the public, he offered to validate all such bills brought to the national treasury, that is, they would be stamped and guaranteed with the seal of his government.[29]

When Villa had gone north earlier in the month to meet Scott he had left behind near the capital a cavalry reserve under General Agustín Estrada. In addition, there were a few troops under Manuel Madinaveitia, Villa's chief of staff in Mexico City. As González Garza assumed control of the government of the Convention on January 16, he dispatched the forces of Estrada to run down the fleeing president, but the Villistas were unable to catch up with Gutiérrez' column, which tarried but briefly in the vicinity of Pachuca. From Pachuca Gutiérrez communicated with Obregón in Puebla for the last time concerning a *rapprochement* with the Constitutionalists. Rebuffed, he then struck north in the direction of San Luis Potosí. As he left the capital of Hidalgo he ordered, through Robles, that all revolutionary troops in the vicinity should attach themselves to his government. Daniel Cerecedo did so, but Roberto Martínez telegraphed González Garza for advice and was warned not to obey the president. Martínez then followed Gutiérrez and Cerecedo north, falling upon their rear at Los Venados, near Atotonilco, inflicting casualties and capturing some prisoners. He could not, however, bring their main body to bay or hinder their retreat.[30]

On the evening of January 17 González Garza arranged a telegraphic conference with Villa, who was now in Querétaro, to ask him to proceed without delay to Mexico City. Villa had already decided against this step, and he asked to "talk" with Madinaveitia. He ordered his chief of staff to leave the capital at once "in order to dominate the North." At the same time, he recalled Estrada from his pursuit of Gutiérrez. Villa could not know that Gutiérrez had failed to interest Obregón in his plan to unify their forces, and he feared that Estrada and Madinaveitia might be caught in a trap unless they left at once. Madinaveitia indicated that he was at the orders of his chief and Villa responded: "Evacuate this very morning. . . . If you have fuel for your trains, move them, even if you have to use firewood. . . . Take precautions, especially in passing through Tula. . . . Bring the Convention and González Garza if they so desire." González Garza replied that he did not believe it necessary for the Convention to leave the capital. But he asked Villa for five thousand troops to protect it, having as little trust as Villa in the competence or inclination of the Zapatistas to defend the city. Villa said that he could not spare that many troops, but offered to leave twenty-five men to protect the Convention. On this wry note the conference ended.[31]

From Aguascalientes Villa sent General Tomás Urbina with forces of the Division of the North to wrest San Luis Potosí from Eugenio Aguirre Benavides and forestall Gutiérrez' setting up his government there. Aguirre Benavides had been designated governor of the state by Gutiérrez. He sent Villa a telegram on January 16 declaring that Gutiérrez represented the only legitimate government in Mexico and had been chosen freely as president. He informed his chief that he "would support the government of Gutiérrez to the last." And at 6:00 p.m. on the seventeenth Aguirre Benavides published a manifesto against Villa and concentrated his troops in San Luis Potosí to await the coming of the president.

For two weeks the city was isolated. Telegraph and rail services were suspended and no news came from the outside world. By the end of the month the troops of Aguirre Benavides were on tenterhooks when word reached San Luis Potosí of the approach of troops from the west. They were Urbina's, not those of Gutiérrez. As Aguirre Benavides prepared to defend the city his men informed him that they would not fight against Villa. The troops were then withdrawn along the rail line toward Celaya, where Aguirre Benavides hoped to encounter Gutiérrez and link their forces. On January 30 Urbina occupied San Luis Potosí without opposition.[32]

When Villa learned that Aguirre Benavides had escaped to the south he ordered Agustín Estrada to cut him off north of Celaya. The two forces met at the historic site of Dolores Hidalgo, and Estrada inflicted a stinging defeat on his adversary. Aguirre Benavides turned tail, retreating across the states of San Luis Potosí and Tamaulipas. His decision to follow the ill-starred Gutiérrez had been a costly mistake, for he was now a revolutionary pariah, unwanted by any faction. He was ultimately captured by Emiliano Nafarrete, Constitutionalist commander in the state of Tamaulipas, as he sought to escape into the United States. Although he bore a *salvo conducto* from another Constitutionalist chief, Aguirre Benavides was shot to death as a traitor in June 1915.[33]

Meanwhile, Gutiérrez and his gypsy government moved slowly through the wildly undulating terrain of the Huasteca, harrassed by the attacks of Martínez upon the rear of the column. Nor did Villa purpose to permit the unhindered passage of the provisional president from Pachuca to San Luis Potosí. He and González Garza kept close track of Gutiérrez' movements, and there were frequent skirmishes (in one of these Gutiérrez was wounded) as various revolutionary bands attacked the rapidly diminishing army. A large part of Blanco's cavalry had already deserted to Madinaveitia near Pachuca. A few days later Roberto Martínez cut off a group of Blanco's soldiers near Actopan, capturing General Andrés Saucedo and his escort. But Gutiérrez shook off defeat and defection and managed to keep his straggling column headed north. By January 24 they had reached Tecozautla and on the next day they were in Tequisquiapan.[34]

By the end of the month, as they neared San Luis Potosí, Gutiérrez received the disheartening news of the capture of his state capital by Urbina. He and his followers then veered north and east, seeking refuge in the vaguely defined no-man's-land between the territory dominated by Villa and that under the control of the Constitutionalists. In the northeastern corner of San Luis Potosí, Saturnino Cedillo had carved out a revolutionary sphere of influence for himself and his brothers around Ciudad del Maíz, while Alberto Carrera Torres exercised a similar hegemony in Tula in the state of Tamaulipas. Difficulties of communication and the lack of importance of their areas permitted them to claim and maintain their independence from all other factions. José Vasconcelos has written in his autobiographical, though sometimes novelized, *La Tormenta* that Cedillo was inclined to recognize the government of Gutiérrez, but refused to commit his troops to a campaign which Gutiérrez hoped to launch into Coahuila. Carrera Torres proved even less hospitable than the Cedillos, and Gutiérrez and his decimated band of faithful adherents were forced to escape into Nuevo León. There they settled in Doctor Arroyo, a town in the most southerly tip of the state, so insignificant and so unimportant that no revolutionary had seen fit to claim it.[35]

The next few months were spent by Gutiérrez in sketching grandiose plans for attacks against the Villistas in Zacatecas and Saltillo, while José Vasconcelos was sent to Washington to plead the cause of his government with the State Department. But the winds of revolution had passed over Eulalio Gutiérrez, and his schemes came to naught. The presidential mantle, which he clutched so obdurately, if pitifully, had been fashioned of cobwebs and no longer served to conceal the heart of a "peddler who sold bedding on installments." On June 2, 1915, he renounced all claims to the presidency. Making his peace with Carranza, he returned, virtually forgotten, to his prosaic civilian status. In the history of Mexico's revolution, however, he had had his day of glory. He had served his country with honor, if not with distinction.

Others among his cohorts were less fortunate than Gutiérrez. General Mateo Almanza, the ex-Villista, was captured by Isaac Arroyo, a brigadier in Villa's Division of the North. He was tried by a summary court martial, charged with treason against the Convention. Condemned for his crimes by the Villistas, he died before a firing squad. Almanza's body was strung from a tree on the battlefield to be picked to pieces by vultures. His skeletal remains were meant to be a mute warning of the ire of Villa. Lucio Blanco made his way across the northern frontier into the United States to be interned in Laredo, Texas, for the duration of the revolution. General José Isabel Robles, on the other hand, returned to the Villista fold as a penitent. On April 2, 1915, he surrendered near Camacho to troops of Villa, together with his entire command, his machine guns, ammunition, and equipment. Abjectly he wrote to his Chief that he recognized his error, promising in the future to remain faithful. In a rare moment of compassion Villa spared the life of his old subordinate and companion.[36]

In the last two weeks of January, as Villa prepared for battle in the North and the West, rumors of the imminent approach of the Constitutionalists became endemic in Mexico City. Manuel Palafox, González Garza's Minister of Agriculture, who also commanded the Zapatista troops in the Federal District, sought to allay public fears by boasting of great, though nonexistent, victories for the Army of the South. And on January 23 he sent a circular letter to all governors loyal to the Convention, announcing that the long-awaited partition of lands would proceed. He said that agrarian commissions for the various states had been, or shortly would be, named by his ministry. González Garza reinforced the optimism of the Minister of Agriculture when he spoke before the Convention on January 25, describing in glowing terms the well-being of his government and stressing its good relations with foreign countries. Many more chiefs, he said, were now adhering to the Convention, despite the defection of Gertrudis Sánchez in Michoacán. On the same day he announced to the press the appointment of Villa as chief of military operations for his government.[37]

To his associates González Garza was extremely skeptical of the alleged successes of the Zapatistas and pessimistic about the future. On January 20 he asked Villa to permit Madinaveitia to march against the Constitutionalists, who menaced the capital from Calpulálpam, less than forty miles away. Villa replied that Madinaveitia's troops were now so far from the capital that it was impossible for them to return. In any event, he said, he was "developing various military plans which I hope will exterminate the enemy in a short time." Mexico City and the South, however, played no part in the immediate plans of Villa, either military or political. By the end of the month he was completely cut off from Zapata and the Convention, and he moved to regularize his already unofficial control of the North. On January 31 Villa announced the appointment of three cabinet ministers for his government. Miguel Díaz Lombardo was designated Minister of Foreign Relations, while Luis de la Garza Cárdenas and Francisco Escudero were named to the posts of Communications and Finance, respectively.[38]

In the first week of February Villa began his campaign in the West. Leaving Agustín Estrada in Querétaro to block any advance to the North by Obregón, he moved the bulk of the division through Guanajuato into Michoacán and Jalisco. The small Constitutionalist garrisons in Yurécuaro and Ocatlán abandoned their posts before the advance of Villa. Diéguez, still supported by Francisco Murguía, did not dare to risk an encounter with the more powerful Division of the North, and he ordered the evacuation of Guadalajara, The Constitutionalist forces in the state were pulled back to Sayula and Ciudad Guzmán. Villa occupied the city on February 13 without a contest. Since Julián C. Medina, the Conventionist governor of Jalisco, was alone no match for the Constitutionalists, Villa ordered Rodolfo Fierro to remain behind to bolster Medina's defenses. Villa then returned to the North to take charge of the floundering campaign against the Carrancistas in Nuevo León and Tamaulipas.[39]

Fully cognizant of the difficulties involved in holding Mexico City, Carranza was determined nonetheless to return the Constitutionalist armies to the capital. For one thing, the diplomatic corps had not followed his government to Veracruz as he had expected. For another, the earlier evacuation of the capital had been so hurried that the Constitutionalists had left behind valuable munitions factories and hospital equipment, needed for their war effort, as well as the presses of various periodicals. Further, if Villa were finally to be defeated, the Constitutionalists had to keep open the rail line which connected Veracruz to Tula and the North, the Antiguo Central, which ran through Ometusco and Pachuca. This would be difficult (though not impossible, as Carranza was to learn) with the enemy in Mexico City. The defection of Gutiérrez and the consequent split in the forces of the Convention gave Carranza his chance. He ordered Obregón to attempt to reoccupy the city immediately.[40]

When on January 25 it became known in the capital that Obregón was as near as San Juan Teotihuacán, the remaining Zapatista troops bolted for the South, leaving the city virtually defenseless. Continuing his optimistic demeanor in public—he informed the press that the Convention still dominated the military situation and that the enemy would be defeated within fifteen days—González Garza told the delegates in a secret session that their cause seemed hopeless, and that they must soon move either north or south. Upon the invitation of the Zapatistas the Convention voted on January 26 to disband and reunite in Cuernavaca. Many of the Villistas would have preferred to go north with Villa, but the possibility that Obregón might already be in or near Tula made this alternative less attractive. Villa telegraphed González Garza on January 27 from Aguascalientes, offering to send a train "with one or two cars" to bring the Convention to "comfortable quarters in Torreón or Chihuahua." But the invitation came too late, for most of the members, Zapatista and Villista alike, had already left for Cuernavaca.⁴¹

The Army of the South set up posts at Xochimilco, San Angel, Tlalnepantla, Tacubaya, Mixcoac, Tlálpam, and Contreras as Obregón was permitted to enter the capital unhindered. It was decided that the members of the Convention should assemble in Contreras and, under the protection of the Zapatistas, proceed to Cuernavaca, thirty-six miles over the mountains from Mexico City. González Garza remained in the city as long as possible to preserve order. After arranging to turn over the political control of the capital to the *Ayuntamiento* as a neutral body, he too left for Contreras before daybreak of January 27.⁴²

The Convention met on January 31 in Cuernavaca's Toluca Theater to confirm the union of North and South. A motion to adjourn their sessions so that the delegates might go forth to do battle with their fellow-revolutionaries was defeated. On the first day of February they began to consider anew the credentials of delegates, and the increment of Zapatistas though the following days slowly, but steadily, sapped the comparative strength of the Northerners. By the end of the month the Villistas were an unhappy minority, and González Garza was experiencing as much difficulty with Zapata as had Gutiérrez before him with Villa. During the sojourn of the Convention in Cuernavaca, Zapata made clear his lack of concern for the revolution outside Morelos, while the Zapatista delegates mirrored the xenophobic spirit of their chief. Although the Convention's program of reform for all of Mexico began to take shape in Cuernavaca, the conversion of the body into a stronghold of *Zapatismo* made the program but a glittering mirage. A successful revolution could not be managed by the men of the South. Only Francisco Villa in the North and West could assure the success of the Conventionist cause.[43]

8

A Hapless City

ON JANUARY 28, 1915, THE CONSTITUTIONALIST ARMY of Operations marched into the capital by way of the Villa of Guadalupe, and Alvaro Obregón took military command of the city in the name of the First Chief. As had González Garza earlier in the month, he decreed martial law, announcing that anyone who spread false rumors against the Constitutionalist government would be shot.[1] With the Army of the South occupying positions in the suburbs, however, Obregón's hold on Mexico City was, at best, tenuous. Zapata did not care to risk a pitched battle with the better equipped Carrancistas, but he was willing to wage a war of attrition, which was cheap in lives and ammunition, the latter an especially dear commodity in the South. That Obregón did not intend to hold the capital permanently is indicated by his failure to deal vigorously with the Zapatistas.

Nor did Carranza attempt to return, preferring the sanctuary of Veracruz for his headquarters. Instead, the military government announced that Mexico City was no longer to be considered the capital of the Republic. Félix F. Palavicini, in charge of public education in the cabinet of the First Chief, came up from Veracruz to arrange for the transfer of all governmental facilities to the port city. He told the press on February 1 that Carranza had decreed the formation of a new state of the Valley of Mexico, encompassing the area of the Federal District. On February 6, Obregón named General Cesáreo Castro as governor of the Valley of Mexico and military commander in Mexico City, now, he said, only a state capital.[2]

Carranza's prime purpose in these maneuvers was to force the diplomatic corps in Mexico City to move to Veracruz, such a move implying recognition of his government. But the ministers realized this and refused to be stampeded until their various governments had decided which revolutionary faction might be recognized. Both Carranza and Obregón disdained to acknowledge the continued presence of the foreign representatives and addressed no communications to them. Cardoso de Oliveira requested the American State Department to "intimate to Carranza" the advisability of leaving an official in the foreign office in Mexico City with whom to deal. In response, Robert Lansing, the Acting Secretary of State, telegraphed Silliman in Veracruz to inform Carranza that the government of the United States "deprecates his action." He said that if Carranza continued to bring pressure upon the representatives so that they left the country, the results might be other than he anticipated. Lansing said that the "most harmful impression [of these actions] abroad is that Carranza cannot maintain his government in Mexico City."[3]

Yet Carranza continued to deal only with Silliman and made no attempt to open the foreign office in Mexico City. Moreover, both he and Obregón were evidently set upon punishing and humiliating the residents of the city for their supposed hostility toward the Constitutionalists. Not only were factories stripped of machinery for transport to Veracruz, and automobiles and horses confiscated from private citizens for the use of the Constitutionalist army, but Palavicini's main purpose in coming from Veracruz was to preside over the dissolution of the educational system of the former capital. Schools were shut down, and the teachers were forcibly transferred to Veracruz. In addition, all public offices still in Mexico City were closed and their employees sent to Veracruz. So long as Obregón remained in Mexico City there was only a military government, and martial law prevailed. The citizens were subjected to the arbitrary justice of military courts with none of the traditional safeguards of civil law.[4]

Until the Constitutionalist forces occupied Mexico City the monetary exchange was the Villista currency, the "sábanas" and "dos caritas," for the government of the Convention was unable to print its own banknotes. It was not to be expected that the Constitutionalists would permit the continued use of these bills. In obedience to the orders of Carranza, Obregón decreed on February 3 the nullification of Villa's currency and the substitution of that of Carranza's government, which was being printed in Veracruz. While it was not surprising, this action of Obregón could not fail to wreak economic havoc in the capital. The outlawed currency had been in forced circulation up to the previous week, and the decree amounted to a virtual confiscation of property. The untimeliness of his action was attested by the fact that the employees of the municipal government and of the tramways company had been paid their wages in Villista currency earlier the same day.[5] The Chamber of Commerce in Mexico City communicated with Carranza to ask him to rescind Obregón's decree, but the reply of the First Chief was noncommittal. On February 4, popular demonstrations against the edict caused Obregón, who concerned himself with the needs of the people, if not those of the business interests, to suspend the execution of his order until he conferred again with his superior in Veracruz. But on the following day, Carranza confirmed the earlier decision, and the circulation of all non-Constitutionalist bills was declared illegal.[6]

Caught in a squeeze between two inexorable forces, many banks and business establishments preferred to close their doors, rather than comply with Obregón's decree. The actions of the Constitutionalists in the short time since their arrival did not presage a long occupancy of the capital. The Zapatistas continued to hold positions less than ten miles from the center of the city and made almost daily incursions into its outskirts.

Obregón did little more than to fend off these raiders, making no attempt to strike at their bases. At the same time, trains were dispatched periodically for Veracruz, loaded with machines and other factory equipment. For the merchants and businessmen to accept Constitutionalist bills when the morrow might see the resurgence of the Conventionist forces to render these bills worthless, was a form of lunacy not common in these classes. When Carranza was informed of the resistance of the merchants and bankers to his order, he telegraphed to his officials in Mexico City that, while some relief might be furnished the laboring classes, he had no concern for the commercial elements.[7] A number of business houses advertised, however, that they would accept Villista bills, despite Obregón's ban, having little confidence in his repeated protestations that the Constitutionalists would not soon evacuate the city. The military government thereupon sent troops, and the merchants were forced at gun point to open their safes. All Conventionist currency discovered was confiscated.

The monetary dislocations in the capital might not have proved insuperable had not the difficulties been compounded by a lack of food and water. After the evacuation of the city by the Army of the South, the Zapatista commander in Xochimilco proposed to the Convention that the pumping station there be destroyed to cut off the water supply to the capital. On February 2, the delegates in Cuernavaca debated sanctioning this act of sabotage, which would bear most heavily upon the populace of the unhappy city. After a member of the assembly compared it with the bombardment of civilians (in the European war) by shell and airplane, the consensus was that it was worth the risk of privation if Obregón might be forced from the city. The Convention gave its consent, therefore, and the pumping machinery at Xochimilco was put out of commission.[8]

By February 6 water was so scarce in the capital and the pressure so low that it flowed only between five and six o'clock in the mornings. To have water during the day it was necessary to fill bathtubs or other containers as reservoirs. While the more important residences or apartment buildings might have *tinacos* on their roofs to husband the precious water, the poorer classes often were forced to queue up before daybreak at public pumps in order to secure a small amount of water. Obregón announced on February 12 that the destruction of the pumping station had been so complete that no further attempt would be made to capture Xochimilco. John Silliman, now in Mexico City, reported to Bryan that the sanitation problem grew worse each day. He noted that there was not sufficient pressure in the pipes to flush out the drainage from houses or from the city's sewer system. Silliman wrote Bryan that the "stench is becoming plainly noticeable." [9]

Not until the end of the month did the Zapatistas, under the influence of Federico Cervantes, relent and notify Obregón that he might send engineers to Xochimilco to repair the pumps. For more than three weeks the city had to rely upon the antiquated aqueducts from the Villa of Guadalupe, which brought an insufficient supply of dirty, unsanitary water into the capital. When Obregón and his Army of Operations retired from the city in the second week of March, the service still had not been restored.

Even more serious than the scarcity of water was the dearth of rations. No one was likely to die of thirst, no matter how noisome or unsanitary the sewage system, though there might be some danger of pestilence. But the peril of starvation among the poor was real and ever-present as the Zapatista blockade shut off the capital from its wonted sources of food, especially breadstuffs. The only possible entry for food into Mexico City, except for the immediate environs, was from the East—from Pachuca, Puebla, or the state of Veracruz. No supplies came in from Morelos, or the larger part of the state of Mexico or from the North or the West. The rail lines from Puebla were operated by the Constitutionalists primarily for military purposes, however, rather than for hauling goods to the city. Many a train left the station full of soldiers or equipment, only to return to the capital with its boxcars eloquently and dishearteningly empty. And the Zapatistas harassed the Constitutionalist communications, frequently blasting rails or bridges, or assaulting the trains. Through February and early March the food situation in Mexico City became increasingly alarming, while the cost of living mounted as hungry citizens bid up the prices of the small amount of food available. To make an example of the businessmen, whom he accused of being "hoarders" of badly needed foodstuffs, Obregón forced a number of Spanish grocers—the Spaniards have always been popular scapegoats in Mexico—to sweep the streets of the capital with crude brooms.[10]

The *Mexican Herald* noted on February 11 the shortage of bread and reported that oatmeal and crackers, as bread substitutes, were rising in price. On the following day, a "meat famine" was announced by the newspaper. Obregón took the opportunity to deny the persistent rumors that an evacuation was contemplated.[11] An even more candid appraisal of the food insufficiency has been left in a dispatch from Silliman to Bryan. On February 12, taking note of the impending exhaustion of fresh meat supplies, he wrote to the Secretary of State that the Constitutionalist government had arrested butchers charged with selling horsemeat. The reluctance of the grocers to accept Constitutionalist currency made the situation more difficult, he said. Many of these, as the banks were doing, refused to open their shops, preferring to keep their commodities until the anticipated return of the Convention. The military authorities attempted to alleviate the sufferings among the poor by distributing new money from government relief stations. Thousands of the hungry, penurious masses gathered daily at these stations, said Silliman, clamoring for money and food. And the scarcity of fuel supplies, coupled with a severe cold snap, had led many people to cut down trees—even those on the fine boulevards—to be burned as fuel. It was to be presumed, Silliman told Bryan, that the Constitutionalist government was "taking advantage of the situation to obtain recruits for the army." High prices were being offered, he said, as lures for enlistment.[12]

In an effort to increase the recruitment of laborers into his army, Obregón had been making concessions to the Casa del Obrero Mundial, the Mexican equivalent of the I. W. W. and the chief workers' organization in Mexico City. When Obregón had occupied the capital initially in August of 1914, he permitted the reopening of the Worker's House, which had been forced to close during the regime of Huerta. Obregón and Antonio I. Villarreal had at that time appealed to the workers to make common cause with the Constitutionalists. Villarreal told an assembly of laborers that the movement of Carranza was not simply political, as many had charged, but was a genuine social revolution. When Obregón found it imperative to withdraw the remnants of his troops from the capital with the schism in the Convention in November, he invited the radical laboring elements to pronounce in favor of the Constitutionalists. But with Carranza's military fortunes at a low ebb and with the natural sympathy within the Casa del Obrero Mundial for the more radical Conventionists (Díaz Soto y Gama and Pérez Taylor had been affiliated with the organization), the workers delayed answering, preferring to await future events. During December and January the workers, many of them strongly anarchical or syndicalist by inclination, worked closely with the Convention.[13]

With Obregón once more in control of the capital, he began to press again the suit of the Constitutionalists upon the reluctant workers. He turned over to them for use as a headquarters the Church of Santa Brígida, as well as the building of the Catholic Colegio Josefino and the printing plant of the periodical, *La Tribuna*. Pious Mexicans were scandalized as the anticlerical workers threw into the streets, or otherwise profaned, many of the sacred objects belonging to the Church. Gerardo Murillo, a quixotic revolutionary painter, known throughout the Republic as Dr. Atl, was entrusted with a large sum of Constitutionalist currency to be distributed by the union to lessen the sufferings of the poor. The leaders of the Worker's House continued to resist the blandishments of the Constitutionalists, although many of the artisans succumbed to the siren call of adventure and a full stomach to join the Constitutionalist army. The organization released a statement charging that the war had degenerated into a political struggle of "bastardly ambitions."[14]

On February 8 the Constitutionalist periodical, *La Prensa*,

stressed editorially the advantages for the laboring classes in the
First Chief's program of reform, as enunciated in the Veracruz
Decrees of the previous month.[15] Still, the hold of the Conventionists upon the labor organization proved strong. On February
18 the military government arrested several radicals for distributing printed circulars to the workers, asking them to join the Zapatista cause.[16] At the critical moment Dr. Atl was thrown into
the breach. He addressed an impassioned plea to the workers to
embrace the revolution of the Constitutionalists, because, he said,
only the First Chief promised the certainty of agrarian reforms, as
well as security for their organization and for themselves. Swayed
by his eloquence, the members agreed to send delegates to Veracruz to arrange a pact with Carranza. "The workers," they said,
"are disposed to take up arms in order to shorten the duration of
the fighting . . . and to safeguard the victory of the poor against
the rich." [17]

The pact between the syndicalist association and the government of Carranza was worked out in Veracruz, although Carranza
showed some reluctance about making an accord with the radical workers. The government of the First Chief reiterated the
resolution of the decrees of December 4, 1914, to "ameliorate
through appropriate laws the condition of the workers, decreeing during the war all laws necessary to fulfill that resolution."
The Casa del Obrero Mundial contracted to recruit troops—
known later as Red Battalions—to aid the cause of the Constitutionalists.[18]

It is probable that, despite the pact made with Carranza by the
labor leaders, the prime reason the workers joined Obregón's
army—and subsequently that of Pablo González—was to get food
and money, not for any ideological affinity with the Constitutionalist revolution. Whatever the circumstances regarding the recruitment of soldiers in Mexico City, it did not cure, or even palliate, the economic distress. Silliman reported to Bryan on February 16 that there were still thousands of unemployed laborers
in the capital. And the food shortages grew worse day by day.[19]

The compact between Carranza and the Casa del Obrero Mun-

dial proved to be of little consequence in the history of the revolution. Carranza never lived up to his part of the bargain to pro-
mote social legislation, while the militarized unionists turned out
to be inadequate soldiers. Silliman told Bryan on March 16 that
Carranza was "having great trouble with the labor unionists
from Mexico City who lately joined the Constitutionalist
army." [20]

Stung by what he felt was the callousness of the propertied
classes toward the sufferings of the poor, Obregón determined
to force from them a monetary contribution to the revolution.
To Obregón there were two sources for money in Mexico City,
each equally recalcitrant toward the Constitutionalists: businessmen and the Church. In a spectacular gesture of hostility toward
the Church Obregón demanded publicly on February 12 a payment of five hundred thousand pesos "to meet the precarious
situation" in the capital. The order was given to Antonio de
Jesús Paredes, the vicar-general of the archdiocese, who had assumed charge of the clergy in the area upon the exile of Arch-
bishop José Mora y del Río. The sum was to be paid within five
days, said Obregón, to Alberto J. Pani or to Dr. Atl.[21]

Both Paredes and Gerardo Herrera, dean of Mexico City's
cathedral chapter, demurred at trying to force such a large contribution from the archdiocese. They made a counter offer to
Obregón, guaranteeing to raise an undisclosed amount of money
among the various parishes for local charitable purposes. They
felt that the curates would know better the needs of their parish-
ioners. Paredes said dramatically that he would sell the "last
chalice," if necessary, but he reiterated to Obregón the refusal
of the Church to pay five hundred thousand pesos to the revolutionary government when no such sum was available. On February 15, Fernando Iglesias Calderón, the ex-Liberal leader, called
upon Obregón at his military headquarters in the Hotel St. Francis, seeking to persuade him to annul the large levy against the
clergy. But the Constitutionalist commander was adamant, tell-
ing Iglesias Calderón that his order was final and irrevocable.[22]

When the five days had passed without any signs of compliance with Obregón's demands, he directed all the clergy in the capital to report to the National Palace at 10 A.M. on February 19. Monsignor Paredes continued to protest to the press that it had been impossible to raise the money. He said that the sole income of the Church was from tithes and that the unsettled conditions in the capital recently had made impossible the collection of these. At the appointed hour Paredes and 167 other priests arrived at the National Palace.[23]

Actually this number represented less than a third of the more than four hundred priests in the area. Many refused to come, not trusting Obregón—as it turned out, with reason. They were met in person by Obregón, who curtly informed them that they were under arrest and that they would be held as prisoners of the military government until the money was forthcoming. When the news of the seizure of the clergymen spread through the city, an excited crowd—mostly women—gathered before the office of the Ministry of War in the National Palace to demand the liberation of their curates. Upon orders by the military commander a squad of cavalrymen wheeled their horses into the throng to disperse the demonstrators.

Because some of the imprisoned priests were foreigners, Paul Lefaivre, the diplomatic representative of France, and Silvio Cambaggio of Italy called at Obregón's headquarters to ask that their nationals be released. Obregón agreed to free all alien clergymen if these priests would bind themselves to leave Mexican soil by February 22. This demand was accepted by the representatives concerned, and the foreign priests held in prison by the military government were sent to Veracruz to be deported.[24]

At about 10 P.M. of the same day, a group of women gathered in the Zócalo to march to the Brazilian legation. They pleaded with Cardoso de Oliveira to use his influence in securing the release of the prisoners. The Brazilian minister was too ill to receive the delegation, however. The priests remained in custody. And during the day Obregón released to the press a notice that within seventy-two hours his government would take measures to insure that both the clergy and the commercial classes would "receive the opportunity to collaborate with the revolutionary junta in aiding the people" of Mexico City.[25]

On the next day another demonstration of women, organized by Antonio Zuñiga, a lay Catholic leader, started from the Zócalo before the National Palace and marched to the St. Francis to repeat their pleas that Obregón free the priests. Zuñiga interviewed Obregón, asking him to release the clergy on condition that they pay the sum within a certain time. He told Obregón that the priests themselves were so poor that they would have to appeal to the Catholic people in order to raise the money. But Obregón pointed out that he had previously given them five days to collect the five hundred thousand pesos, and that they had made no effort to do so. Now he refused Zuñiga's request, alleging that the priests would "extort" the money from the poor. The deluded people, he said, would "give all of their resources to the curates" instead of buying food for themselves and their children.[26]

In an interview with a correspondent for the *Mexican Herald*, Obregón admitted that he had not expected that the priests would pay promptly the sum demanded of them. He had only imposed this levy, he said, in order to show the clergy in its true light, that in reality the priests had no concern for the physical well-being of their charges. Asked in what way the Church might do good, he responded sarcastically: "I have never believed the clergy capable of anything good. That body, which excommunicated Hidalgo and Morelos, applauding their murder, which curses the memory of Juárez, which is leagued with Porfirio Díaz to violate the Reform Laws, which applauds the assassin Huerta . . . , and which today proclaims itself with Villa, never can accomplish any good for our suffering country, whose curses it must receive always. A cancerous tumor has never done any good to the patient suffering from it. That body gave forty millions to the execrable assassin Victoriano Huerta and today has not even half a million . . . [for] our needy classes." Asked if he made any exceptions to this broad indictment of the Church, he admitted: "There might be some well-intentioned members of the clergy, but so small must be their number that the wickedness of the rest neutralizes their actions, and they can do no good so long as they do not break with [that] accursed association." [27]

February 21 was a Sunday and a pall of gloom lay over the city. Few churches were open and all but two of these for rosary services only. The doors of most, in prudence, were kept tightly locked. At the churches of San Felipe de Jesús and San Francisco, both on the Avenida Madero, low Masses were offered. Thousands crowded into these two as staunch Catholics gathered from all over the city. When the short services were concluded, many of the worshippers gathered in the Zócalo, conveniently near the two churches, for another popular demonstration of protest. The day was clear and the sun warm as they marched westward from the National Palace, down Madero and Juárez. Debouching from the narrow Avenida Madero in front of the "House of Tiles" (today Sanborn's Restaurant), the marchers were waylaid by a hostile group of "Liberals" from the Casa del Obrero Mundial, who had organized a counter demonstration at the foot of the monument to Benito Juárez on the south side of the Alameda. Taunting, angry words led to fisticuffs and canings, and soon the sabbath was profaned as the two demonstrations merged into a roiling contest between two rival philosophies. The clash at the monument dedicated to the great Liberal president was an ironic re-enactment of Mexico's years of State-Church problems. The police of the Federal District finally forced an end to the rioting, but not before two demonstrators were killed and many others injured.[28]

Meanwhile, the priests were removed from the National Palace to jail cells, where the turnkeys attempted to persuade them to purchase their freedom. The asking price dropped day by day until a *mordida* of five pesos was considered sufficient to permit the release of a priest. A few, including Monsignor Paredes, refused on principle to pay even a nominal sum. When Obregón prepared to evacuate the capital in the first week of March he ordered the release of the aged and infirm priests. Only 26 of the original 168 remained in custody. Obregón was stubborn enough to make an example of these, and they were herded into decrepit boxcars and shipped to Veracruz. En route the train ground to an unscheduled halt, and the 26 priests were ordered to march around the cars and to line up in a field. Certain they were soon to be the victims of the *ley fuga,* the unhappy priests fell to their knees, made a hurried sign of the cross and prepared themselves for death. But their fears came to naught, for it was only a joke. They were put back in the boxcars and arrived safely in Veracruz. Ultimately they were released by order of Venustiano Carranza, who was embarrassed that foreign newspapermen had reported their presence in Veracruz. The priests made their way back to the capital after that city had been reoccupied by the Convention.[29]

Obregón had not intended that the Church assume sole responsibility for ameliorating the sufferings of the poor. On February 22, as he had hinted in an earlier public statement, he decreed a capital levy on all businesses in the "state of the Valley of Mexico." It is interesting that the levy was to be calculated in terms of dollars, not pesos. He had no need for Carrancista currency, for his government could print all he required. The Villista notes, which the merchants had accumulated during the period the Convention was in Mexico City, were useless. Few had Mexican gold pieces or were willing to admit that they had. It may be that Obregón was fomenting a huge practical joke and fully expected that the merchants, as the clergy, would be unable to pay. It is now evident that he knew at this early date that his troops would soon be withdrawn. He may have looked upon whatever sum he could wring from the Church or the propertied classes as a fine for their opposing the revolution. At any rate, the attempt to get money to buy food was a farce, for the problem was the shortage of food, not of money. Obregón announced that the levy must be paid before 6 P.M. of February 26 and that foreign as well as domestic business concerns were liable.[30]

By February 22 the food situation was critical. All of the *molinos de nixtamal,* the shops which usually supplied *masa* for the city's tortillas, were closed for lack of maize. Late in the afternoon many persons, without food all day—tortillas provided the bulk of the diet for most lower-class Mexicans—made desperate attempts to find beans or rice in the markets as substitutes. Some were reduced to eating *piloncillos,* cone-shaped masses of crude sugar, the crusty leavings after cane sugar is refined, full of impurities and vile tasting. Many less fortunate than these passed the night with no food at all.

On the following morning crowds gathered at the government's commissaries only to be informed that there was no food there. A few vendors at the San Juan and Dos de Abril markets offered tortillas at exorbitant prices and these were soon sold out, despite the cost. The prices of foods had doubled or trebled or more since the Constitutionalists had come. Lard was two dollars a kilo, the highest price in Mexico City's history. On the last day of the month the food shops were still closed. There were by now no tortillas at all, no breads, *bolillos,* or *pambazos* (a type of roll). Many people, in desperation, sought bananas or other fruits in place of breads. But there was little food of any kind to be had. Bulk milk was also scarce, and that which was sold was liberally adulterated with water or flour, or both.[31]

Since Obregón's capital tax was directed against alien as well as national enterprises, the representatives of foreign powers interested themselves in the matter. On February 23 the diplomatic agents of France, Japan, Italy, Austria-Hungary, China, Sweden, England, Belgium, and Germany sent a joint telegram of protest to Carranza, calling his attention to the existence of treaties between their own countries and Mexico which banned extraordinary levies, such as this of Obregón, unless they were made throughout the Republic. The shops and offices of foreign firms had already closed their doors, sealing them shut with the waxed imprints of their respective consulates. Thus any attempt by Obregón to force open these businesses would be, *ipso facto,* a matter for diplomatic action.

Carranza responded to these protests by ordering Obregón to suspend the collection of the tax so far as foreigners were concerned. Obregón complied and at the same time extended to March 7 the deadline for the Mexicans to pay the tax. But as he announced to the press the modification of his earlier decree, he was bitterly critical of the "foreign capitalists" in Mexico City. When his derogatory words were relayed to Washington, Bryan was moved to address a stern protest to Jesús Urueta, who had taken the place of Zubarán Capmany in Carranza's foreign office in Veracruz. The American Secretary of State requested Carranza "to take immediate steps to prevent further statements of this character." But the protests of the government of the United States were to no avail. Obregón remained vociferously contemptuous of the foreigners under his jurisdiction.[32]

To combat the impression that they had no concern for the sufferings of the poor, the foreign colony in Mexico City organized an International Relief Committee in late February, obtaining an initial subscription of 125,000 pesos from two banks alone. Arrangements were made to purchase a quantity of food in Pachuca, San Juan del Río, and Apam, and on March 1 a member of the committee approached Obregón about the possibility of using the Constitutionalist rail facilities to haul the food into the capital. Obregón spurned the request and the offer of food, saying that the "Mexican people [do] not require any help from foreigners." When the Committee appealed over Obregón's head to Carranza, he too rejected the gift, alleging that the trains were being used solely for military transportation.[33]

The business and professional men of Mexico City had joined together to appoint a committee to interview Obregón, asking him to annul the noxious decree. On March 3 about 150 of these gathered at the Hidalgo Theater to hear a report of the committee. To their surprise and chagrin Obregón attended the meeting to render his decision in person. Taking note that his decree had been termed immoral, he asked the group: "Is there anything more immoral than a group of monied men and merchants who close their doors to a hungry people . . . ? The Constitutionalist army does not come to beg good will. It comes to impart justice." He warned his listeners that they "need not be alarmed over this decree, for others soon will be published which will alarm you more. . . . You have refused to pay the tax, but I have no intention of letting myself be outwitted. I am determined that my orders shall be obeyed." As Obregón finished his excoriation the merchants attempted to leave the theater only to find their exit barred. Obregón had stationed troops with machine guns at the doors of the theater, and all of the merchants were taken into custody. Those who could not show receipts to prove that they had paid the tax were remanded to prison cells.[34]

After the arrest of the merchants Obregón granted an interview to the press, and for the first time in public he admitted that the Constitutionalists were contemplating withdrawing their troops from the capital. He insisted that there was no valid reason for remaining. "I give no importance to this city from a military standpoint," he said. "It is not a strategic position; neither is it a railroad center. . . . For these reasons, whether to hold this city or not, it is all the same to us." At the same time Luis Cabrera in Veracruz told Silliman that Mexico City was "a white elephant" to the Constitutionalists which would soon be abandoned. The troops now tied up there, said Cabrera, would be used in a campaign being planned against Villa. To give credence to these words of Cabrera, Carranza ordered all train traffic suspended between Mexico City and the coast, except for troop movements.[35]

As Obregón proceeded toward the complete evacuation of Mexico City he exhibited his contempt for the niceties of diplomatic relations. His attacks upon foreign businessmen and the Church were sufficiently vexing so as to move even mild-mannered men such as Wilson and Bryan to anger. If in less than a week from the last part of February into the first few days of March the already weakened ties between the United States and the Constitutionalist government were stretched to the breaking point, it was primarily due to the words and deeds of Obregón in Mexico City.

Certainly all diplomatic and newspaper reports cast Obregón in a poor light. Although he had refused to accept an offer of food from the International Relief Committee, it could be seen by all in the capital that there were many unoccupied boxcars and idle engines in the stations and yards. That these were being held in readiness for the impending departure of the troops of the Army of Operations did not palliate the bad appearances. His public utterances seemed to be incitements of the lower classes to violence, and they were so interpreted by the government of the United States. On March 2 Obregón warned: "At the first attempt at riot I will leave the city at the head of my troops in order that they might not fire a single shot against the hungry multitude." And on the following day he told the merchants assembled in the Hidalgo Theater: "I will not punish hungry people who try to get bread and do justice to themselves. If my children had no bread I would go out and look for it with a dagger in my hand until I had found it!" [36]

There were rumors in Mexico City that Obregón had deliberately provoked the crisis by shipping food from the city in order to force the hungering populace to join his army. While thoroughly unsubstantiated and later denied by Carranza, rumors such as these had a profound influence in Washington. It is true that the Constitutionalists had stripped several hospitals in the capital of their beds and equipment. But in justice to Obregón it must be admitted that he and his men were soon to need these much more acutely than the civilians who remained behind.[37]

Robert Lansing asked Silliman and Cardoso de Oliveira to relay to Carranza and Obregón that the American government took an "alarming view of these actions." The seriousness with which Wilson regarded the situation is evidenced by his advice to Americans on March 6 "to leave Mexico until conditions become settled." And on the same day the president wrote to Bryan about "the extraordinary and unpardonable course pursued by General Obregón," which had "renewed talk of joint action by several of the governments of the world to protect their embassies and nationals. . . ." The antipathy felt in Washington toward Obregón in the first week of March 1915 might well have brought about another occupation of Veracruz. Wilson ominously requested Bryan to ask Josephus Daniels, the Secretary of the Navy, "if he has ships with long range guns, . . . which he could order at once to Veracruz. . . ." [38]

An American note was delivered to Obregón on March 7 by the Brazilian minister bearing the concern of the United States for the recent happenings in that city, and especially for Obregón's "utterances to the residents of Mexico City." He was informed that the American president could not "endure" these conditions, and that the government of the United States would "take such measures as are expedient to bring to account those who are personally responsible for what may occur." Obregón refused to accept the note, holding that such matters "of international character are not within his jurisdiction." Instead, he sent it to the First Chief in Veracruz.[39]

Wilson and Bryan thought seriously enough of intervention to ask Lansing to present his opinions on the subject. On March 8 Lansing wrote to Bryan advocating that American troops be used in Mexico to put an end to the troubled conditions in the capital. Anticipating that such a unilateral action would reflect unfavorably upon the United States in world opinion, he suggested that the State Department might explore the possibility of a joint venture with the ABC powers.[40]

In Veracruz the government of Carranza bristled at any hint of American intervention in Mexican affairs. Bryan's note to Obregón displeased Carranza, and he told Silliman privately that Bryan was "misguided!" He said that the American Secretary of State must sooner or later answer to him personally for this threat to intervene once more in purely Mexican affairs. Despite his oral belligerency, the First Chief directed a more tactful, if still forceful, communication to Wilson, denying all the allegations made by Bryan. "I point out," he said, "that [Obregón] has been in possession of Mexico City since January 26 without mobs, assassinations, looting, or other outrages. When we leave Mexico City, proper care will be taken of foreign rights, and they [the foreigners] can leave if they wish. . . ." He added that he had already addressed a note to the diplomatic corps in Mexico City inviting them to come to Veracruz when Obregón evacuated the city.[41]

Wilson's letter of reply to Carranza was written on March 11, although it did not reach Veracruz until many days later. The president thanked Carranza for the personal message, but he was blunt in his warning to the Mexicans: "I beg that you will understand that if our messages are occasionally couched in terms of strong emphasis, it is only because they concern some matter which touches the very safety of Mexico herself and the whole possible course of her future history. . . . To warn you concerning such matters is an act of friendship, not of hostility, and we cannot make the warning too earnest. To speak less plainly or with less earnestness would be to conceal from you a terrible risk which no lover of Mexico should wish to run." [42]

Yet while President Wilson was writing this letter Obregón had already begun to pull his troops from the beleaguered city, and the occasion for the displeasure of the American government and its possible intervention in Mexico was removed. The twenty-six imprisoned priests had been sent ahead by special train to Veracruz. On March 9 all the merchants and other businessmen, who had been arrested for failure to pay their taxes or to keep their shops open, were released. At the last moment Obregón turned the administration of the city back to the *Ayuntamiento,* which took control until the expected return of the Zapatistas. In the early hours of March 11 the last military train quit the capital, and by dawn the city was rid of the Constitutionalists.[43]

Carranza had designated the small but vital railroad center of Ometusco as a rallying point for the Army of Operations, but because a band of Zapatistas had severed the rail line of the Mexicano near San Juan Teotihuacán, Obregón moved his troops to Tula and Pachuca instead. During the rest of March Obregón prepared for the long awaited offensive against Villa's Division of the North. Weapons and ammunition were brought to Tula from Veracruz, and Obregón's army was reinforced by Constitutionalist troops from the state of Michoacán under Joaquín Amaro and Alfredo Elizondo.[44]

As the rearguard of the Constitutionalists pulled back through Mexico City the troops of Amador Salazar, Antonio Barona, and Genovevo de la O moved in cautiously on the morning of March 11 by the now familiar routes from San Angel, Xochimilco, Tacubaya, and Tlalnepantla. As the first Zapatistas were sighted they were greeted by the populace with hearty "Vivas," while the church bells of the capital sounded a clangorous welcome. The depredations and assaults of the past were now forgotten in the exquisite relief that Obregón and the Constitutionalists had at last departed. The joy of Mexico City at its deliverance probably had no ideological or factional implications, but rather was a reflection of the anticipated end to hunger pangs. It was expected that food supplies in the Federal District would soon be normal. To aid in the rehabilitation of the capital the Convention, still in Cuernavaca, voted to appropriate five million pesos to buy food and supplies for its inhabitants. It was a different Convention, however, which returned from Cuernavaca after a month and a half of Zapatista catalysis. The Southerners now possessed a sizable majority in the assembly, and the Convention's president, González Garza, found his political authority and his influence with the delegates severely curtailed.[45]

9

The Eclipse of Francisco Villa

GONZÁLEZ GARZA CAME TO CUERNAVACA AT THE END
of January bearing an olive branch for Emiliano Zapata. The
chief of the Liberating Army, however, took no heed of the
Convention or its government and withdrew to his mountainous
eyrie at Tlaltizapán. There he conducted at a considerable distance the amorphous and lackadaisical campaign against Obregón
in Mexico City. Zapata showed no inclination to take on the
Constitutionalists in a pitched battle, and the frequent armed
encounters between the rival forces for the next month and a
half were little more than raids in force by the Zapatistas
against the outskirts of the capital. The movements of the various
units of the Army of the South were entirely uncoordinated. A
band would push forward to engage the enemy in a fire fight,
only to fall back pell-mell at darkness or when the Zapatistas
had exhausted their scant store of ammunition.

On February 20 Zapata wrote to Villa, though the letter
was not received in the North until nearly a month later, asking for troops and ammunition to aid the campaign in the South.
Had Villa had a surplus at that moment it is improbable that
he would have sent any to Zapata. The spirit of union manifested
between the two chiefs at Xochimilco had been long since

dissipated. As it was, Villa stressed in his reply to Zapata the necessity of capturing equipment and ammunition from the enemy. In the end, the food and water blockade of Mexico City proved the only efficient weapon possessed by the men of the South.[1]

While the Constitutionalists occupied Mexico City communications between North and South were severed, except for occasional hazardous trips by mounted couriers. The principal rail lines all ran through the capital, and a possible connection with the north, a narrow-gauge road by way of Toluca, Acámbaro, and Celaya, was obstructed by the hostile neutrality of Gertrudis Sánchez and Alfredo Elizondo in Michoacán. In an effort to secure an alliance with the revolutionaries in Michoacán, González Garza authorized Colonel Gustavo Baz, the Conventionist military governor in the state of Mexico, to treat with Elizondo, even to the extent of handing over to him the town of El Oro Hidalgo. On the borders of Mexico and Michoacán, El Oro had long been disputed between the two rival forces in that area. But Elizondo refused to come to terms with the Conventionists and eventually came to Mexico City instead with Joaquín Amaro to join Obregón's Army of Operations.[2]

Rebuffed by Villa, Emiliano Zapata looked to the government of the Convention to furnish his army with two commodities: ammunition and money. Shortly after his arrival in Cuernavaca, González Garza agreed to turn over to the Zapatista paymaster general two hundred thousand pesos every ten days. Yet without an assured income, the government faced the certainty of bankruptcy within a few weeks, unless the Convention could return to Mexico City. González Garza had no means in Cuernavaca to issue more paper money, and he had brought with him less than two million pesos in the treasury, all of it the Villista "sábanas" or "dos caritas." To make matters worse, a large part of this paper money did not bear the stamp of the Conventionist government, and González Garza had forgotten to bring the "revalidating" machine with him to Cuernavaca.

In Guerrero the Zapatistas controlled silver mining areas from which they extracted a limited amount of the precious metal, converting it into a crude but valuable coinage. The people of Morelos preferred these coins to the alien bills from Chihuahua and refused to accept the latter, while hoarding the former. As early as February 2, González Garza found it necessary to decree that this paper currency be accepted in Morelos by force, if necessary, though no bills but those stamped by his government in Mexico City would be valid. In the next five days González Garza received numerous queries from the Zapatista commanders of various towns about the forced circulation of the Conventionist currency—a niece of Zapata was among those reported to have refused to accept the paper money. On February 8, in order to have enough money to finance his government, the Convention's president decreed the prorogation of his earlier order concerning revalidated currency. He announced that the unstamped bills would be in forced circulation as well.[3]

The financial quagmire into which the government of the Convention was slipping was responsible for a serious misunderstanding between Zapata and González Garza. In the first week of February, Zapata left Tlaltizapán for Iguala to bolster the revolutionary movement of Encarnación Díaz and other chiefs in the state of Guerrero. A "Revolutionary Bank" in that state had issued more than a million pesos in paper currency, so poorly fashioned that they were known popularly as "tordillos" (grizzled). Zapata had wrung an agreement from González Garza to furnish him eight hundred thousand pesos from the Convention's fast dwindling store to take the bills of Guerrero out of circulation. On February 9 Zapata wrote to González Garza from Iguala complaining that, though a commission had arrived from Cuernavaca with the money, more than five hundred thousand pesos were unstamped. The people of Guerrero, said Zapata, would no more accept these "sábanas blancas" than their own "tordillos." He asked that González Garza send an equal quantity of "good currency" immediately to replace that which was unstamped and, in addition, to make available the machine with which to revalidate the "sábanas blancas" now in circulation.[4]

Although he had on the previous day decreed the unlimited circulation of all Conventionist currency, stamped or unstamped, for a period of three months, González Garza hastened to comply with the request of the Southern leader. He wrote to Zapata on February 9, informing him that the money had been sent. He insisted, however, that all of the "sábanas" were valid, though some might be "inconvenientes." [5]

For a month and a half González Garza was harassed by the flat refusal of the state government in Morelos to assume the responsibility for its own finances. Although requiring a constant supply of paper money, which its citizens were reluctant to accept, the state declined to print any money of its own. The Zapatistas seemed to González Garza to desire that the whole Republic shoulder the liabilities of the small state of Morelos. Aware that the decrees of the forced circulation of the Villista bills would not cure the grave monetary shortage in the South, González Garza urgently requested Gustavo Baz in Toluca to procure linen paper "of a good quality" and inks of various colors, as well as hand presses, in order to print a new Conventionist currency.[6] Because of the constant attrition from the treasury without any source of revenue for his government, González Garza, in accord with the assembly, decreed on February 25 a new emission of twenty-five million pesos.[7] He wrote to Villa in explanation that these bills would be guaranteed and amortized by a forced "contribution from the mortgage bankers, the majority of them money grabbers, who have lived on their mortgage loans, without any risks or losses on their part and without hardships of any kind." [8]

The Convention met for the first time in Cuernavaca on January 30. The early sessions were given over to the examination of the credentials of more Zapatista delegates. As January gave way to February the Convention accomplished little. Debates were heated and full of personal allusions. The Zapatistas vented upon the Villistas their anger over the paucity of ammunition available to the Liberating Army, while the men of the North taunted the Zapatistas for the inactivity of their fighting forces. On one occasion a mob of Zapatistas broke open the door of the Toluca Theater, seeking to intimidate the Northern delegates.[9]

There were, nevertheless, occasional instances of harmony. At the end of February the delegates of North and South united in a humanitarian gesture in voting to reopen the water mains between Xochimilco and Mexico City. On another occasion the Convention took note of the rumors that many Yaqui Indians in the Constitutionalist armies were, when taken prisoner by the Zapatistas, summarily shot. It was agreed that many of these "unfortunates" had been tricked by Obregón into supporting Carranza, and that they should be treated with consideration "and shown that the cause of the Convention was their own." And on February 24 the assembly received for its consideration a 25-point program for revolutionary reform, which a joint committee of Zapatistas and Villistas had been preparing in Mexico City and Cuernavaca. The program was debated article by article and by the time the Convention reassembled in Mexico City the first 13 points—which dealt primarily with parliamentary government—had passed the muster of the Zapatista majority.[10]

While the Convention deliberated and Zapata dallied in Tlaltizapán, González Garza tried to make the most of his role as executive for the Convention. But he was plagued by the same troubles as Gutiérrez before him—both the Zapatista majority in the Convention and Zapata wished upon him a debility which frustrated his desire for a vigorous executive. In all the correspondence between Zapata and González Garza there was no indication of a single act of loyalty or friendship by Zapata toward the Convention's president. To the Southerners he was a financial milch cow, useful when affluent, but expendable when dry. González Garza suffered daily complaints from men in high and low office about shortages of ammunition and clamorings for increased allotments of paper money from his treasury.

On February 19, unable to endure his situation any longer,

González Garza submitted his resignation to the Convention. He told the delegates that he had originally been elected their presiding officer on January 9 and that more than a month had passed since that election, despite the rule adopted earlier by the Convention that the *Mesa Directiva* should be renewed each thirty days and that the president could not be re-elected. Although the Convention persuaded him to remain in office, assuring him that the rule applied solely to the vice-presidents, a disagreement ensued which led to the temporary withdrawal of the two Zapatista vice-presidents, Díaz Soto and Otilio Montaño. González Garza remained in charge of the executive power, but only with the sufferance of the Southern members of the Convention.[11]

González Garza found himself hamstrung by the inability or disinclination of the Zapatistas to see law, order, and regular government restored in Morelos. No elections had been held in the state since 1912, although the area was now at peace and there was no threat there from the Constitutionalists. Nor was there a civil government, either state or local. Civil law gave way to the caprice of military courts. The children were growing up unencumbered by education, for there was not a single school in the entire state. The peasants tilled their fields, the *hacendados* had been dispossessed, and the revolutionary chiefs played at war, drank pulque in the cantinas, and saw themselves enriched at the expense of the former masters of haciendas and factories. No taxes were collected, for the revolutionaries refused to concede to the Convention's government the right to levy them. Nor could González Garza exercise any control over the railroads, for these were administered by Eufemio Zapata, irresponsible brother of the Southern commander. The trains were used only for "military purposes," a euphemism for the whims of the revolutionary chiefs.

The president of the Convention wrote on February 21 to Díaz Soto and Montaño, complaining about the Zapatista domination of the railroads. He said that although the Army of the South required a subvention of more than twenty thousand pesos each ten days to operate the rail lines, no passengers or freight could be hauled. "There are military chiefs," said González Garza, "who deem themselves the owners of the forests and refuse to permit the cutting of fuel wood or crossties. When I say to you that there have been some armed men who have refused to let the engines take on water, I believe it will give you an idea of the situation. . . . Every chief asks for a train at whatever hour he wants and takes it wherever he wishes to go, without consulting anybody, while threatening the employees with death and committing actual assaults upon them. . . . For another thing, nobody pays on the trains, and it is difficult to recover the subsidy which is given them, so that instead of getting any use from the railroads, they are a liability to the government." [12]

In their reply, written on February 24, Montaño and Díaz Soto rejected the accusations made by González Garza against the Zapatistas, insisting they "desired only friendship between the North and the South." [13] They obtained some measure of revenge upon González Garza when, on February 27, the assembly accepted their proposal to make its presiding officer ineligible for the office of constitutional president. At the same time he was stripped of any veto power, even of a suspensive nature, over the actions of that body for the duration of his term. The question of the executive veto was debated furiously between North and South before the will of the Zapatistas prevailed.[14]

González Garza's difficulties, severe enough with the friction in the Convention between North and South, were compounded by the lack of discipline among the soldiers of the Liberating Army. As in Mexico City under the occupation of the Villistas and Zapatistas, brawls were frequent in Cuernavaca and other towns in Morelos, and some of these ended in a flourishing of pistols. Unable to exert any personal control over these troops, González Garza was forced to petition Zapata to ban the sale of alcoholic beverages among the members of the Southern army.[15] In this, however, as in most other matters concerning the government, Zapata paid no attention to the wishes of González Garza. As a result, excessive drinking led, on February 17, to a serious altercation between two generals of the Army of the South and open hostilities between the forces under their command. This senseless warfare within the Zapatista army demonstrated clearly the impotency of the Convention and the Convention's president to impose law and order in the areas they supposedly governed.

General Juan M. Banderas, who had shot to death General Rafael Garay two months earlier in Mexico City, had incurred the enmity of Zapata's most malign bully, Antonio Barona. The forces of Barona and Banderas were each attacking Mexico City near Churubusco, and it had been brought to Barona's attention that Banderas had disparaged him in a report to González Garza on the military activity in their sector. Banderas was supposed to have written that Barona had acted in a most cowardly manner in withdrawing his troops from the Hacienda de Coápam, which they had just captured. During the afternoon and evening of the seventeenth, Barona, who was in a cantina in Xochimilco with Santiago Orozco and Astrolabio Guerra, nursed his venom against Banderas, drinking innumerable glasses of pulque. As he became increasingly intoxicated, others in the cantina heard him cursing Banderas, accusing him of causing the death of Barona's brother. Late in the evening Barona decided to assemble his troops and to go to Tepépam, where Banderas' headquarters was located, to kill him. Orozco, who was his representative in the Convention, accompanied Barona part of the way and made no move to stop him or to warn Banderas.

At about 10 P.M. Banderas was asleep in his tent—the account by the participants in this imbroglio does not indicate any seriousness among the Zapatistas about capturing Mexico City —when Barona burst in to awaken him. Barona accused Banderas of calling him a coward and brandished a pistol before him. Banderas was not intimidated and insisted that he had reported Barona's actions correctly to González Garza. The angry words gave way to violence, and shots were exchanged. Barona was either a poor marksman or was befuddled by pulque, for he failed to hit Banderas at close quarters. He fled from the tent leaving one companion dead and another a prisoner. The cessation of fire was only temporary, however. Banderas' encampment was surrounded by high rocks, and Barona gathered his men behind them to engage Banderas' forces in a fire fight which lasted until three o'clock in the morning. Barona brought into action an 80 mm. gun, as well as several hand arms. A number of soldiers were killed in each party and many more injured. Banderas escaped injury, although his hat was pierced by a bullet and his headquarters was destroyed. In the end, Barona was forced to withdraw to his own sector.[16]

Banderas drew up a protest which he presented the next day to Santiago Orozco, who ignored it. He then reported the incident to González Garza and asked the Convention's president to take action against Barona. In the meantime, Banderas prudently withdrew his own forces from the Churubusco sector in order to avoid more trouble with Barona. On February 20 Banderas came before the Convention to decry the unprovoked attack made upon him and entreated the delegates to punish his adversary. The Convention refused, however, to accept the responsibility for enforcing order on the ground that this was purely a military affair. And Zapata, despite the intervention of González Garza, was unwilling to see Barona punished. It was clear that Zapata would not concern himself with law enforcement in the state of Morelos or in the Liberating Army of the South. Arguments must needs be settled by recourse to arms, not to the law. On February 24 the festering ill feeling erupted once more as one of Barona's officers shot to death a major in the forces of Banderas. In the end, González Garza took it upon himself to shift Banderas to the northern sector to obviate further trouble. Thenceforth, Banderas operated between Toluca and Mexico City.[17]

For the next two weeks relations between the Zapatistas and the executive office deteriorated even further. Santiago Orozco and General Zapata brought increasing pressure upon the government of the Convention to increase the allotment of funds for the Army of the South from two hundred thousand to two hundred and fifty thousand pesos each ten days. But González Garza refused, maintaining that it was better to give an insufficient amount gradually than to exhaust the treasury prematurely. The result was that González Garza, with his tight purse strings, became the scapegoat for the Zapatista anger at their lack of military success. And González Garza, for his part, did not seek to hide his contempt for the Zapatistas as soldiers.[18] On March 4 González Garza wrote Villa to say that "the situation has changed unfavorably for us. . . ." He said that he was sending Lt. Colonel Juan Antonio Acosta, his own chief of staff, to request personally that Villa give ammunition and troops to help the Convention. "We are not dejected or humbled," he wrote, "but we really do need your help. . . ." But by the time Villa received this request, he was in the North busying himself with plans for a campaign against Tampico, and he made no effort to aid the Convention or the Zapatistas in any way.[19]

Within a few days, however, González Garza and the Convention were back in the capital and the need for aid from Villa and for more paper money was less acute. Though the assembly continued to be dominated by the Zapatistas and grew increasingly hostile toward its presiding officer, the government could collect taxes in Mexico City and so had some source of income. The Convention held its last session in Cuernavaca on March 11. During the previous night word had been brought from Mexico City that Obregón's forces were evacuating. Not without a fervid debate in which many of the Zapatistas expressed opposition to leaving Morelos, the members of the assembly finally voted themselves in recess for a period of ten days, after which they would reconvene in Mexico City.[20]

In Washington, President Wilson and the Department of State continued their efforts to bring about a peaceful solution to the conflict in Mexico. During the first week of March Wilson sent Judge Duval West of San Antonio to Mexico to visit the several factions and to make recommendations which would help shape American policies toward the revolution. At the same time,

Robert Lansing conferred with the president concerning intervention in Mexico to end the hostilities. Both Wilson and Lansing remained unfriendly toward Obregón and the Constitutionalist First Chief, even though the troops of Obregón had evacuated Mexico City. On March 18 Wilson wrote to Bryan that he did not allow himself "to think of intervention as more than a remote *possibility* [the italics were Wilson's], but I suppose I must admit it is at least a possibility, and the possibility is worth preparing for. . . ." [21]

West met Villa for the first time on March 6 and found him affable and completely friendly toward the United States. Villa at once renounced any political ambitions for himself, preferring that the presidency go to Felipe Angeles. According to West, Villa's attitude toward Zapata was patronizing. He said he could "control" Zapata, but, while granting the good intentions of the Southern chief, he depreciated his military accomplishments. The trouble with Zapata, said Villa, was that he was surrounded by men of evil influence, such as Benjamín Argumedo. Because Villa was unable to assure West safe passage overland to the south he recrossed the border into Texas in order to go by sea to Veracruz. In his written report to Bryan, West stressed the good order maintained in the territory under Villa's domination. But the stable conditions were, he said, at the price of harsh and unjust military courts. If the United States were to recognize Villa and furnish him arms, said West, the chief danger would lie in Villa's own personal lack of respect for laws, property, and women. Until June the United States limited its diplomatic activity in Mexico to the routine day-by-day protection of American interests, and no moves were made toward overt intervention to favor any particular faction. [22]

On March 11 González Garza and the forces supporting his government re-entered Mexico City hard on the heels of the departing Constitutionalists to be greeted with popular acclaim. To spare the inhabitants further privation González Garza ordered the immediate repair of the pumping station in Xochimilco and the restitution of water service to the capital. Before long the severe distress of the city was alleviated, though food-stuffs continued in short supply for the duration of the revolution. As the merchants had anticipated, the Conventionist government immediately voided the Carrancista currency which had been in forced circulation since January. Once more only the "sábanas" and "dos caras" which were revalidated by the treasury were to be legal tender. Manuel Padilla, the official in charge of the Treasury Department, promised to seek means to lessen distress among the poorer classes with the change of the cur-rencies. Although martial law was continued in the capital, the consular seals, which had barred the doors of foreign establish-ments to the soldiers of Obregón, were removed. Business activity in Mexico City took on a semblance of normality.[23]

González Garza's hopes for regaining his independence from the Zapatistas upon the transfer of his government from Morelos to Mexico City were shattered almost immediately. He was informed on March 13 that Gildardo Magaña, a colonel in the Army of the South, had been designated governor of the Federal District by "a junta presided over by Zapata." When he arrived in the capital Magaña began to decree orders concerning the forced circulation of the Conventionist currency. González Garza responded with vehemence to this trespass upon his own prerogatives as the Convention's executive. He informed Magaña tartly that the designation of public officials lay within the province of the executive, not of Zapatista generals.[24] But his protest was in vain. Not only was the Convention itself dominated by the men of the South, but all officials in the capital with any authority were Zapatistas, as well. The three most powerful men in Mexico City were Santiago Orozco, in charge of the head-quarters of the Army of the South, Gildardo Magaña, who kept his post despite González Garza's opposition, and Amador Salazar, the Zapatista military commander. None heeded the Convention's president, except to direct impudent and vilifying communications to him. The Zapatistas could not forgive him for his frankness concerning the lack of valor of the Liberating Army of the South.[25]

Yet, whatever his private feelings, González Garza was the eternal Pollyanna in public, manifesting an optimism calculated to gloss over the weaknesses behind the façade of the Conventionist union. On March 19 he released a statement to the press of the capital stressing that Villa and Zapata together still controlled the greatest part of the Republic. Further, he said, relations between his government and foreign countries were good, in contrast with the harsh words the government of the United States had directed toward Carranza.[26]

In accordance with the decision made in Cuernavaca, the Convention reconvened in Mexico City on March 21. In the first session, although no important business was transacted, tempers flared as the Zapatistas and Villistas debated a minor, seemingly innocuous question. A proposal was made by a delegate from the North that the assembly adjourn for the day in honor of the birthday of Benito Juárez. Díaz Soto opposed on the technical ground that the Convention in Cuernavaca had laid down the rule that the first two hours of debate in each session would be devoted to a discussion of the program of reform. José Castellanos accused the Zapatista leader of tyranny against the rest of the delegates in refusing to let them address themselves to the people of Mexico City. Federico Cervantes could not lose the opportunity to gibe at his opponent by reminding the Zapatistas that in Cuernavaca Montaño and Díaz Soto had given many "florid discourses" to the people of Morelos. Should it not be prudent now to permit those who desired, to speak to the public? Even Pérez Taylor, the erstwhile companion of Díaz Soto, was at a loss to explain his vagaries. "Licenciado Soto y Gama," he said, "is the delegate of Cuernavaca, and therefore he desires that speeches be made only in that city. I am surprised that he does not want us to express our hatred for the bandit of Sonora, Alvaro Obregón!"

Díaz Soto answered his antagonists, holding that Cuernavaca was a city of liberties, while "Mexico is one of tyrannies." "The metropolis has never complied with its duties," he charged. When the public in the galleries manifested its displeasure at Díaz

Soto's attacks on Mexico City, he retorted: "It is of little importance to me if the galleries hiss me, because they are composed of the reactionary elements. Mexico City is the courtesan who applauded the triumph of Huerta and many other tyrants. I am glad to say that I am not a son of courtesans." In the end, the Convention was adjourned as the Villistas had requested, but the debate showed that, unless there was a radical change in temperament among the leaders, a rocky road lay ahead for the union of North and South.[27]

During the sessions which followed, the members of the Convention began to consider the articles of the proposed program of reform. Led by Antonio Díaz Soto y Gama, the Zapatista majority approved measures which would assure the juridical personality of syndicates and other workers' organizations. The Villista delegates, who represented a regime in the North which seemed synonymous with rapine and disorder, found themselves defending in the Convention the traditional nineteenth-century rights of private property and the individual. By the end of the regular session of March 27 the radical course of the Convention's government seemed assured. For the first time in Mexican history a national legislative body had gone on record as favoring social reform. But when the assembly was hastily reconvened later the same day the program of reform seemed suddenly of little importance. The military situation, which the delegates had blithely ignored in their fanciful flights of oratory, had worsened, and they were brought face to face with harsh reality. They were not to meet again, except for a brief session that same night, for nearly a month. In the last week of March the Convention was forced to consider the evacuation of Mexico City once more.[28]

On March 22 González Garza received from Gustavo Baz in Toluca the news that telegraphic communications had been reopened to the North and that Villa was reported to be in Monterrey.[29] González Garza immediately sent a telegram to his chief, informing him of the occupation of Mexico City by the Army of the South and asking Villa's opinion on the proposed

cabinet he was submitting to the Convention for its approval.
On the next day Villa replied, offering his felicitations for the
capture of the capital, but he had caustic words about the
Zapatistas. Villa complained that though there were but six
thousand enemy troops between Mexico City and San Juan del
Río, the Army of the South had been unable to do anything
about it. "Frankly," he said, "I think that the Convention will
find little advantage in remaining in that city, for the enemy
forces can attack them from one or another side, and you will
find yourselves obliged to flee again . . . to Morelos." Villa
said that he was the first to recognize the "patriotism, loyalty,
and good intentions" of the Liberating Army. But its "lack of
organization and discipline" had, he felt, reduced its accomplishments considerably. The solution to their problem, thought
Villa, was for the Convention to move its capital to Torreón
or Chihuahua in his own territory. There, at least, the delegates
would be safe from the Constitutionalists.[30]

Villa gave no consideration to a return to Mexico City. From
Monterrey he was organizing a three-pronged attack on the
remnants of the Constitutionalist troops in the Northeast. By
the end of the month his forces had captured the coalfields of
Coahuila and were bearing down upon Tampico and the oil-
fields in twin drives from Monterrey and Ciudad Valles. And
with Obregón in Tula, Villa could not afford to venture South
of Celaya, even to occupy the capital. His plan was to safeguard
the North by defeating Pablo González, who protected Tampico
at El Ebano, before turning south to confront the army of
Obregón. Despite his public attestations of respect for Zapata,
Villa was certain that the Army of the South could not handle
the Constitutionalists in Tula. He preferred that the Convention
come north while it could.

González Garza replied on March 24 to Villa's invitation by
refusing to contemplate a move from Mexico City at that time.
While he conceded that the capital had no military importance,
he maintained that the Convention could gain a moral and
political advantage by remaining. He recalled that the diplomatic

corps had refused to follow Carranza to Veracruz and would certainly refuse to follow the Convention as well. To do so, he said, would imply recognition of the Conventionist government, and no country had as yet made such a move. Moreover, said González Garza, as its president he was at the orders of the assembly. Now that the majority of the members were Zapatistas, they would without doubt oppose that course, he said. In conclusion, González Garza, while conceding the transcendent importance of the campaign in the North, asked Villa if he might spare two thousand soldiers. He felt that with this number from the Division of the North he could organize a "resistance of the people of Mexico City against the Carrancistas." Like Villa, he was under no illusions that the Army of the South could protect the Convention in Mexico City.[31]

On the following day, March 25, González Garza conferred with the Brazilian minister, Cardoso de Oliveira, and intimated for the first time that the Convention might evacuate the city, after all. Cardoso de Oliveira broached a plan prepared by the United States government for the neutralization of Mexico City and of the communications between the capital and Veracruz. González Garza responded favorably to this suggestion and promised that his government would be "removed to a site chosen by the Convention."[32] But when Villa in Monterrey was told of these negotiations he strongly disapproved of them as "a sign of weakness." He informed his representative that if he and Zapata wished to carry out such plans they might, but "tengan la bondad de no mezclarme en nada!" He reiterated his opinion that the possession of Mexico City was not worth the trouble of staying there, despite the presence of the diplomatic corps. He suggested again that the Convention and the government of González Garza come north to be with him in safety. It was better, he said, to abandon Mexico City to the Carrancistas than risk losing the greater part of the Republic by "foolish actions."[33]

At the urgent request of its president the Convention was reassembled in the Chamber of Deputies on the night of March

27. Because of the nature of the matter to be considered, the public galleries were closed and no reporters were permitted to enter the salon. González Garza laid before the Convention the danger that Mexico City might soon be cut off from the north of the Republic, for Obregón had begun to move his troops from Tula toward Celaya. For two weeks the Constitutionalist Army of Operations had lain menacingly inactive in the area of Tula and Pachuca, drawing reinforcements from Veracruz. But by the end of the third week of March Obregón confidently opened the long awaited campaign against north and central Mexico. On March 21 he arrived at Cazadero with the bulk of his forces, and on March 24 his advance guard reached San Juan del Río, just thirty miles from Querétaro. Thirty miles beyond Querétaro was Celaya, and it took no military acumen to see in Mexico City that within a few days Obregón would choke off the chief rail communications linking Villista and Zapatista Mexico. By March 27 there was no longer time for parliamentary dallying. The Convention must decide whether to make a dash for safety in Villa's North or to risk being forced back to Cuernavaca. Dramatically, González Garza repeated Villa's invitation to all of the members of the Convention to join him in Torreón or Chihuahua. With surprising concord the delegates agreed to accept his offer of haven.[34]

Yet on the next morning many of the Zapatistas began to regret their generous gesture of friendship toward the Villistas. Santiago Orozco issued an "urgent call" to the members of the Convention to assemble in the Chamber of Deputies at 8 A.M. "The matter to be treated," he said, "is so delicate that by not attending the meeting the delegates may meet with difficulties transcendental in character for the future work of the Convention." Although Orozco did not reveal the nature of the "matter" and González Garza publicly denounced the calling of such a meeting, it was evident that many Zapatistas, and even Zapata himself, did not wish the Convention to leave. Manuel Palafox, the most influential Zapatista in the Conventionist government, indicated to González Garza his reluctance to go north. Ignoring the critical shortness of time, he told the president of the Convention that he was unable to fix any definite time for his departure, "because of military and agrarian matters." [35]

The Southern leaders were especially concerned over the finances of their army should the Convention move from the capital. Santiago Orozco sent a complaining letter to González Garza on March 29 indicating that the Army of the South had no money with which to maintain itself. He also demanded the resignation of Genaro Amezcua, the paymaster for the Conventionist armies, who in the eyes of the Zapatistas shared with González Garza the odium for the government's parsimony toward the Army of the South. The Convention's president, undoubtedly pleased with the prospect of ridding himself of his most persistent critics, replied sharply to Orozco. Although he agreed to give Orozco two hundred thousand pesos immediately for the ensuing ten-day period, he flatly refused to ask for the resignation of Amezcua. Moreover, he accused Orozco of threatening him in every communication the Zapatista had directed to him. He concluded: "It would be very convenient if you would change your attitude toward me, for my comportment toward you, toward the headquarters of the South, and toward General Zapata does not merit, in my estimation, such letters as you have been sending to me. . . ." [36]

González Garza acted with dispatch in preparing for the new exodus of the Convention. By now the only avenue of escape from Mexico City was the narrow-gauge railroad through Toluca and Acámbaro to Celaya, and the rapid advance of the Constitutionalists indicated that the Conventionists had, at the most, a day or two to get by Celaya, unless a strong Villista force was sent to cover their flight. González Garza requested Villa to order General Agustín Estrada to move south of Celaya with two thousand troops to protect the area between Acámbaro and Toluca. Villa, from the security of Monterrey, assured his representative that there was "no need to worry about the enemy." He did, however, promise to do as González Garza asked. At the same time, González Garza requested

Francisco Estrada, who had moved a few hundred troops into El Oro, to advance toward Acámbaro from the south. The proximity of the Constitutionalists and the danger of entrapment for the Convention were brought home to González Garza by a report on March 29 from General Andrés Pérez in Tlalnepantla that a band of Carrancistas had advanced as far as Huehuetoca. Although he said that they had been ejected by the inhabitants of that town, their presence within twenty-five miles of Mexico City was alarming.[37]

When González Garza sought to commandeer a train for a trial run from Mexico City to Acámbaro, he found that the Zapatistas had placed armed soldiers in the railroad station with orders to prevent anyone's leaving the city. Outraged, he asked Zapata to withdraw the guard. Zapata, still in Morelos, acquiesced, but he assured González Garza blandly that he was simply making certain that the Convention left in a body, not helter-skelter as though in flight. His concluding words were a scarcely veiled threat to González Garza. He telegraphed that he had "recommended" to his chiefs in Mexico City that they not countermand the orders of the executive power "unless there is reason to do so." [38]

By the penultimate day of the month, all obstacles seemed cleared away. The Zapatistas dragged their feet, but made no active opposition to the plans of the Convention and González Garza. Even Manuel Palafox had ceased his obstructionist tactics. On March 30 he ordered the military chief in charge of the railroad to Toluca and Acámbaro to furnish five trains with six coaches each in the Estación de Colonia "for the disposition of the Sovereign Revolutionary Convention." González Garza assured Cardoso de Oliveira that the full facilities of the government would be maintained in Mexico City, while Zapata was mollified with the promise that money and supplies would be furnished regularly to the Army of the South.[39]

Though González Garza sought to keep secret the plans of the Convention, it was evident in the capital that a change of governments was near. He denied to the press that a general evacuation was planned. It was, he said, part of a plan to ensure the neutralization of the Federal District "with the sole and exclusive purpose of preventing the people of Mexico from again suffering materially the horrors of war." Nevertheless, the rumors continued that the Constitutionalists would soon return, and the anticipation of this had an unsettling effect upon what passed for a stock market in Mexico City. On March 30 there was a sharp drop in the prices of all Mexican stocks listed on the exchange.[40]

The State Department in Washington, which had been plagued by protests from American nationals in Mexico City, alleging mistreatment, confiscatory taxes, and even famine, was now confident that the area of the Federal District would soon be neutralized. Since González Garza had agreed to take the Convention from the capital, Bryan requested his agents in Mexico to secure the approval of Villa and Carranza to this neutralization and their acquiescence to the free movement of trains between Veracruz and Mexico City. Carranza would have no part in any peaceful dealings with his enemies, however. On April 5 he reminded Silliman in Veracruz that the American nationals in Mexico City had been repeatedly advised by Bryan and Wilson, and given every opportunity by Obregón, to leave if they desired. As for the railroads, Carranza said, they were being used for a far more important purpose than the provisioning of Mexico City. The First Chief expected that a victory for Obregón over Villa would present the American government with a *fait accompli* and wring from the State Department, however reluctantly, the recognition he felt was his due.[41]

On the same day Carothers conferred with Villa on the matter. Like Carranza, Villa was both recalcitrant and optimistic. He told Carothers that "after the coming battle tomorrow, such neutralization would not be necessary. . . ." He boasted that he intended to "annihilate the enemy." His anticipated success would leave only three isolated pockets of Constitutionalists in Matamoros, Veracruz, and Tampico, which he would soon surround, said Villa.[42]

In the end, the American hopes to neutralize Mexico City and the rail communications fell through, not only because of the refusal of Villa and Carranza, but because the Convention was unable to leave the capital in time. By March 31 it was already too late, for on that date the Constitutionalist Army of Operations reached Querétaro, much too close to Celaya to risk the passage of five trains loaded with Conventionists. On April 3 Obregón's troops occupied Celaya, as the Villista garrison there withdrew to Irapuato without a fight, and the last feasible escape route for the Convention was jammed shut. The fate of the assembly and the social program it supported rested squarely on the shoulders of Villa as the two mightiest chiefs of the revolution met in combat for the first time.

The news of the advance of Obregón's army caused Villa in Monterrey to break off his campaign plans in the North and to hurry south to meet this new Constitutionalist threat. That Obregón in Celaya would cut off his division from Mexico City did not concern Villa. He no longer cared what happened to Zapata. But Obregón in Irapuato would trap Rodolfo Fierro and Pablo Seáñez in the West. To Villa, this campaign in Jalisco was second only in importance to his own in the North. Villa assembled his troops in Aguascalientes and moved his division south. By April 4 he was in Irapuato, preparing for an assault against Obregón's army, which was encamped in Celaya, thirty-five miles due east.

Meanwhile, González Garza in Mexico City received an urgent request from Felipe Angeles, who had come with Villa only as far as Torreón, to secure Zapata's consent to an attack upon Obregón's rearguard. Angeles correctly anticipated the great importance of the impending clash between Villa and Obregón, and he asked that the Zapatistas cut the communications of the Constitutionalists with Veracruz. His plea for cooperation by the Army of the South was reinforced by two telegrams from Villa to Zapata to the same effect. Zapata agreed to launch attacks on the railroad between Querétaro and Tula and at Ometusco, but he complained to González Garza of a lack of ammunition. He seemed pessimistic about the outcome of such a venture, saying that he feared to use his forces at that time without an adequate supply of ammunition, lest he expose them to a "fracaso." González Garza reported to Villa in Aguascalientes on April 3 that the troops of the South had won a "signal victory" at Tula. Though this claim was later proved to be false, for there were no Zapatistas near Tula, it must have increased Villa's optimism at the outset of his engagement with the Constitutionalists. Cockily, he told Carothers that he intended to "crush Obregón and deliver a staggering blow to the Carranza [sic] movement." [43]

Celaya was a small city in 1915 with a population of approximately twenty-five thousand, known in Mexico principally for its candied fruits, the *dulces de Celaya*. Once Villa had initiated his attack several of Obregón's subordinates importuned their commanding general to pull back to Querétaro. But he saw correctly that Villa's superior cavalry and greater numbers in infantry would inflict severe punishment on the withdrawing Constitutionalist troops. Moreover, Celaya possessed in its many canals and drainage ditches an excellent terrain for defense. During the next ten days the events at Celaya made the twin battles there the turning point in the revolution, and for those few days it was the most important site in all of Mexico.

Between April 4 and 6 Villa concentrated his troops in Irapuato. His battle plans were twofold: to defeat Obregón at Celaya and to come to the aid of the Villistas in Jalisco. But Villa underestimated Obregón as an enemy, for he remained in Irapuato instead of advancing with his division. His troops were committed piecemeal by their individual commanders as they arrived at the line of fire. The battle took shape in a helter-skelter fashion, growing from a small fire fight between the advance guards into a full-scale battle without Villa's maintaining reserves or taking the other normal precautions of an attacking commander. Villa and his subordinates continued to show their predilection for massed cavalry and infantry attacks, regardless of their own losses, in the hope of driving the enemy back by sheer weight. It was to be a costly and ruinous tactic.[44]

At about 10 A.M. on April 6, Villa's scouts, probing forward from Irapuato, reached Guaje and engaged the Constitutionalist advance guard of Fortunato Maycotte. As more Villistas appeared, Maycotte's cavalry, offering little resistance, fell back precipitously toward Celaya. Through the day the build-up of the Division of the North continued before Celaya. As attack followed attacking wave against the Constitutionalist positions, Obregón's well-entrenched riflemen and his machine guns took a high toll of lives. Nevertheless, the fighting raged unabated through the night of the sixth and into the morning of the seventh. Despite the withering fire of Benjamín Hill's infantry, a single Villista charge in the early morning hours carried troops of the division into the center of Celaya. They jubilantly mounted into a church tower to ring out on the bells the news of Obregón's defeat. But this was but a premature and empty boast. The invaders were ejected, and during the day Villa's initial superiority turned into a Constitutionalist advantage.[45]

Obregón seized the opportunity of a lull in the fighting to throw the full weight of Cesáreo Castro's cavalry on Villa's flank to drive back the now dispirited soldiers of the North. Villa's division had been too reckless in its expenditure of men and, perhaps even more, of ammunition. By the evening of April 7 the Villistas were back in Irapuato, licking their wounds. The Constitutionalist army was itself too spent to exploit its victory, and the issue between Villa and Obregón was still to be decided.[46]

The published claims of the two parties to the battle were extravagantly at odds. On April 9 the *New York Times* headlined: "Villa Men Routed, Carranza Reports." And the First Chief announced that "Obregón is in pursuit of the fleeing army." Obregón asserted that Villa had lost three thousand killed, wounded, and captured, while he insisted that his own losses were only about five hundred. On the other hand, Carothers contended from Irapuato that the fighting was only a "skirmish in which the Carranzistas [sic] were forced to retreat toward Querétaro." Villa telegraphed Enrique C. Llorente, the Convention's agent in Washington, that the enemy was completely demoralized. The newspapers of Mexico City carried not a word of the battle, perhaps because it was a reverse for Villa, but more probably because telegraphic communications with the North had been severed when the Constitutionalists occupied Celaya, and the lines between Veracruz and the capital carried only diplomatic dispatches.[47]

Yet it is inconceivable that reports of the great battle at Celaya, however garbled, should not have found their way to Mexico City. In the days which followed, the Convention marked time. No sessions were held, as though the delegates were awaiting a decision from Celaya. But the ill feeling between North and South, always a danger within the government of the Convention, erupted to imperil the position of González Garza and the existence of the Convention itself. The Army of the South failed to aid Villa in any way. The promised attacks upon Obregón's rear did not materialize, and the second battle of Celaya began with the Constitutionalist lines of communication unimpaired from Celaya to Ometusco and Veracruz. Despite the exhortations of Villa, Angeles, and González Garza, the Zapatista commanders dawdled or made picayunish thrusts at the enemy outposts. The small successes they achieved, though much trumpeted in Mexico City, came long after the second battle of Celaya had ended. Zapata still did not care enough about Villa to venture out of the mountains of Morelos to lead his troops against the Constitutionalists.

A week's respite following the first encounter at Celaya gave both sides the opportunity to regroup and reorganize their forces. Villa was now deadly intent upon victory at any cost, and he put aside notions of launching a simultaneous attack on the enemy in Jalisco, drawing together his strongest forces in Irapuato. Obregón wisely remained on the defensive in Celaya and reinforced his entrenchments. Fortune smiled upon the Constitutionalists as a shipment of one million cartridges arrived from Veracruz in time to be used in the battle. Villa again scorned to take the defensive, hoping to retrieve victory by the same means which had brought him success against the federals at Torreón and Zacatecas. Before the battle was concluded, Villa was to miss sorely the sagacious counsel of Felipe Angeles, who had not come south with the division.[48]

On April 11 Villa asked four consular officers in the city of Irapuato to pass through the enemy lines under a flag of truce, bearing a message for Obregón. It was a plea, coupled with a threat, that Obregón come into the open to fight, or Villa would bombard the city "within two or three days" with sixty pieces of artillery. He asked the Constitutionalist commander to consider the inhabitants of Celaya and to save the town itself from destruction. Obregón was not to be drawn from his prepared positions, however, on a humanitarian ruse. He had learned from the European war what Villa seemingly had not—massed attacks could not succeed against trenches, machine guns, and barbed wire. He spurned Villa's challenge to meet his division in the open, knowing that the Northern cavalry and infantry would cut his numerically weaker forces to shreds.[49]

As he promised, Villa opened his attack upon the Constitutionalist positions at 6 A.M. on the thirteenth. His artillery, 75 and 80 mm. guns, boomed out its support for the charges of the division's infantry and horsemen. To belie his boast of two days earlier, Villa evidently could count on no more than thirty guns for this engagement. Obregón's troops were in their trenches in readiness, the infantry under Hill and the artillery under the charge of a German officer, Maximilian Kloss. Obregón stationed Castro's cavalry brigade and a force of infantrymen well behind Celaya in reserve. The Constitutionalist lines were now in a broad semicircle, embracing the western outskirts of Celaya. For more than twenty-four hours, as the men of Villa and Obregón fought each other with unabated fury, the flower of Mexico's revolutionary armies was despoiled. Villa mounted attack upon attack, determined to ram through the enemy lines. But the trenches held, and this time there was no penetration. In the end, Obregón picked the psychological instant of an exhausted

Villista charge to order his reserve cavalry against the division's left flank. It was the same tactic which had won the first engagement. As the cavalry charged, the infantry reserve enclosed the enemy's right flank and the Northerners wavered, then fell back in a general, disastrous, pell-mell retreat. The heavy guns were abandoned, and the foot soldiers flung aside their weapons and other encumbrances in their mad scramble to save their own lives.[50]

Castro's cavalry pursued the Villistas, inflicting heavy casualties and rounding up the dispirited enemy, who now surrendered in droves. Obregón's infantry pushed forward as far as Guaje before the decimated Villistas were able to break contact with their pursuers. From Aguascalientes Villa telegraphed his brother Hipólito in El Paso to rush ammunition and supplies from the United States as quickly as possible. Villa set aside a large sum of money in dollars to pay a bonus for the first shipment to reach him. The moment for reinforcements and aid had passed, however, for Villa was never able to redress the losses he suffered at Celaya.[51]

J. R. Ambrosins, an American who passed through the area immediately following the second defeat of Villa, has left a vivid account of the destruction wreaked on the Division of the North. In a telegram to a friend in Mexico City he called the battlefield "a terrible sight." Dead bodies, he said, "were strewn on both sides of the track as far as the eye could reach." Ambrosins asserted that he had personally seen five thousand Villista prisoners entering Celaya and that there must have been at least four thousand killed. Obregón claimed to have captured eight thousand enemy soldiers and at the same time minimized his own losses. He fixed his casualties at five hundred killed and wounded, probably far too low an estimate, however, even for an entrenched army. Villa admitted to George Carothers after the battle that he had lost six thousand men at Celaya. In any event, it was a crippling blow to Villa, one from which he never recovered.[52]

Barragán Rodríguez has felt that the subsequent encounter at León de las Aldamas was more important than Celaya in sealing the fate of Villa.[53] Yet the double victory of the Constitutionalists at Celaya undoubtedly marked the end of an era in the revolution. From then on Villa's fortunes ebbed. Obregón at Celaya not only blasted the legend of Villa's invincibility and drove a Constitutionalist spearhead into the vitals of Villa's own territory, but he forced Villa to recall his scattered forces from Jalisco and elsewhere in the Republic. The success of the Constitutionalists at Celaya relieved the pressure on Matamoros, Nuevo Laredo, and especially on Tampico. And if the Constitutionalists under Diéguez, Murguía, and Pablo González were able to hold these important sites, it was due not only to their own prowess at arms, but also to Obregón. This is not to depreciate the valiant seventy-two-day stand of Jacinto B. Treviño's army at El Ebano, which held off the Villistas under Manuel Chao and later Tomás Urbina from the oil-rich lands around Tampico. But it is clear that without the victory at Celaya, there could have been none at El Ebano, Matamoros, or Nuevo Laredo, or perhaps, in Jalisco. The month of April 1915 saw the fortunes of the First Chief and his Constitutionalist government suddenly in the ascendancy.

Secretary of State Bryan early recognized the importance of Celaya for American foreign policy. On April 18 he released a statement to the press in Washington indicating that the "failure of Villa . . . has about convinced administration officials here that the men upon whom hopes had been pinned for the pacification of Mexico cannot be relied upon to save the situation. . . ."[54] Thereafter there was no likelihood that the United States would either support Villa or recognize the Convention as the *de facto* government in Mexico. Instead, the policy followed by Wilson and the Department of State was to work for a peaceful settlement among the various factions which would terminate the bloody and costly civil war. It may be true, as Barragán Rodríguez contends, that Villa was not irreparably damaged. But he had lost twice at Celaya because he could not learn from adversity. The Villa of León de las Aldamas was the same Villa as at Celaya. He simply could not defeat Obregón. From the middle of April, because of the military impotence of Villa and the inactivity of Zapata, the Convention was living, debating, and wrangling on borrowed time.

10

Discord in the Convention

JUDGE DUVAL WEST ARRIVED IN VERACRUZ DURING during the first week of April 1915 to confer with Venustiano Carranza. If they met the fact is unrecorded, for West did not mention the First Chief in his reports to Secretary of State Bryan. Although President Wilson attached great importance to this mission and subsequently relied upon West's advice in revising American policies in Mexico, Carranza steadfastly refused to interest himself in Wilson's special representatives. Judge West found Villa, González Garza, and even Zapata easier to deal with than the First Chief. Wilson's emissary did not tarry long in Veracruz, leaving by train for Mexico City on April 5, accompanied by Arnold Shanklin. Shanklin was the American consul-general in the capital, and he was to act as West's interpreter. West was received in Mexico City with full diplomatic honors. It was a particularly inopportune time for the Convention, however. Not only was González Garza's cabinet rife with dissention, but during West's visit Villa suffered his two disastrous defeats at Celaya. Nevertheless, the Conventionists sought to impress him with the strength and justice of their cause and with the certainty of their ultimate victory.

On April 7 West conferred with González Garza for three

hours, and at the conclusion of their meeting the Convention's president presented him with a copy of the program of reform, which the delegates had been considering until the suspension of sessions in late March. On the following day Dr. Miguel Silva, acting for González Garza, repaid West's courtesy call upon his chief. At the moment of Obregón's victory over the Division of the North, Silva spoke optimistically of the strong leadership given the Conventionist forces by Villa. West provided a hint of later American policy shifts when he asked Silva if it were possible to achieve peace in Mexico through conciliation of the various factions, rather than through the use of armed forces. In the evening González Garza held a banquet in honor of Judge West at the San Angel Inn, attended by all the principal members of his government and of the Convention.[1]

As West prepared to go to Morelos to visit Zapata, he was made aware by Zapatistas in the capital that their chief had never received a reply to the letter he had sent to Woodrow Wilson in the previous August. West cabled Bryan on April 10 asking whether any action was taken as a consequence of Zapata's message. He said that "Zapata has been expecting a reply and feels hurt." The American president's concern for West's mission was indicated by the fact that he answered the query personally. On April 12 he telegraphed West that he had read Zapata's letter "with the deepest interest." "I am deeply sorry," he said, "that it was not acknowledged as I had instructed and can only ascribe this to a misunderstanding. The letter gave me a new and gratifying insight into the purposes of General Zapata and a new understanding of the Revolution." He told West that Zapata "may regard you as deputed to discuss the very matters he set forth in his letter and to hear any suggestions he may have to make that he would wish conveyed to me in the light of recent and existing circumstances." [2]

West was taken to Morelos by General Alfredo Serratos, and on April 16 he met Zapata in the headquarters of the Army of the South at Tlaltizapán. He found Zapata friendly, but incredibly naive, a rustic for whom the cosmos was circumscribed by the state boundaries of Morelos. Although West saw Zapata but briefly and his stay in Morelos was short, his assessment of the Southern leader was penetrating and accurate. No American agent before West had seen Zapata for what he was—a simple-hearted countryman with little chance or concern to influence the subsequent course of the revolution.

West wrote to Bryan that the peon classes in Morelos "look to him as a savior and as the Father." But as for Zapata's role in the greater revolution, West predicted that "his influence will eventually be narrowed to the people in the country he represents." Zapata told West that justice lay in seizing the property of the rich and giving it to the poor. He conceded, though, that he had little education and no experience beyond those matters pertaining to his life in Morelos. Zapata said that he found it impossible to live in the city, that his home was among his people, on their farms and ranches. In the state of happy anarchy he envisioned for his Mexico, he saw no need for a government or a standing army. All men, he said, should carry their arms as they tilled the fields. If the enemy should come, then the men must leave their occupations to defeat him. Life to Zapata was the soil, the air, the mountains of Morelos. And for these ideals —land and liberty—he led his revolutionary movement. But his interest was only with Morelos. Let the rest of Mexico secure its freedom and happiness in the same way.[3]

West returned to Mexico City on April 19 and informed Bryan that Zapata intended to send a commission to Washington to explain to President Wilson the "facts relating to the Revolution." He hoped to secure American aid and recognition for his movement. West had told Zapata in Tlaltizapán that he believed that Wilson would receive such a commission, if it were sent. But Bryan quickly exorcized the Zapatistas of such phantasms. On April 19, the day following his statement indicating a re-evaluation of American policies toward Villa and the Convention, Bryan asked West to tell Zapata that Wilson could not consistently receive a delegation from the Zapatistas, when he had rebuffed similar advances of the Constitutionalists. The

Secretary of State suggested that he would be personally pleased to see an informal delegation, if Zapata cared to send it to Washington.[4]

As a result of this invitation the Convention voted on April 27 to commission eight of its members to go to the United States to discuss the question of recognition with the American government.[5] No delegation was sent for several weeks, however, for the occupancy of Celaya and Irapuato by Obregón had shut off all avenues from Mexico City to the exterior. When a group of Conventionists, headed by González Garza, reached Washington in September of 1915, it was too late to influence the course of American policy.

As West prepared for his departure, the Convention's president requested the Zapatista chief in Mexico City in charge of the railroads to furnish the American agent with a Pullman car. But the matter was referred to Eufemio Zapata, who flatly refused to grant the request. "In the first place," he said, "there are no cars available. And even if there were, I do not think I would send one, for foreigners must realize that when they are on our soil they have no supremacy over the noble Mexican race. . . ." Toward the United States the Zapatistas exuded honey and bitter gall at the same time. The matter of a Pullman car was of slight concern, however, for West could have travelled toward Puebla no more than forty miles without crossing the lines of battle. At that time he would have to dismount. Without incident West reached Puebla by automobile and arrived on a Constitutionalist military train in Veracruz on April 29.[6]

After the return of the Convention and its government from Cuernavaca, Zapata remained in Tlaltizapán, indifferent to the proceedings of the assembly and the operations of the Conventionist troops north and east of the Federal District. The repeated requests of Villa, Angeles, and González Garza for the cooperation of the Zapatistas against Obregón went unheeded, and the Army of the South was virtually immobilized. During the month of April, González Garza sent almost daily telegrams to the various Zapatista commanders, rousing them to renewed effort against the enemy. But as frequently he received reports from all sectors: "There is nothing new." Only Almazán, J. M. Bonilla, and Porfirio Bonilla, east of the capital, were able to claim small victories; they blew up rails and blasted Constitutionalist trains whenever possible. But this activity was sporadic and uncoordinated. Communications between North and South remained closed, and Obregón was permitted to continue his advance almost unhindered.

When it became apparent that the Convention would remain in Mexico City, González Garza experienced increasing difficulty with the men of the South. The generals of the Liberating Army, particularly Santiago Orozco, continued to press him on the matter of paper currency, demanding that he make available to them an unceasing flow of money, which would cost the South nothing, yet would find wide public acceptance. González Garza was now determined to issue no new currency. On April 1 he ordered the derogation of the earlier decree of February 25 in Cuernavaca, which had provided for the emission of 25 million pesos. He asserted that his government, through its powers of taxation, had a means of postponing a new issue indefinitely. When the Zapatista El Radical attacked González Garza and published "false information" about the decrees, he reacted with vigor and ordered its suspension for a week.[7]

Next to Antonio Díaz Soto y Gama, Manuel Palafox was the sharpest thorn in the side of González Garza. Emiliano Zapata had insisted since the previous December that both Eulalio Gutiérrez and González Garza give the post of Minister of Agriculture to his secretary, Palafox. The Zapatistas saw in Palafox' position in the government the realization of their dreams of land reforms, the fulfillment of the Plan of Ayala. Consonant with the ideals expressed in this plan, lands were being confiscated in the areas under the domination of the Army of the South. Some estates reverted to the Indian pueblos. But many of the best properties were being expropriated by the military chiefs themselves. It was a phenomenon not limited to the Zapatistas, and the revolution was creating, thereby, a class of *nouveaux-*

riches landowners. Palafox, who was to preside over the despoiling of the *hacendados,* was known to be a *bribón,* not averse to feathering his own nest.[8]

In January Palafox, as a member of the cabinet of Eulalio Gutiérrez, had made arrangements with a clothing firm in the capital, Veyan, Jean, and Company, to purchase twenty thousand uniforms for the Army of the South at nineteen pesos apiece. In the light of future developments, Palafox would probably receive a *mordida* for his part in the deal. Shortly thereafter, the Convention left Mexico City for its month-long sojourn in Cuernavaca. Upon the government's return to the capital, Veyan, Jean delivered some of the uniforms to the Zapatistas and, on April 3, presented a bill to González Garza for 250,000 pesos. Since the treasury was virtually exhausted and he felt himself obligated to advance to the Army of the South no more than two hundred thousand pesos for each ten-day period, González Garza refused to honor the request for reimbursement. Through his secretary, Francisco Lagos Cházaro, he alleged that his government was not responsible for any contractual agreements made in the name of Gutiérrez. On the morning of April 7, as Villa was suffering his first reverse at Celaya, Palafox came with Díaz Soto to the office of the Convention's president. A stormy exchange of words ensued as Palafox accused González Garza of refusing to pay for legitimate army equipment. He alleged further that González Garza had deliberately withheld funds from the Department of Agriculture and the Army of the South, in order to cripple their activities.[9]

González Garza refused to back down, even in the face of the ire of the two most influential Zapatistas. He saw in his minister's breach of discipline a dangerous and unwarranted assault on his position as executive for the Convention's government, and he became convinced that drastic action was necessary. Later the same day he wrote to Zapata that relations between Palafox and himself were "worsening." He recounted to the Southern chief the happenings of the morning and categorically denied the accusations made by the Minister of Agriculture. González Garza offered to meet with Zapata and to present documents to him which would prove the rectitude of his case against Palafox. He had by now decided to seek a showdown with the Zapatistas by demanding the resignation of Palafox. He saw correctly that unless the excesses of Palafox and other Zapatistas in the capital were curbed, his position as head of the government was endangered. But he also knew that Zapata would take the dismissal of Palafox as a personal affront, and the letter of explanation to Zapata was an attempt to batten down the hatches before the expected storm broke.[10]

When González Garza intimated to leaders of the Convention —no word of the incident had been made public as yet—that he intended to exact the resignation of Palafox, Díaz Soto, as Zapata's personal representative, sought to forestall such a move. On April 9 he visited González Garza with Adalberto Hernández, the Zapatista Under Secretary of Agriculture, to ask him to "reconsider the delicate matter of the resignation of . . . Citizen General Manuel Palafox." But the president proved adamant and insisted that it was a question of honor. He said that he had been repeatedly insulted by Palafox and that this was but the culminating incident of many others like it. González Garza reminded Díaz Soto that he had been present when Palafox had come to the presidential office and had personally witnessed the latter's violent attacks. The two Zapatistas continued to insist on the withdrawal of González Garza's demand, threatening retaliation which would destroy the coalition of North and South. Still the president refused, maintaining that he had had sufficient provocation. He said that if he backed down now his action would be interpreted as "lack of energy or excessive weakness" on the part of the executive.

Unable to break the president's determination by threats, Díaz Soto sought to appeal to his patriotism. At that moment, he said, Duval West was in the capital seeking information upon which to base the policies of the United States toward Mexico. Would not the consequences, he insinuated, of an open rupture between North and South be calamitous for the Convention?

The specter of an ugly quarrel and the washing of soiled Conventionist linen before the eyes of Duval West proved too much for González Garza. With the utmost reluctance, he agreed to revoke his demand for the resignation of Palafox, but only on condition that both Díaz Soto and Hernández bind themselves to assure that Palafox would make no more trouble for his government. It was with evident satisfaction and in high spirits that the two Zapatistas signed the agreement to act as nursemaids for the volatile and unpredictable Minister of Agriculture.[11]

It is probable that they had no intention of complying with their commitment to González Garza, that they would seek the ouster of the president before they would consent to the elimination of Palafox. González Garza's troubles continued with his Minister of Agriculture, with Díaz Soto, and with other Southern chiefs in the capital. On April 22 Amador Salazar, the Zapatista military commander in Mexico City, ordered the arrest of all those Huertista members of the 26th Congress still in that area and their confinement in the penitentiary until they had reimbursed the government for salaries they had received from Huerta. The money, said Salazar, would be used to help the widows and orphans of dead revolutionaries. When informed of the action, González Garza branded it illegal. He requested Salazar, if he desired to proceed against those enemies of the revolution, to do so within the law.[12] On April 24 González Garza received a report from Gustavo Baz in Toluca that a week earlier Antonio Barona had seized the lands of several pueblos and an hacienda in the state of Mexico. Baz, as governor of the state, asked by what right Barona made these seizures. González Garza replied that his government did not sanction such actions and asked Baz to deal with Barona personally. But González Garza did nothing himself to enforce compliance with the orders of his government. Indeed, he could not. And as for Baz, Barona's reputation for savagery impelled him to take no course on his own which might lead to trouble with the Zapatista chief.[13]

By April 21 the long delayed sessions of the Convention were resumed, and debates began anew on the program of reform. During the next several sessions the Zapatista majority steam-rollered through the assembly several articles of the program dealing with the betterment of the lot of the laboring classes. The Villistas, particularly Federico Cervantes, protested, but without success. Workers were guaranteed the right to strike and even to employ the boycott. *Tiendas de raya* (hacienda or company stores) and payment of wages in *vales* (chits) were outlawed. Other articles were adopted to improve working conditions in factories and rural areas.[14]

On April 29, with labor reform out of the way, the Convention began to consider measures dealing with marriage and divorce. Most members of the Convention, like Carranza at Veracruz, were determined to keep the institution of marriage and its dissolution under the control of the civil government. As the debate began, however, Northern delegates José Nieto and José Casta opposed these proposals. Casta held that in supporting them the majority were in actuality defending "free love." "Just because Don Venustiano Carranza has introduced divorce," he scoffed, "we feel we must adopt it in order to say that we too are revolutionaries. I myself do not fear divorce, even though I am married, and it does not matter to me. But what I do fear is that this article . . . will constitute a grave menace for the future. . . . If there are men who get married without knowing what they are doing, why should the majority become the victims of those individuals?"[15]

The debate was carried over into the next session when Pérez Taylor spoke in favor of a divorce law and castigated Nieto as "Friar José," an epithet which elicited laughter from the assembly and hisses from the public galleries. "I saw with sorrow," he said, "that here we have been discussing the woman solely from a utilitarian point of view, as a machine to produce children. And for that we must blame the damned Church." This Church, he continued, declared "in a famous council that the woman does not possess a soul, committing the same blasphemy as Señor Casta, who assures us that love does not exist

. . . Who is the enemy of divorce? It is the priest, the accursed priest, who in the confessional tells a woman she should not leave her husband, lest she live in mortal sin forever—and in all this invoking the name of God." He concluded his malediction of the clergy amid a riotous mixture of applause from the delegates and catcalls from the galleries. As order was restored, the presiding officer, José Quevedo, announced that the rest of the session would be held in secret and that the public would be required to leave the galleries.

José Nieto immediately jumped to his feet to oppose this action, declaring to Quevedo that he must have the opportunity to answer the personal allegations made against him by Pérez Taylor. When Nieto was ruled out of order, he protested, insisting that his only honorable recourse was to leave with the public, rather than remain in the salon with the assembly. The spectators, who were being evicted by the Convention's guards, applauded him vigorously, while the Southerners shouted protests and insults against the public and against Casta and Nieto.

Quevedo left the rostrum to signal the conclusion of the public session, but Nieto would not be denied his protest. He climbed to the platform of the Chamber of Deputies to shout that the Southerners would not let him be heard. People in the galleries, still being forced out the doors of the salon, continued to applaud him, while the Zapatista delegates, to avoid listening to Nieto, left as well. Some of the Zapatistas, incensed at the obvious public hostility toward them, climbed into the balcony to abuse the spectators. When the galleries were finally cleared, Quevedo resumed the chair, and the Convention, with order restored, went into secret session. The matter to be considered, so important as to interrupt debate on the program of reform, was the renewed demand of González Garza for the resignation of Manuel Palafox.[16]

Despite the assurances of Díaz Soto and Hernández that they would assume responsibility for the continued good behavior of Palafox, relations between the chief executive and his minister had grown steadily worse. On the last day of April, in secret so as to obviate a public scandal, the Convention heard the charges of its president against Palafox. The question of the removal of Palafox was a difficult one, for Zapata could not fail to interpret it as a personal affront. Yet the charges were serious enough and sufficiently substantiated by González Garza so that the Convention, with the Zapatistas firmly in control, voted his dismissal.[17]

The reaction of Emiliano Zapata was immediate and vehement, and certainly not unexpected. On May 2, as the news of the action of the Convention reached him in Yautépec, he telegraphed González Garza: "I will not permit you to continue molesting General Palafox." He insisted that his friend must remain in his post. In a scarcely veiled threat against the Convention's president, he added: "I am coming personally to arrange the matter. In the meantime, you will take no action." González Garza assumed the position that the sole responsibility was that of the Convention, which had voted to remove Palafox. He sent Zapata's message to the secretary of that body and, at the same time, informed Zapata that the assembly alone was accountable for "resolving the matter." [18]

An incident of such importance could not long be kept secret. On May 3 the newspapers in the capital published the news of the "resignation" of Palafox. These stories elicited from him a letter to the editors of the *Mexican Herald* and *El Monitor,* denying their accuracy. Palafox said that he had not resigned, that the Convention had moved against him illegally. Under the rules of parliamentary government, adopted by this same Convention, he said, a minister could not be removed until the charges against him were aired fully, and he had had an opportunity to reply to these charges. This had not been done, he stressed. Palafox wrote: "I shall remain at my post and shall continue to do so, until the legal requisites have been filled for the removal of a minister responsible for his acts, and a duly justified decision is made." [19]

Upon receipt of this letter the editor of the *Herald* sent a reporter to interview González Garza about the accusations made against him by the Minister of Agriculture. González Garza expressed surprise that the newspapers had received information about the secret session. But since Palafox' letter was to be made public, he decided to release to the press a complete account of the affair from its beginning.[20]

The publication of González Garza's statements brought a second letter from Palafox, enlarging upon his earlier somewhat general charges. While he admitted that on April 7 he had expressed himself "in harsh terms before the chief of the executive power," his demeanor was, he said, "due to the marked hostility which [González Garza] has always manifested toward the affairs of the Liberating Army. . . . As I am here to defend the interests of the revolution of the South, I was by no means submissive to the hostile and impolitic manifestations made by the executive." Palafox contended that González Garza had on many occasions "threatened the revolutionary principles" for which the Zapatistas had struggled. As an example, he cited the marked interest of the president in the restoration of the estates of the Braniff family, which the Ministry of Agriculture had confiscated for the revolution. In his turn, González Garza gave to the press copies of the correspondence between his office and the clothing firm, Veyan, Jean, in order to prove his charges of corruption and insubordination against Palafox.[21]

Zapata was not to be put off the scent by González Garza's denial of responsibility in the affair. He knew that the Convention, on its own initiative, would not have cared to remove Palafox. On May 4 he telegraphed González Garza from Jojutla that he was "leaving today for that capital with all my forces." It was a dangerous moment for the Convention's president, and he met it with the unflinching courage and forthrightness which had characterized his entire revolutionary career. With but a single aide, he rode out to meet the Southern chieftain. Zapata's railway car had been brought from Cuernavaca as far as Los Reyes, and it was there that the two conferred. Although at one point Zapata drew his pistol and threatened to take González

Garza's life forthwith, the latter refused to be intimidated. He insisted upon his good faith in dismissing Palafox and said that he, as president of the Convention, must give orders to Zapata. Unable to break González Garza's determination, Zapata accompanied him as far as the Zócalo and the National Palace. Zapata did not remain long in the city. He commandeered a flat car of the street railroad system, rode his horse into the car, and was carried out to Xochimilco. By way of Los Reyes, he returned to Morelos and never, thereafter, saw Mexico City again.[22]

The incident was not closed, however. On May 8 Zapata telegraphed the Convention from Ayala to express his displeasure at the delegates' part in the demission of Palafox. He said: "May I be permitted to propose the following solution? If the Minister of Agriculture leaves the cabinet, you shall secure the immediate resignation of González Garza. But if González Garza is permitted to remain in power, General Palafox will keep his post as well." Zapata added illogically: "I am disposed to see that these two proposals are carried out." [23] The results of this ultimatum to the Convention were not immediately apparent in the recorded debates, except that during May Díaz Soto and the other Zapatistas became ever more scurrilous in their attacks on the executive. Palafox continued to occupy his offices and refused to accept his dismissal, and González Garza was powerless to oust him by forcible methods. The Zapatistas were content with the *modus vivendi* which left Palafox in control of the expropriation and distribution of lands.

The month of May saw no improvement in the military situation of the Zapatistas. There were a number of skirmishes to the north and the east, most of them inconclusive, and nowhere was the enemy forced to withdraw, except briefly. The greatest success for the Army of the South was the seizure of Ometusco, and the Zapatistas held the junction for a few days, blocking temporarily Carranza's communications with Obregón. But reinforcements were sent from Veracruz under General Agustín Millán, and on May 17 the Constitutionalists retook that site.[24] Because of the lack of any large-scale activity and the sporadic nature of the campaigning, the officers of the Liberating Army were enabled to spend much time in Mexico City. The frustrations at constant defeat, the jealousies among various revolutionary leaders, and the availability of spirituous liquors with much time to consume them, all combined to make breaches of the peace frequent in the capital. And González Garza found no means of curbing these excesses. The most serious incident occurred on May 7 and cost the life of one of the Convention's leading generals, Francisco Estrada, who was murdered by Antonio Barona in a drunken brawl. When Zapata was informed of Barona's crime he contented himself with ordering the withdrawal of Barona and all of his troops from the Federal District. Again Barona escaped punishment or retribution.[25]

Later the same day the Convention met to consider a course of action in the death of Estrada. The division between North and South was so complete that the Zapatistas, whatever their personal feelings in the matter, felt constrained to oppose any measure providing for the censure of Barona. Nieto and Cervantes insisted that Barona be brought to justice, but the presiding officer, José Quevedo, laughingly passed off the entire affair as a "boyish escapade." Díaz Soto supported Quevedo, maintaining that it was no more than a personal quarrel. Since the case was not political, he said, the Convention had no right to judge Barona. The men of the South seemed unconcerned about the death of Estrada, who was a Villista. At the conclusion of the debate, the Zapatista majority prevailed, voting to take no action. Rather they would refer the case to the military authorities in the capital.[26]

This affair was only the most spectacular breach of the peace at a time when crimes and assaults committed in the capital by the Army of the South had become frequent. The assembly, from the ideological heights of Cloudcuckooville, preferred to ignore matters as mundane as crimes of passion. The delegates whiled away their time planning for the utopian end of the revolution —a revolution, however, which the forces of the Convention were fast losing. González Garza had no authority to arrest or hold a member of the Army of the South. His sole recourse was to petition Zapata once more to exercise closer control over his troops. Zapata promised to do so, but the excesses were terminated only by the expulsion of the Southern army from the Valley of Mexico.[27]

By the end of April 1915, with the Zapatistas firmly in control, the Convention steered a more radical course than at any time in its history. The articles of labor and social reform in the proposed Program of Government were adopted, despite the objections of the Villistas. And on April 28 a group of Zapatistas, headed by Antonio Díaz Soto y Gama, introduced a measure to create a Committee of Public Safety within the Convention to deal with those "enemies of the Revolution," the Porfiristas and Huertistas, still at large and unpunished. The similarity to the institutions of the French Revolution was more than coincidental, for the men of the South saw themselves as the reincarnation of the Mountain, while Díaz Soto fancied himself another Robespierre. There is no indication that the Southerners anticipated or favored a reign of terror, although their opponents in the assembly, the principal spokesmen of the North, composed a picture of Mexican guillotines and tumbrels. The majority of the Conventionists merely wanted more vigilance than the revolution had shown so far.

The Villistas were determined to resist the formation of such a committee, which, they feared, would be dominated by the radical Zapatistas. As debate on the proposal began on May 3, Genaro Palacios Moreno termed it a dangerous step toward dictatorship. In retaliation, Sergio Pazuengo charged that Palacios Moreno was a Felicista. In a heated exchange of insults between the two, the words "liar" and "calumniator" were among the many epithets recorded by the reporters present. Throughout the session there was no attempt made to preserve decorum. José Nieto, to the accompaniment of the galleries' applause and hisses from the Southern benches, took issue with the proponents of the measure, maintaining that it endangered the traditional rights of the Mexican people. Holding to nineteenth-century Liberal values, Nieto said that if a Committee of Public Safety were formed and given broad powers by the Convention, "there would be no more law than the caprice of a majority, headed by Licenciado Soto y Gama, who intends by this means to wreak personal or partisan vengeance upon his enemies." [28]

The debates were carried over from May 3 to the seventh. Though there were caustic charges and countercharges between Díaz Soto and Cervantes, in the end the measure was accepted overwhelmingly. It only remained to designate the members of the Convention who would constitute the Committee of Public Safety.[29]

In its regular sessions, the Convention continued to take up new articles of the Program of Government. On May 6 the proposal to introduce a divorce law in Mexico was approved by a vote of 65 to 12.[30] On the following day the delegates began to untangle the knotty problem of Article 25, which provided for a thorough overhauling of Mexico's faltering educational system. In general, they followed the Constitution of 1857, in that lay instruction would be mandatory in the public schools. But their thinking proved to be more radical than that of the leading Constitutionalists and foreshadowed, to a large extent, the reforms built into the Constitution of 1917 at Querétaro. The assembly proposed that religious groups be forbidden to operate any schools whatsoever. The members of the Convention showed their impatience with the traditional literary education of the Mexican schools by insisting upon a strong emphasis on physical culture and the manual arts.

The currents of anticlericalism ran deep in Mexican society, and the irreligious spirit was manifested in the Convention among Zapatistas and Villistas alike. A small group of diehards, headed by Nieto, Mejía, and Zepeda, stood upon their Liberal principles. Mejía opposed any restrictions upon religious bodies. He advocated complete freedom of education, for the Church as well as for the civil government. Cuervo Martínez supported the measure, alleging that the "hand of the Church has three claws—the confessional, the pulpit, and the school." The national character, he said, could not be developed "while the priests have control of education, for they have turned the pulpit into a means of propaganda." He called for reform of Article 3 of the Constitution of 1857, which still permitted the Church to operate its own schools. José Nieto then sought to interpellate Díaz Soto on his concepts of liberty. Did he not, asked Nieto, believe in freedom of thought? Díaz Soto's reply was brief, but eloquent. "Yes," he said, "but not to teach lies."

The debate on this article was unique in that it saw, for the first time, Cervantes and Díaz Soto arguing in support of the same principles. Cervantes, though no radical, was a deep-dyed clerophobe. He told the delegates: "The school is something that must be kept untainted by anything religious. The role of the teacher is to educate the pupil within a system of pure morality, not of religious morality. From his first years in school the child is inculcated by the priests, who teach him lies, such as that of the dead spirits which return to haunt us. And they teach him ideas which keep him in ignorance and throw stumbling blocks in the path of his development. . . . I would a thousand times prefer that they teach philosophy and sociology in the schools, instead of religion. . . ." [31] The discussion was resumed in the session of May 8, but proved to be very brief and without an untoward incident. After Sergio Pazuengo moved that the article be amended to provide that instruction in all schools in the Republic, primary or secondary, be laical, it was accepted by a vote of 45 to 28. Ten delegates abstained.[32]

Though it was not the intent of the Convention, this was the last constructive act in Mexico City, for two matters of grave importance intervened to cause the delegates to suspend debates on the Program of Government and even the Committee of Public Safety. There was a worsening of the food situation in the capital which necessitated quick action on the part of the assembly. And when Roque González Garza seemed unable to solve the economic crisis the Zapatistas sought to remove him as the Convention's president. The Villistas resisted by leaving the sessions and deliberately breaking the quorum. By the end of May 1915 the assembly had virtually ceased to function and there was no possibility of further discussion of the desired reforms.

The Federal district, in the past, had drawn a good portion of its foodstuffs, grains especially, from the area around Acámbaro in the state of Michoacán. But the military successes of the Constitutionalists in April and the occupation of Acámbaro by Elizondo were reflected in a sudden and noticeable diminution of the amount of grain coming into Mexico City. By May 8 the government of González Garza was forced to announce that there was no corn at all in the city. Lacking tortillas or any other forms of maize, Mexicans of the lower classes would find survival difficult. With the shortage of all types of food, prices started to climb, and the populace began to relive the harrowing January days when Obregón had held the capital. Wherever, or more accurately, whenever, bread or *masa* was available, long lines would form. But only the first few persons could count on being lucky enough to secure food. The same conditions prevailed when wood or charcoal was offered for sale. And not only the indigent felt the pinch. In the front windows of fine residences along the Paseo de la Reforma or Avenida Chapultepec signs appeared offering to exchange a piano or a Chihuahua dog, an automobile or a phonograph for food. Many citizens, unable to find food within the city, went into the country to pick tunas, xoconostles, or nopales, the fruits or prickly leaves of wild cactus plants. Some, in a desperate attempt to stifle their hunger pangs, stuffed themselves with alfalfa or other animal fodders. And others, driven to violence, raided stores or looted the shops at various markets in the city.[33]

On May 17, after a long and rancorous argument in which Díaz Soto turned his heaviest salvos of opprobrium on González Garza, the Convention voted to give its chief executive fifty thousand pesos immediately to buy foodstuffs for the poor in the city. Díaz Soto called González Garza a friend of the bourgeoisie and a reactionary. With heavy sarcasm he said that there seemed to be plenty of money for subsidies for *El Monitor,* for a luxurious school of medicine, and a presidential guard.

The delegates also authorized the president to spend as much as five million pesos in relief work and directed the *Ayuntamiento* of Mexico City to fix maximum prices for all basic necessities. In order to secure an equitable distribution of foodstuffs, the government was ordered to buy them up and to sell them to the public at the lowest possible prices.[34]

Three days later the problem of the acute food shortage was literally thrust into the laps of the Conventionists. Mexico has always had a considerable portion of the population whose only mode of existence is the practice of the fine art of mendicity. The wheedling cry of the beggar—until recently—has been a common street noise in the Mexican capital. At this time the ranks of the legitimate beggars were swelled by destitute citizens unable to find enough to eat. When the Convention met on May 20, a crowd of hungry women and children gathered before the building of the Chamber of Deputies clamoring for relief. As their numbers increased and no one appeared to answer their pleas, they pushed open the doors and burst into the salon, interrupting the session of the Convention. Some brandished empty food baskets. Others held out their crying babies. All complained of their hunger.

The plaints of these women and their children touched the delegates and moved them to attempt personally to ameliorate the lot of the poor. Rafael Pérez Taylor proposed that each delegate give fifty pesos to buy maize for these starving people. Díaz Soto added that each should give all the money he had with him. This was not enough, said delegate Chargoy. He suggested that every member of the Convention give half his property to the poor. This gesture of excessive generosity found no seconding voice. Instead, a collection was taken, and more than six thousand pesos were distributed among the women in the salon. The good fortune of these few assured that a large number of persons would be on hand on the following day. But although a crowd of women and children again besieged the door of the chamber, there was no repetition of the previous day's largesse. The assembly prudently decided not to meet.[35]

Yet the crisis had to be met in some way. Later the same

evening the Convention was convoked to hear a report by González Garza on the state of the government and especially on possible measures to relieve the food shortages. It was, in reality, a long jeremiad against the Zapatistas. After four frustrating months as the Convention's executive, he made no attempt to conceal his resentment against the men of the South. Taking note of the charges by Díaz Soto and others that he was personally responsible for the sufferings of the poor, González Garza insisted that his conscience was clear, that he could refute any such accusations made against him. It was most unjust, he said, that Díaz Soto continued to attack him, while steadfastly refusing to accept a post of responsibility in the government. The Convention, itself, he said, had made it impossible for his government to function effectively by refusing either to accept or reject the cabinet he had proposed more than a month earlier. He spoke derisively of Francisco Pacheco, who, at the insistence of Zapata, had been named Minister of War. González Garza said that he had hoped that the appointment of Pacheco would "stem the waves of anarchy which threaten to envelop us." But he complained that Pacheco came to his office only when he "deemed it convenient," and was of little value to his government.

If the government was in a state of anarchy, the condition of the treasury was worse, he reported. There was not a single centavo left. Until recently, he said, there had been 234,000 gold pesos which had been hoarded by his government. But it had been necessary now to give it to the banks in trade for 400,000 pesos in Villista currency, in order to stave off bankruptcy. González Garza reviewed the monetary vicissitudes of the government of the Convention since Gutiérrez had made off with the larger part of the treasury. Although the Army of the South had agreed to receive 200,000 pesos each ten days, they had insisted that González Garza name a paymaster from their own forces, and, as a result, they had been collecting more than a million pesos in each period since the return of the Convention from Cuernavaca.

His government had attempted to keep on an even financial

keel, he said, by taxation, but the importunities of the Zapatistas had driven it to disaster. Although in the past he had resisted the demands that he print more paper currency, González Garza now asked permission of the Convention to issue notes in the denomination of one hundred pesos—an evidence of the spiraling inflation in Mexico City. For, he asked, unless he was permitted to issue paper money, how could he comply with the directive of the Convention to spend up to five million pesos to aid the poor? He recognized that the food situation would not be solved by the mere expedient of printing more bills. But he placed part of the responsibility for shortages on the Zapatista military chiefs, who were abusing their positions —those who refused to allow the railroads to carry anything but military supplies. The Convention, said González Garza, must take strict measures against those men who "without scruples or conscience" were causing misery among the poor.

In conclusion, González Garza made it clear that he was weary of the abuse heaped upon him by his nominal allies. He intimated that he might soon hand back to the Convention the executive power which had been entrusted to him. But as long as he was in office, he said, he would never permit Palafox in his cabinet. Nor would he change his course of conduct to please his detractors. He expressed the pious hope that there would soon be a genuine "closing of the ranks" among the revolutionaries of the North and the South, and that such a concord might include even General Carranza and bring peace to Mexico. Nowhere did he hint, however, that the cause of the Villistas and Zapatistas was waning. Any concord with the Constitutionalists, González Garza implied, would be on the terms of the Convention, not of Carranza.[36]

If González Garza really expected or hoped for peace with the Zapatistas, he was soon disabused of the notion. On the following day, May 21, the session of the Convention began with the Southern delegation seething with anger against the executive. A Northern delegate, Francisco R. Velázquez, who claimed to represent the Yaqui tribe in Sonora, asked to be heard, in order to make "a clarification." But Díaz Soto could not contain his ire toward González Garza and the Villistas, and he interrupted on a point of order to demand that Velázquez not be permitted to speak. When Velázquez remained standing and refused to give way to Zapata's representative, the latter accused him of being "servil" and "adicto al Ejecutivo." Ignoring Velázquez' protests, he delivered an indictment against the Northerners, singling out A. G. Castellanos and Federico Cervantes as "aduladores" of González Garza. Díaz Soto remonstrated that González Garza, as "acting executive," should have been permitted to address the Convention on the previous night. As he waxed more violent, and the charges against the Villistas became even more bitter and personal, several Northern delegates joined in exchanging invectives with him. To add to the furor, some stamped their feet or beat upon the tables, while the galleries, always hostile to Díaz Soto, howled insults at the Southern orator.[37]

When the bitterly passionate accusations and mutual recriminations seemed about to erupt into fisticuffs, the Northerners withdrew from the salon to meet separately in the Green Room of the Chamber of Deputies, thereby breaking the quorum. As they left, Díaz Soto heaped further scorn upon their heads, calling them "potbellies, scoundrels, rascals, bandits, and milksops." The Villistas returned shortly to hand José Quevedo a protest against Díaz Soto. They requested that he be examined by two doctors, and that if he were judged sane, he should be "required to give satisfaction" to the assembly for his actions. A few of the Northerners appended a second petition, asking that, in the event he was found to be unbalanced, another delegate be named by Zapata "until he had regained his faculties." [38]

A possible physical clash between the Villistas and Zapatistas was averted when, at the moment the Northerners returned to make their protest, the hall was invaded by a mob of hundreds of hungry women, who pushed their way past the doorguards and ushers. According to the correspondent for the *Mexican*

Herald, they cried: "Corn! Corn! We want corn! In the name of the Virgin Mary, do not deceive us! We want to eat! We want to live!" As the clamoring women milled through the salon, pleading with the members of the Convention for help, the delegates retreated with assurances to the crowd that they would soon have cheap corn. The lights were extinguished in order to drive the women out, and the abortive session, with no quorum present, was declared adjourned. But the passions aroused by the shouting orators of North and South could not be so easily turned off. There seemed, thereafter, no possibility of a rapprochement.[39]

The rules of the Convention provided for the election of a new *Mesa Directiva* every thirty days. They had not been enforced, however, in the case of González Garza. The result was that he had remained as the assembly's president, in charge of the executive power, since January, while the Zapatista vice-presidents acted as presiding officers. On May 24 a resolution was introduced by Villistas José Nieto, Genaro Palacios Moreno, and Alberto B. Piña to provide for the election of two new vice-presidents and four secretaries. The Zapatistas immediately seized the opportunity to rid themselves of González Garza. Díaz Soto moved that the entire executive committee be replaced, and that the assembly elect a new president, as well, as provided in the rules. It was at once apparent that this proposal was a ruse to evade the rules governing parliamentary government. These stipulated that the president could be removed only by a two-thirds vote in the Convention. The chairman decided that the Villista motion took precedence and must be voted upon first.

The debate was opened as the Zapatistas made the by now familiar charges that González Garza and the Northerners were reactionaries or Huertistas, and that they depreciated the soldiers of the Liberating Army. A long harangue by Díaz Soto led the exasperated Cervantes to echo Cicero: "In heaven's name, Catiline, how long will you abuse our patience? How long will that madness of yours mock us? To what limit will your unbridled audacity vaunt itself?" He called the accusations of the Southerners "infantile and mendacious," and insisted that González Garza was the "trait d'union" between North and the South.[40]

The discussion continued into the session of May 25, and it was clear that the real issue was the permanence of González Garza, not the replacement of the two vice-presidents. Otilio Montaño took the floor to castigate the executive as a non-revolutionary and a violator of the Plan of Ayala. "I come," he said, "to sustain the agrarian principles, the distribution of lands. . . . Eight months have passed and we have done nothing practical. . . . Nothing has been done about the agrarian question." Montaño called for the replacement of González Garza by a stronger executive, one chosen in conformity with the Plan of Ayala. Cervantes defended the Convention's president as an old revolutionary and a brilliant soldier. "I do not say that Roque González Garza is indispensable," he admitted. "For us of the North, who are not personalists, no one is indispensable." But the Villistas would insist, he said, that his removal be legal and not by the irregular manner, the subterfuge, contemplated by the Zapatistas.[41]

At the conclusion of the debating, a vote was taken on the motion to replace all of the Convention's officials, except González Garza. It was defeated by the Zapatistas, 53 to 38, far short of the two-thirds necessary to remove a president by the assembly's parliamentary system. The delegates of the South then attempted to interpret this vote to mean that their counter-proposal had been approved. Determined to block the summary dismissal of González Garza in a manner which was contrary to the spirit of the Convention's rules, yet knowing that the Zapatistas had enough votes to push through their own measure by a simple majority, many of the Villistas left the hall and deliberately broke the quorum. When a voice vote was taken on Díaz Soto's motion it was declared approved by Quevedo. But a demand by the Northerners for a roll call showed that there was no quorum, and the delegates recessed.[42]

For the rest of the month the Convention met sporadically, but enough Villistas absented themselves each time to assure that there would be no quorum. By this means the men of the North effectively blocked the elimination of González Garza. But it was only at the price of sabotaging the Convention itself. For without official sessions no business could be transacted. It was a stalemate which could not long continue without imperiling the existence of the Conventionist government.

11

Victory in Defeat

IT WAS NOW MORE THAN TWO YEARS SINCE WOODROW Wilson had become president, and Mexico's problems seemed as far from solution as ever. Though Villa's defeats at Celaya had demonstrated that the Division of the North was not winning the revolution, it was still not certain that Villa would lose ultimately. His forces were powerful and well equipped; his hold on the North and the Northwest seemed unassailable. Whatever the immediate military situation might be, it was apparent to the government of the United States that months or even years of fighting might be necessary before one side or the other emerged completely victorious. In the meantime Mexico was tearing itself apart. Men died in battle; women and children died in hunger and want. It was a prospect that the humanitarian Wilson could not endure. At the end of May 1915 he decided to take a more personal hand in bringing hostilities to an end. Once again there was a strong possibility of American intervention in Mexico. At this moment Judge Duval West arrived in Washington from Veracruz.

West presented to the State Department a long, detailed report of his meetings with Villa and Zapata. He had reached the not too surprising conclusion that most Mexicans did not want American intervention. But he did not consider any of the factions worth supporting. He saw that *Zapatismo* was too parochial to be of any value to Mexico as a whole. While he was favorably impressed with Villa's attitude toward the United States, he feared that there would be repercussions if the American government should decide to back the Division of the North because of widespread confiscations and especially of the personal proclivities of Villa in forcing respectable women to submit to his wishes. To Judge West the best solution seemed to be to "examine the situation from a constitutional point of view," so as to decide who was the legal successor of Madero and Pino Suárez. Then the United States could "use its influence to back the rightful claimant to power." Nowhere did West indicate that recognition should be accorded the Constitutionalists.[1]

West supplemented this written report in a personal conversation with President Wilson. Although it was announced after their conference that the president contemplated no changes in his policies toward Mexico, American diplomacy did veer sharply at the end of May, and this shift of direction seems clearly due to West's influence. He stressed to Wilson the disastrous economic conditions in Mexico as a result of the years of revolution. There was a widespread food shortage throughout Mexico, he said, and many fields lay fallow, as few cared to plant their crops. West feared that pestilence would sweep through Mexico unless conditions were alleviated and that such a pestilence would threaten the United States, as well. But there was no chance, he told Wilson, for a quick end to hostilities. To avoid a long-drawn-out, costly stalemate he recommended that the United States use its influence to seek a reconciliation among the various revolutionary factions.[2]

For many weeks almost daily reports had appeared in United States newspapers of the havoc caused by the revolution, of starvation and food riots, especially in the unfortunate Mexican capital. There were accounts that the inhabitants of Mexico City were eating rats, that a starving mob had fallen upon a dead mule and had torn it to pieces. Although many of the stories were gross exaggerations, there was a solid core of truth in them, for large parts of Mexico were in dire need of food. Transportation had broken down or was monopolized by the military. Starvation was possible in sectors only short distances from areas where food abounded. The repetition of these reports in diplomatic dispatches, in newspaper stories, and in statements from refugees, both Mexican and American, had a disquieting effect on Woodrow Wilson. He was particularly irked by reports from Mexico that Carranza's government in Veracruz had held up and diverted a shipment of five hundred tons of corn bought by the International Relief Committee and destined for Mexico City.[3]

A child of the Enlightenment and a nineteenth-century humanitarian Liberal, Woodrow Wilson thought in terms of the reasonability of mankind and of the necessity of resolving all differences by means of calm and sedate discussions. If only the contending leaders might be brought together around a conference table, they would end the revolution forthwith. In the last days of May he drafted a note to the Mexican factions which was to be released to the press in the United States at the same time it was delivered in Mexico. There were many rumors current in Washington, which were promptly relayed to Mexico, that the United States would soon intervene in Mexico, that a period of a month or two would be granted for attempts at reconciliation. If these failed, the United States would take unilateral action.

These rumors brought Eduardo Iturbide, who was living at that time in New York City, to Washington for fevered conferences with State Department officials on this proposed intervention. According to the *New York Times*, some of these officials were so "impressed by his personality" that they considered offering his name as a compromise candidate for the Mexican presidency.[4] If such an attitude was prevalent in the department, it demonstrated a thorough unawareness of the true conditions in Mexico. Iturbide, as a member of Huerta's government, was completely unacceptable to all revolutionaries. In fact, had it not been for the vigilance of American agents, who had spirited him out of Mexico under the nose of Villa, Iturbide might well have been dead.

Wilson presented a draft of his note to his cabinet members for their approval on June 1. The consensus was favorable, except that Bryan suggested a change in phraseology to make the note less a commitment on the part of the United States, and more an invitation and a warning to the Mexicans, leaving the door open to any one of several courses. Wilson had written that if the contending factions did not find a solution, the United States "would be constrained to look elsewhere" for its own solution. Here is a clear indication that Wilson was at least toying with the idea of going outside the ranks of the revolution to find a compromise candidate, a man such as Iturbide or Manuel Vázquez Tagle. It was thought in Washington that Vázquez Tagle, Madero's Minister of Justice, had been the only member of the cabinet who had refused to resign upon the usurpation of Huerta and so had a tenuous legal claim to the presidency. When Wilson substituted "for other means" for "elsewhere," Bryan asked him to change this to read "to decide what means should be employed," so that the United States would have more leeway to make its ultimate decision. Wilson accepted this suggestion of his Secretary of State and incorporated the change in his final draft.[5]

In his message Wilson took the attitude of a stern, but loving, father toward his prodigal son. In his recitation of the evils brought on by the revolution, the destruction of crops, the unseeded fields, the confiscated cattle, he showed how much West's report had moved him. In Mexico, Wilson said, "no man seems to see or lead the way to peace and settled order." He disclaimed any intention to interfere in Mexican affairs, but he said that his government could not see Mexico fall into utter ruin. The United States must now "lend its active, moral support to some man or group of men." The factions must unite, he warned, "within a very short time" or the American government

would be "constrained to decide what means should be employed
. . . in order to help Mexico save herself and serve her people." [6]

Wilson's note clearly showed Mexico a mailed fist beneath
the tendered glove of friendship. On June 2 it was telegraphed
to Silliman in Veracruz, Carothers in Aguascalientes, and Cardoso de Oliveira in Mexico City for delivery to Carranza, Villa,
and González Garza. With the publication of the note, the
Argentine ambassador to the United States, Romulo F. Naón,
called upon Bryan to give his approval. He suggested that whenever the United States decided to recognize a faction, it might
be wise for the ABC countries to grant simultaneous recognition. This suggestion pleased Wilson, for such an action would
imply inter-American cooperation, rather than singlehanded
intervention on the part of the United States.[7]

In Mexico Wilson's note was received with mixed feelings.
There was some hostility, some indifference, and even some
amusement. A Carrancista commander at Mazatlán remarked:
"What a witty man Mr. Wilson is!" [8] The Constitutionalists,
who were winning the war, were by and large disdainful of
Wilson's intentions. The American president seemed to expect
the Constitutionalists in the moment of victory to halt the war
and negotiate with the defeated enemy. The Zapatistas, with
characteristic disregard for the greater world outside Morelos,
refused to be bothered about it. Only the Villistas in the North
and within the Convention, now that they were losing ground,
clutched gratefully for the chance to conclude the uneven
hostilities upon favorable terms.

The newspapers in the Mexican capital carried stories on
June 1 concerning the impending note of the American president,
which stressed the strong likelihood of intervention by the
United States if an accord were long postponed. González Garza
immediately alerted all of the governors and military commanders
under his government to the dangers inherent in these reports.
The replies from the Army of the South—there were, of course,
no direct communications with Villa—were disappointing, but
not surprising, evidence of the narrowness of the Zapatista

spirit. Eufemio Zapata was scornful of the American threat. He recalled his earlier rejection of a request for a Pullman car for Duval West and informed González Garza: "We are not afraid to defend our country. . . . It does not matter if they send millions of soldiers. We shall fight them, one against hundreds. We may have no army or ammunition, but we have breasts to bare to their bullets. . . ." [9]

Emiliano Zapata said that when the moment came for American intervention he would "take such measures" as he deemed convenient. "But for now," he chided the Convention's president, "you should not worry about such picayunish things [pequeñeses] and devote your attention to matters of greater interest to our country. . . ." In his reply, González Garza expressed disappointment at Zapata's lack of concern, "for, as you shall see, the matter is really very delicate." Having already received Wilson's note and delivered it to the Convention, González Garza asked Zapata to direct his delegates "to cooperate in a very patriotic and disinterested way in the resolution" of the problem. [10]

On June 2 Wilson's note was brought by the Brazilian minister to Ismael Palafox, the official in charge of foreign affairs for the Conventionist government in Mexico City. As González Garza prepared a message indicating it had been received, the Convention held an informal session to consider the new development. Only about fifty members attended the meeting so that there was no quorum. But the Northern delegates agreed at last to the removal of González Garza. In that way, they felt, a harmonious front could be maintained by the Conventionist forces in the face of Wilson's insistence upon negotiations between them and the Constitutionalists. Thus the first fruit in Mexico of Wilson's new policy was the reluctant concession of the Villistas that González Garza was expendable, while Manuel Palafox was not. Meanwhile, González Garza, through Ismael Palafox, thanked Wilson for his interest in Mexico's problems and promised an answer as soon as the Convention decided upon a course of action. He "noted with regret that the final portion of this note contains remarks not in accord with the policy which up to the present has been followed by the government in Washington. . . ." He objected to Wilson's minatory attitude, which portended active intervention, possibly of a military nature, in Mexican affairs.[11]

Despite the need for quick action, there was no meeting of the Convention until June 5, when the delegates met in secret session. The atmosphere was charged with hostility, and the mood of the men of North and South boded ill for the prospects for peace. Antonio Díaz Soto y Gama ran the gamut in his attack on all those who were not Zapatistas. He railed against Wilson, against Wall Street, the Jews, the Villistas, the *Científicos,* and American diplomats and politicians. He accused Cardoso de Oliveira of altering the text of Wilson's note before it was delivered to the Convention. When Cervantes tried to speak in defense of the Brazilian minister, the Zapatistas would not permit him to be heard.[12]

Díaz Soto continued his reprobation of President Wilson and Duval West. He saw correctly that the American note had been the direct result of West's recent visit to Mexico. Díaz Soto accused West of demanding a bribe from the Zapatistas. He alleged that West had intimated to Zapata that Carranza had offered him and Silliman several million pesos to support the Constitutionalist cause. According to this thoroughly apocryphal account, West had become indignant when Zapata would not cross his palm with a single centavo. "From the understanding had between the venal West and the adventurous Jews of the International Relief Committee, resulted a report which will be an eternal insult and perennial infamy for our revolutionists," he said.

The foreigners in Mexico City, Díaz Soto insisted, "were spreading lies and calumny about revolutionaries and deserve to have Article 33 applied to them." (This was a reference to that part of the Constitution of 1857 which permitted the government to expel without a hearing "pernicious foreigners.") "If we really wish to be revolutionists and patriots," he told the delegates, "we should give that bigoted and ill-intentioned, unsuccessful professor of Princeton a severe lesson [by] hanging from our legendary cypress trees in Chapultepec the compilers of this report." He admonished the Conventionists not to "become alarmed with this ridiculous and childish note, which confines itself, as everything coming from Wilson, to words, and words, and words. . . ." When Cervantes again requested the floor to answer Díaz Soto, he was refused, the Zapatista majority holding that the note of Wilson had been sufficiently discussed in private.[13]

In the evening, when the session was thrown open to the public, Cervantes finally managed to be heard. He refuted the charges made against the Brazilian minister by reading from both the English and Spanish texts of Wilson's note. In conclusion, he called the attention of the delegates to the fact that Wilson had specified "a very short time" for the settlement of Mexico's difficulties. Others spoke of errors in the American note and insisted that Mexico was capable of governing herself without foreign intervention. Nowhere was there any sign that the Convention would seek a realistic concord with the Constitutionalists. The Conventionists, like their president, González Garza, still lived in a geocentric universe, in which the various revolutionary factions were all satellites, albeit errant ones, of Mexico City and their sovereign assembly.[14]

Francisco Villa proved more receptive to Wilson's suggestion of conciliation than either Zapata or Carranza. On June 10 he released a statement, through Miguel Díaz Lombardo, placing the blame for the intra-revolutionary hostilities on the shoulders of Carranza and the Constitutionalists. Grandiosely, he claimed to control the largest part of Mexico and made it appear that he would negotiate as a superior with the enemy, or at least as an equal. But what Villa did not care to say, perhaps would not acknowledge to himself, was that the area under his control was shrinking at an alarming rate. Michoacán and Jalisco had long since been abandoned to the Constitutionalists. By the end of May, the army of Carlos Treviño had begun a counterattack from El Ebano which drove the Villistas back toward Valles. And on May 23 the troops of General Vicente Dávila occupied Monterrey, forcing the Villistas to withdraw to Saltillo. Even more disastrous for Villa was his own defeat during the first week of June.[15]

After his twin losses at Celaya, Villa had dropped back to Aguascalientes to regroup his shattered Division of the North. Joined by the troops of Seáñez and Fierro from Jalisco, as well as other Conventionist chiefs in the North and East, he concentrated perhaps as many as 35,000 men at León de las Aldamas to renew his duel with Obregón. Felipe Angeles now counseled Villa to abandon the foolhardy tactics of charges of massed infantry and cavalry. Angeles insisted that Villa should take the defensive, forcing Obregón to fight him upon his own terms. Obregón must be drawn further from his base of supplies, said Angeles, and then cut off from Veracruz. But Villa proudly scorned to give up the initiative and failed to heed the warning of his "grey lieutenant." He prepared to attack Obregón once more.

On June 1 the Division of the North opened an assault on Obregón's Army of Operations, which was entrenched between Silao and León. In the battle which ensued Obregón lost an arm when he was struck by a shell fragment. But victory lay once more with the Constitutionalists, as Obregón's subordinates, especially Francisco Murguía, took the match of the once invincible Villa. The defeat of the Division of the North could not have come at a less opportune time. Villa's weaknesses were now confirmed and revealed to the world. The welcome news at Veracruz on June 6 that the Constitutionalist cause had again triumphed strengthened Carranza's hand in his dealings with Wilson. He need no longer consider the possibility of negotiating with the Conventionists. Ultimate victory was now certain.[16]

Characteristically, Venustiano Carranza did not answer Wilson directly, for he would not recognize the right of the American president to mix in Mexican affairs. Instead his reply came obliquely, by means of a manifesto to the Mexican people, which was released to the press on June 11. A copy was given to Robert Lansing by Eliseo Arredondo, the Constitutionalist agent in Washington. (Lansing had become Secretary of State, *ad interim*, only two days earlier, when Bryan resigned rather than face up to a sterner policy toward Germany with the sinking of the *Lusitania*.) In his manifesto Carranza pointed out the increased strength of his movement and called upon all the warring factions to submit "in order to expedite the establishment of the peace and to consummate the work of the Revolution." He directed the attention of the Mexican public to his Veracruz decrees and promised land reforms, but reforms which would not involve confiscations. The First Chief stressed the claims of his government to legitimacy and expressed the hope that it would soon be granted the recognition it deserved by the foreign powers.[17]

On the same day, Villa, who was now back in Torreón, sent through Carothers and the State Department a message to González Garza, Zapata, and Carranza. He asked all the chiefs to discuss their peace and unification terms, as Wilson had asked. He hoped in this way, he said, to forestall American intervention, which might bring the *Científicos* back to Mexico. Carothers talked with Villa at great length in Torreón and found him earnestly desirous of peace. The American agent informed Lansing that Villa would "accept any reasonable proposition." He frankly summed up to Lansing the desperate situation of Villa. His money was worthless and the treasury was empty. "Military commanders everywhere," said Carothers, "are grafting to the full extent of [their] ability." Although there was not a serious shortage of food, the lack of transportation, except for the army, and the reluctance of the producers to sell goods for fiat currency caused real distress in many parts of the North. Carothers concluded: "I don't see how existing conditions can last much longer without a collapse. If any agreement can be brought about . . . , it will have to be soon, or the country will be confronted with an anarchy that only military intervention could stop." [18]

Wilson was already becoming aware of the overwhelming strength of the Constitutionalist faction. On June 17 he wrote to Lansing to suggest unofficial feelers toward Carranza on the matter of granting him recognition. But Wilson could not relinquish his hopes for a negotiated peace. He thought all factions might be persuaded now to accept Carranza. The president told Lansing that the Constitutionalist leader must at least attempt a course of "conciliation and conference." "He cannot in our view," wrote Wilson, "afford to insist upon establishing his own dominion, unless he first makes a genuine effort to unite all groups and parties." [19]

Following Wilson's suggestion, Lansing requested Silliman in Veracruz to "say to General Carranza casually and in an unofficial and personal way that the government of the United States is watching with the greatest earnestness for indications that the leaders of the principal factions in Mexico are assuming a conciliatory attitude toward each other. . . ." In the fence-straddling jargon of diplomats, Lansing asked his agent to "intimate cautiously that it is within the possibilities . . . that the United States might recognize . . . Carranza, in view of the way things appear to be shaping themselves. . . ." But when Silliman approached Carranza with these intimations, he found himself in a diplomatic cul-de-sac. The First Chief made it immediately clear that the Constitutionalists would "under no circumstances" treat with Villa. If the United States conditioned recognition upon a conciliation with the enemy, then Carranza did not desire to be recognized. He promised Silliman that if the United States remained neutral, however, the Constitutionalists would soon subdue the opposition and recognition would follow as a matter of course.[20]

Throughout June the reports on conditions in Mexico continued to be depressing. There were more food riots in Mexico City. In the North Villa, pressed for money and supplies, redoubled his depredations against property owners, especially the cotton producers and foreign mining companies. Yet despite these provocations the possibility of American intervention receded daily. Mexico, which had been a mote in Wilson's diplomatic eye, was becoming less and less important. The president's attention was shifting to the European war. By the end of the month, with no appreciable progress toward factional reconciliation, Wilson was pleased to embrace the plan of inter-American cooperation first broached by the Argentine ambassador. Wilson asked Lansing to begin consultations with the ABC representatives in Washington to seek some other means of halting the revolution.[21]

In Mexico City the full Convention met on June 9 for the first time since May 25. In the morning the delegates held a secret session to work out the means for electing the new executive. Díaz Soto, supported by other Zapatistas, moved for a reformation of that section of the program for parliamentary government which stipulated that a president could be removed only by a two-thirds vote of the assembly. But the Villistas resisted this change—as they had when the issue originally came up—which would leave the tenure of the president subject to the whims of a temporary majority. The Zapatistas then abandoned that course, and the two factions agreed that the rules of parliamentary government need not apply to González Garza, but only to a constitutionally elected president. When the method of replacing the president had been decided, the consensus of the assembly was that the Convention itself should exercise the executive power, but that this authority should be delegated to one of its members. Thereupon the Convention settled upon Francisco Lagos Cházaro, former governor of Veracruz, as the virtually unanimous choice for the now further emasculated office of the chief executive.[22]

In the afternoon session, which was now open to the public, the members of the Convention duly cast their ballots for Lagos Cházaro. Only three votes were recorded against him. While the new executive was being notified of his election, General Alfredo R. Serratos spoke in favor of a unification of all the revolutionary factions under the banner of the Convention. Serratos, and the Convention with him, seemed insensible to the realities of the military campaigns. He hailed the election of the new executive, but said that Lagos Cházaro would serve only until the time when all the different revolutionaries in the field should lay down their arms and come to the Convention as brothers. Then a permanent president would be elected, he said.

At that moment, Lagos Cházaro entered the hall to address the Convention. His speech lacked the fire of González Garza. He was a man of little distinction in the revolution, and this was, of course, the reason the Zapatistas had agreed to accept him. He made a simple recital of his aims. He would, he said, work for the union of Villa and Zapata in the Convention. He promised that on the next day he would present his cabinet choices for the approval of the delegates. As Lagos Cházaro took his seat the brief concord was ended as Díaz Soto launched an attack against the Villistas, calling them personalists, and urging a radical course upon the Convention. In reply, the mild-mannered Lagos Cházaro promised to give his full support to the Committee of Public Safety.[23]

With the delegation of the executive authority to Lagos Cházaro, parliamentary government became a reality, for he drew his cabinet ministers almost entirely from among the members of the Convention. Moreover, unlike González Garza, he was not the assembly's president. On the day following his election, the entire *Mesa Directiva* was renewed, and a Zapatista, Francisco Alfonso Salinas, was elected to that office. To the nine cabinet posts to be filled, Lagos Cházaro named five Villistas and four from the South. Of these, all but Palafox, again the Minister of Agriculture, and Pacheco, the Minister of War, were delegates to the Convention. Lagos Cházaro offered the post of Minister of Justice to Antonio Díaz Soto y Gama.[24]

On June 12 the cabinet of Lagos Cházaro was completed as the Convention gave its approval to all but Díaz Soto. Consonant with his anarchistic philosophy, he steadfastly refused to accept any position with the government. He urged that his appointment be rejected, commenting bitingly—and with complete truth—that those Northerners who had sought his appointment were merely trying to remove him from the assembly. With the business of the cabinet terminated, the Convention turned to the pressing problem of a belated reply to the note of President Wilson.

It was much too late for diplomatic notes. As the delegates debated a fitting reply to the American president, González Garza interjected the alarming news that the Constitutionalist troops were converging upon Mexico City from several directions to lay siege to it. The enemy wished, he said, to take the capital first and then enter into peace discussions later. For himself, he announced dramatically that he was willing to defend the Convention with his companions until they were all shot to pieces by the enemy. Although Díaz Soto minimized the danger of an attack and professed himself to be optimistic about the future, the threat was real. A Constitutionalist Army of Operations was in Puebla, preparing to move on Mexico City. In the middle of June 1915 the Mexican capital seemed destined to be a revolutionary battlefield for the fifth time.[25]

Although Venustiano Carranza had depreciated Mexico City as a military base and had in February decreed it to be no more than the capital of the Valley of Mexico, by June 1 it was patently necessary for the Constitutionalists to recapture the city. For as Obregón pushed farther north following his victories at Celaya and León, his line of communication became longer and more vulnerable to attack. Despite the ineptitude of the Army of the South, Carranza feared that a concerted attack by a large force of Zapatistas at Ometusco or Tula could damage the Constitutionalist cause grievously. On May 12 the troops of Juan Andrew Almazán blew up a section of the railroad tracks between Apam and Ometusco to interrupt traffic between Veracruz and Obregón's army temporarily. It is true that small successes such as this attack proved more annoying than dangerous to the Constitutionalists. In May, as in April, González Garza received daily reports from the Zapatista generals east of the capital indicating that their scope of operations was extremely limited. North of the city Andrés Pérez and Juan Banderas seemed more interested in feuding with each other than in waging war against the enemy. Nowhere in the area controlled by the Army of the South was a battle fought or even planned. Nevertheless, the potential threat posed by the Zapatistas could be met only by driving them from the Valley of Mexico.[26]

A second reason for Carranza's concern to reoccupy Mexico City was the report from Washington on June 1 that President Wilson contemplated active intervention in Mexico to end hostilities if the revolutionaries could not find a peaceful solution themselves. Probably nothing disturbed Wilson more in the Mexican situation than the flood of reports from the Mexican capital of starvation and disorders. Had it not been for the troubles in Mexico City it is doubtful if intervention would have become an issue. It was only by capturing the city that Carranza could remove this sore spot in his relations with the American government. It was no coincidence that immediately after the announcement of Wilson's note was received in Veracruz, Carranza ordered General Pablo González to move on the old federal capital at once.

For the projected attack Carranza formed an Army Corps of the East under the command of González, who was transferred from the Tampico campaign. Included in the corps were the division of Francisco Coss, the brigades of Máximo Rojas, Juan Lechuga, and Carlos Tejada, and smaller units under Alfredo Machuca, Nicolás Flores, Amado Azuara, and Agustín Millán. Shortly thereafter, with the end of the Villista threat at El Ebano, more troops were brought from Tamaulipas to Veracruz to reinforce the army corps of General González. The enlarged force, based at Puebla, was designated an "Army of Operations against the Capital of the Republic." [27] During the first two weeks of June González planned with his staff the attack against the Zapatistas guarding Mexico City. It is significant that no thought was given to an attempt to drive behind the garrisons of the Army of the South to cut them off from Morelos. The aim of González was to capture Mexico City, not to defeat Zapata.

Holding in mind Wilson's plea for a peaceful settlement in Mexico and hoping to avoid a protracted siege of the capital with possibly heavy losses to his troops, González issued on June 13 an ultimatum to the Convention to surrender the city within forty-eight hours. He demanded that the Conventionists accept the Plan of Guadalupe. It was, he said, the only means of unifying all revolutionary factions. By surrendering, the Convention might avoid the useless shedding of blood, González said.

After fully discussing the ultimatum and the consequences of rejecting it, the members of the assembly drew up their own counterproposal. González' plan for unification was inadequate, they felt, because the Plan of Guadalupe made no reference to social reforms. It referred only, they said, to political matters, important at the time of the usurpation of Huerta, but now a dead issue. The Convention asked instead that all factions accept a period of armistice for thirty days and that during this time all commanders should remain in control of the areas they now occupied. The armistice would allow time for discussions of revolutionary union by all chiefs. But it was stipulated that every faction must accept a program of "politico-social reform" embodied in the additions to the Plan of Guadalupe, the Plan of Ayala, and the Convention's Program of Government. A preconstitutional regime would be formed from all three factions, with a provisional president, to be a civilian, chosen at the end of the thirty days by an enlarged Convention. The president would serve through December 31, 1915, and his cabinet would be made up of three members from the North, three from the South, and three Constitutionalists. An amnesty would be proclaimed for all revolutionaries, but the Committee of Public Safety, now containing elements from all factions, would act with renewed vigor against all "enemies of the revolution." [28]

General González rejected the counterproposal of the Convention as "completely unacceptable." It would, he said, only serve to delay peace, not to hasten it. González said that the election of a provisional president with a cabinet composed of members of the three factions would create "an impossible government without cohesion." And to leave the military men in charge of the areas they then occupied would, he added, "implant a state of anarchy." González saw correctly that such an armistice would benefit only the Villistas and Zapatistas, who were losing the revolution. He repeated that any agreement must of necessity be based on the complete submission of the Conventionist faction to the First Chief. He concluded: "All of us are therefore at liberty to proceed as we may think best. . . ." [29]

The Convention now determined to resist, rather than accept the harsh terms of González. During the evening of June 16 the cabinet of Lagos Cházaro met and agreed that the forces of the Convention would fight in the streets of the capital, if necessary. There would be no unconditional surrender to the enemy. Many members of the assembly thought it more prudent to leave the city while they might, finding refuge outside the battle areas. Others, of more martial spirit, left to join their troops on the lines of combat.[30]

Emiliano Zapata manifested some interest in the developing campaign for the Federal District, though he did not bestir himself from his mountain retreat at Tlaltizapán. On June 18 he ordered all the "generals, chiefs, and officers of the Liberating Army, who are passing their time in Mexico City in theaters, cantinas, and houses of ill fame, to report at the front for duty." [31] But beyond such exhortations, Zapata did nothing to influence either the progress or the outcome of the skirmishing around the capital.

During the rest of June conditions inside Mexico City grew increasingly bad. The proximity of the Constitutionalists and the evident skittishness of the Zapatista soldiers made it abundantly clear to the populace that the city would soon change hands, despite the public assurances of Lagos Cházaro and members of his cabinet that it would be held at all costs. Anticipating the return of the Carrancista authorities and remembering the difficulties with monetary exchange which accompanied previous Constitutionalist occupations, the merchants became suddenly wary of accepting any Conventionist currency. Many refused outright to receive the bills, while others hiked their prices to discourage transactions. The government found it necessary, therefore, on June 19 to decree once more the forced circulation of the "dos caras" and "sábanas." But continued public resistance to the Villista currency led Lagos Cházaro on June 25 to declare the "sábanas" no longer legal tender. They were to be exchanged at the treasury for other Conventionist currency, the "revalidados" or restamped notes. This expedient also failed to break down the natural reluctance of the merchants and businessmen to accept money which would soon be valueless.[32]

As the troops of Pablo González invested the city, the economic situation became completely anarchical. Rioting mobs of hungry citizens broke into the closed stores and markets to obtain food and other supplies. On June 25, in trying to halt the looting of a market, the police shot to death a woman rioter. On the next day the police broke out fire hoses to disperse mobs in the market areas, and another woman was killed and many others wounded by gunfire. The Conventionist government sought to alleviate the food shortages by distributing grain from its own commissaries. Thousands milled around these points to be doled the little corn obtainable. In the pushing at one station a baby, carried in its mother's *rebozo,* was crushed to death.[33]

When the Convention had not accepted Pablo González' ultimatum by June 16 he began to deploy the troops of his Army of Operations in preparation for the attack on Mexico City. González planned a concerted move on the capital from three directions. From the North, General Alfredo Machuca was to proceed by way of Cuautitlán and Tlalnepantla. In the East, González' left flank, the division of Francisco Coss would advance along the rail line from Texcoco to Los Reyes. In the center, the main body under the personal command of González was to drive from Ometusco along the Mexicano toward San Juan Teotihuacán and the Villa of Guadalupe. Although progress was slow, all of the Constitutionalist troops moved forward against light opposition without a hitch. Only Machuca had any real success, however. By June 18 his forces had rolled as far as Atzcapotzalco, but six miles from the capital, before they were halted by the Zapatista garrison in that town. On the following day González' troops passed through San Juan Teotihuacán to Tepéxpam, which fell without resistance. Francisco Coss was at the same time in Texcoco. The Zapatistas in that sector fell back to positions at Los Reyes and Ayotla along the road from Cuautla to Mexico City. Those in the center retreated as far as the Gran Canal del Desagüe, the ancient drainage ditch for Lake Texcoco, and took up positions along that natural embankment.

González' troops in the center continued forward slowly until, on June 23, they ground to a rude halt before the Gran Canal, fifteen miles from Mexico City. For the first time the Constitutionalists came under enemy artillery fire. The Zapatistas were woefully weak in artillery and short of ammunition, but they had dug in five fieldpieces in the Cerro Gordo, the heights behind the Gran Canal. Here the Southern troops under General Rafael Eguía Lis made a courageous stand. Eguía Lis, like Zapata's most effective commanders, was an ex-federal, rather than a revolutionary from Morelos. González' forces were halted completely and were unable to span the wide drainage ditch. This engagement reflected little credit upon the Army Corps of the East, for not only did the attack bog down under sparse enemy fire, but the troops of General Amado Azuara fell back in dismaying retreat. On the next day, June 24, the Zapatistas launched a counterattack in a torrential rainstorm to push the Constitutionalists back as far as the hills which surrounded Tepéxpam.[34]

Except for the capture of Puebla in the previous December, which the Liberating Army had accomplished with a much larger force, this was probably the most successful engagement for the men of Zapata. Untrained, poorly armed, and without competent leadership, these troops gave some scant hope for the success of the Zapatistas at Mexico City. It was, however, a false hope, for whatever the shortcomings of Pablo González as a military leader, he had sufficient force to take the capital whenever he desired.

During the first phase of González' operations against Mexico City the Convention met sporadically, but the members showed little stomach for the realities of the military situation. While the Zapatista commanders in charge of the defense of the capital pleaded for supplies and reinforcements, the assembly busied itself in the discussion of ceremonies for the installation of the Committee of Public Safety, or the punishment to be meted out to those "reactionaries" responsible for the *cuartelazos* of Félix Díaz and Victoriano Huerta. The sessions were characterized by an almost moribund serenity, and the occasions were few when the flash of tempers recalled the earlier days of scathing accusations and threats of violence between the Zapatistas and Villistas.[35]

On July 5 the Convention made its last overtures for revolutionary unity, voting to invite all Constitutionalist leaders to come to the assembly or to send their representatives within thirty days. But in the midst of the appeal for peace, there were rumblings of continued hostility toward Carranza. When Pérez Taylor warned that American intervention was imminent, "based on starvation," he was interrupted by Díaz Soto, who minimized this threat. He insisted that the matter of revolutionary unity was not urgent, saying that the Convention must stand on its dignity. Since its earlier proposals for peace had been sarcastically and insultingly rejected by Carranza, said Díaz Soto, the Convention must not now crawl at his feet. Pérez Taylor agreed that the Constitutionalist First Chief was a "traitor and a lackey of the Yankees," but he recommended that the new peace offer should be made to the army leaders, not to Carranza.[36]

The moment for such propositions had passed, however. Pablo González had already begun to commit his forces for an all-out assault on Mexico City. While the Committee of Public Safety plied its trade, searching the capital for "enemies of the revolution," the Convention met once more on July 7 and then only to raise the pay of the Zapatista soldiers at the front. It was, though the Conventionists could not have known it at the time, the last full meeting of the assembly.[37]

After several days of light skirmishing, the Constitutionalist Army of Operations initiated the final push for the control of the Valley of Mexico on July 6. Francisco Coss had already moved his division up to Los Reyes from Texcoco, and he began an advance along the narrow-guage line toward Peñón Viejo and Mexico City. In order to meet this threat in the Southeast, the Zapatistas shifted troops from the area of the Gran Canal del Desagüe to oppose Coss. In so doing, they dangerously weakened their forces northeast of the capital. Without material reinforcement from Zapata, which never arrived, the Army of the South could not cope with an enemy on more than one front. There was too little ammunition, too few cannons, and above all, no competent general in charge of the over-all operations. On July 10 González reached the outskirts of Mexico City.

The collapse of the Zapatista defense at the Gran Canal showed the leaders of the Convention the futility of further resistance. Some delegates had already left the capital for Cuernavaca with the fleeing troops of the Liberating Army. Those who remained in Mexico City voted, after a hasty conference, to disband and reassemble in Toluca. The Villistas entertained the bizarre hope of going north from Toluca to find salvation with Francisco Villa. In response to the earnest pleas of Cardoso de Oliveira and other foreign diplomats, the Conventionists agreed on July 9 to pull out all Zapatista troops and to permit the Constitutionalists an unopposed entry into the city.[38]

Despite the concern of the foreign colony that the Zapatistas would vent their anger and frustration upon the foreigners as they departed, these fears proved unfounded. There was only the normal amount of looting, as individuals or groups tried to take with them the household goods from the residences they had been occupying and automobiles or other vehicles. The garrison at Xochimilco cut off the water supply to Mexico City, as the Zapatistas had done six months earlier.[39]

On July 10 the *Ayuntamiento* assumed temporary control of the capital, pending the arrival of Pablo González. But with the Conventionist government gone and no police force to maintain order, mobs of hungry citizens broke into shops and markets and ransacked the barracks, which the Zapatista soldiers had occupied, in search of food. The merchants kept their establishments closed in the anticipation of a change in currency. Pablo González entered the city on July 11 without an incident, taking charge of the National Palace and other governmental buildings. He directed Francisco Coss to proceed against the Zapatistas south of the capital, but the garrisons at Xochimilco, Contreras, Tlálpam, and other points in that area, showed no desire to resume hostilities. Instead, they retreated over the Cerro de Ajusco into Morelos. By July 14 Coss had cleared the Valley of Mexico of all forces of the Army of the South.[40]

Economic conditions in the capital continued unsettled, as González made no immediate decision on currency circulation. Most businesses remained closed and the large amount of Villista paper money was without value. Again, as under the Convention, mobs rioted demanding food. The fronts of stores and markets were smashed in as the hungry citizenry seized foodstuffs from merchants who would not receive their money. González did little to stop the disorders. Not until July 15, four days after his occupation, did he decree the forced circulation of Constitutionalist bills, voiding the "sábanas" and "dos caras" which had been used in the capital since March 11.[41]

To the consternation and dismay of the populace of Mexico City, the tenure of González was short-lived. It is perhaps indicative of his character as a military commander that a bold strike toward the capital by the enemy caused him to fly in confusion. He has been much maligned as a general, called a man who never won a battle. This was untrue. González was honest and well-intentioned and, though a bumbling commander, he did win battles. He was undoubtedly not a bold and aggressive warrior like Obregón, or even Villa. But in the case of a man of little talent, perhaps discretion was the better part of valor. On July 17 González' army left Mexico City as suddenly as it had come. Once again the *Ayuntamiento* took charge of the capital, awaiting with resignation the inevitable return of the Zapatistas under Amador Salazar. The stores in Mexico City, which had begun to open on the fifteenth, now closed their doors once more to await the outcome of this latest shift of revolutionary fortunes.[42]

While Pablo González had been advancing upon Mexico City during the first week in July, Obregón, too, was making steady progress against the enemy. With decreasing Villista resistance, his Army of Operations pushed north along the rail line from León de la Aldamas. On July 10 his troops occupied Aguascalientes, capturing many prisoners, as well as a considerable quantity of weapons and ammunition.[43] In desperate straits, Villa conceived the stratagem of sending Rodolfo Fierro and Canuto Reyes with a strong force of cavalry to cut behind Obregón, severing his communications with Veracruz. Whether Villa hoped in this way to achieve complete victory is problematical. At the most, he seems to have wanted Reyes and Fierro to link up with the Zapatistas and harass Obregón's rear so as to impede his further progress north. It was also possibly in Villa's mind that success in this daring venture might prolong the hostilities and make the Constitutionalists more willing to compromise, as President Wilson demanded.

The Villista cavalry crossed the northeast tip of Jalisco and, surprising the small Carrancista garrison at León, tore up a section of the tracks of the Mexicano. They proceeded south along the line through Celaya, Querétaro, and San Juan del Río, the defenders in these towns evacuating with no resistance. On July 17 the raiders reached Tula. After a sharp engagement, the troops of Agustín Millán withdrew toward Pachuca. But at Pachuca a force of Zapatistas materialized to attack Millán, and he was forced back still further, removing his troops to Zempoala. It was this double threat to the Constitutionalists' communication line to Veracruz, and the danger that the enemy might capture the key junction of Ometusco, which caused González to give up the capital so hastily. He drew back his Army of Operations to Ometusco to guard that important site.[44]

In contrast with González, Alvaro Obregón reacted to the danger to his rear with decisiveness. Not trusting González to hold Ometusco and determined to have a supply line to the coast, he ordered General Gabriel Gavira to move on San Luis Potosí and, if necessary, drive a wedge across the Republic to the seaport of Tampico. Gavira reached San Luis Potosí on July 18 to find that the city had been occupied two days earlier by the forces of Herminio Alvarez. Alvarez had operated in the northern sector of the state for the First Chief and moved into San Luis Potosí when Tomás Urbina deserted the city after Villa's loss at Aguascalientes. The Constitutionalists made no attempt at that time to move on to Tampico. In the meantime, another column of Obregón's troops under Francisco Murguía continued north and, on July 17, captured Zacatecas. The Villista defenders split; some fled toward Torreón, while the rest went west to Jerez.[45]

Pablo González' exodus from the capital was a cruel blow to the hopes of its inhabitants for peace and an end to the economic dislocations. Cardoso de Oliveira wrote to Lansing on July 18: "I really consider the situation hopeless in the true sense of the word." [46] For Mexico City the next two weeks were the most harrowing of the revolution. It was completely without a government. Instead anarchy reigned supreme, the only law being the whim of the Zapatista soldiers. The few Conventionists who remained in Toluca recognized the futility of relying further upon the protection of the Army of the South and made no effort to return to the capital. In Mexico City the matter of a legal tender became critical as most merchants refused to open their shops. Only a few were found who would risk accepting once more the "revalidados," and prices in these establishments soared. Some hedged against the return of the Carrancistas by buying Constitutionalist currency at a discount. These businessmen, termed "coyotes" by the Zapatista military officials, were arrested and imprisoned without the semblance of a hearing.[47]

Not only was there no effort by the military government to curb the passions of the individual soldiers, but the Zapatista commanders made their own lawlessness a standard for the rank and file of their troops. On June 21 the members of the *Ayuntamiento* were arrested and remanded to prison cells. And there were many other acts of violence and depredation against private citizens.

The lack of food, the day-to-day uncertainty of what to expect from the Zapatistas, and the hostile attitude of many toward the Americans caused Cardoso de Oliveira to complain to Lansing that people in Mexico City seemed to hold him personally responsible for their sufferings. He wrote: "It is really an unbearable situation, after all." Never in the history of the revolution did the diplomatic dispatches from the Mexican capital reflect such utter despair.[48]

Between July 26 and 30 the troops of the South evacuated and reoccupied the capital three times. Each time, as the approach of the Constitutionalists was rumored, the Zapatista soldiers would dash in a disorderly fashion through the streets toward San Angel, Tlálpam, or Xochimilco, firing their rifles and pistols in complete abandon, only to return when the alarms proved to be false. The Brazilian minister reported to Lansing that these helter-skelter retreats caused the deaths of many noncombatants and the wounding of many more. When Villa, now in Chihuahua, heard of these disorders in Mexico City, he asked Carothers and the State Department to relay a plea to Zapata to "see that they are suppressed." Villa feared that such reports would hinder his chances of bringing about a negotiated peace.[49]

When Pablo González' initial trepidation at the advent of Fierro and Reyes had worn off, it became apparent that their movement was nothing more than a raid in force. Despite the occupation of Pachuca and Tula, the threat against the Constitutionalists was slight. Zapata failed to cooperate with the Villistas, who were too weak, themselves, to hold out against a sustained attack. They had no artillery, for all the troops were cavalry. Failing to accomplish their mission, Fierro and Reyes evacuated Tula, after holding the city for a week. Passing through Mexico City and Toluca, where they were joined by the troops of González Garza and Juan Banderas, they turned north and west in order to rejoin Villa without being trapped by the Constitutionalists. Many of the Villista members of the Convention in Toluca took the opportunity to leave for the safety of the North.[50] A rump Convention remained in Toluca with Lagos Cházaro, discussing fruitlessly the Program of Reform for a nonexistent government and hoping against all reason for a resurgence of the fortunes of their faction.

On July 27 the troops of Agustín Millán and Abraham Cepeda moved up to Pachuca, and on the following day, after a heavy shelling, the town was recaptured by the Constitutionalists. The Zapatista defenders retreated to Mexico City. From July 29 to August 1 the Army of Operations retraced the familiar route to the capital. There was no opposition and progress was rapid. Unaccountably, the troops of Amador Salazar put up strong resistance in the streets of the capital, and fighting was heavy before the Zapatistas were driven back across the mountains and out of the Valley of Mexico. On August 2 the Constitutionalists reoccupied Mexico City and were never thereafter dispossessed.

It was to be several weeks however, before Carranza deigned to return with his government. Veracruz remained, to the Constitutionalists, the capital of the Republic, although the diplomatic representatives still refused to leave their stations in Mexico City. The city was placed under martial law by González, and General Francisco de P. Mariel was named military commander. General César López de Lara became governor of the Federal District.[51]

Despite the overwhelming military success of the Constitutionalists, the American Department of State and President Wilson attempted throughout the months of July and August to effect a peace of their own making in Mexico, that is, a termination of hostilities through the elimination of Venustiano Carranza. There is little doubt that Wilson meant well, but his policies were ineffectual. For all the special agents he had sent to Mexico, he found it difficult to see the obvious—that Carranza was winning and would be Mexico's next president, regardless of the wishes of the American government. When Wilson received word of the First Chief's polite, but firm, rejection of the principle of mediation, he found the actions of Carranza "not only disappointing, but disgusting." He wrote to Robert Lansing on July 2: "I have never known of a man more impossible to deal with on human principles than this man Carranza." [52] This one sentence epitomized Wilson's attitude toward Carranza. He did not see eye to eye with the American president, and therefore to Wilson, with stern Calvinistic self-righteousness, Carranza was completely unreasonable.

The new Secretary of State, too, seemed resolved upon the exclusion of Carranza. On July 5 Lansing wrote to Wilson that "the Mexican situation has been much in my mind and I have been seeking to map out a course of action which will lead to definite results." The problem continued to be, he said, the harmonization of all the factions of the revolution. Since Carranza had rejected the earlier overtures toward peace and would, presumably, continue to do so, he need no longer be considered in the policies of the United States. Lansing proposed that the ABC countries, together with the United States, should call for a conference of the "lesser chiefs" to choose a government which would preclude Carranza or any other factional leader. This government would be recognized by the United States, which would then furnish it arms and ammunition, while preventing "such from reaching hostile parties." [53]

President Wilson found these suggestions to be an "excellent foundation" for planning the government's Mexican program. As though he were manipulating toy soldiers, Wilson played with the names of various compromise candidates for the provisional presidency which the United States might prefer, men such as Iturbide, Angeles, Vázquez Tagle, or Manuel Bonilla. That each was unsatisfactory to the dominant revolutionaries did not seem to cross the president's mind. Iturbide showed himself a strong suitor for American favors, visiting Washington or keeping in touch with Wilson from New York. Writing to the Secretary of State on July 1, Iturbide stressed Mexico's need for "strong man rule," though he conceded that he did not mean a dictatorship such as Huerta's. He did not specifically advance his own candidacy—in fact, he suggested Pedro Lascurain, Madero's Minister of Foreign Relations, as a possibility—but his demeanor in conversation with members of the State Department led them to feel that he would not shirk the responsibility if it were thrust upon him.[54]

Felipe Angeles also came to Washington for conferences on means of settling the revolution. Ostensibly he had entered the United States to visit his family in Boston. But there were rumors in Mexico that Angeles had left the Republic when he and Villa split following the battle of León. It was true, however, that Angeles' presence in Washington coincided with the increased concern of the Conventionists that the fighting be ended on the basis of Wilson's note of June 2. In any event, the rumors of the defection of Angeles were denied by the Villistas in Mexico.

Woodrow Wilson, while accepting the principle of Lansing's program, thought he saw the flaw in a policy which demanded the elimination of all factional leaders. Would not the United States, he wrote Lansing, "be in a wallow of weaknesses and jealousies down there?" A possible alternative, he thought, would be for the American government to back a man such as Felipe Angeles. Above all, Wilson now wished to avoid the consequences of unilateral action on the part of his government. He insisted that the United States continue to work closely with the principal Latin American republics in proposing a new factional conference in Mexico. Following the suggestion of Lansing, Wilson designated Paul Fuller as his agent in the negotiations, asking him "to be our eyes and ears" in dealing with the various factions.[55]

The urgency with which Wilson viewed the Mexican situation in June 1915 was not reflected in the actual peace negotiations. It was not until August 5, more than two months after the president had threatened American intervention if the war were not concluded, that a conference of Latin American ministers was held in Washington.[56] Fuller sat in with Lansing to represent the views of Wilson. The guiding hands of Lansing and Fuller are seen in the unanimous agreement of the conferees that "Carranza was impossible, that even if he triumphs, it would mean continued disorder." All accepted Lansing's suggestion that the secondary chiefs be called upon to choose a government excluding all the factional leaders, particularly Carranza. On August 11 the ministers dispatched identical notes to all revolutionary leaders, offering their good offices to end the war and bidding them to a conference in Washington. Carranza had already been apprised of the ministers' conference, and he told reporters derisively on August 9 that it was an attempt to "meddle in matters" which were exclusively the concern of Mexicans.[57]

The response to this second appeal to a peace parley was not unexpected. Those who had the most to gain by negotiation accepted with alacrity. Villa, with a show of reluctance, assured the ministers that he had "the power and resources to continue the struggle in defense of the rights of the Mexican people." But in view of the "praiseworthy and fraternal attitude" of the signatories to the note, he was disposed, he said, to accept their invitation. Zapata, too, penned up in Morelos, found the principle of mediation palatable, though he preferred that such mediation be carried out through the Convention. For the languishing government of the Convention in Toluca, Ignacio Borrego, the Minister of Foreign Relations, accepted the invitation also.[58]

The Constitutionalists' reception of the bid to come to Washington might have been anticipated, but the unanimity of opinion came as a surprise to the American government. All secondary chiefs referred the mediators to Carranza in Veracruz. And the First Chief met the situation with the same impassivity which had characterized his dealings with the United States since 1913. Jesús Acuña, now in charge of Foreign Relations for the Constitutonalist regime, delayed answering the ministers' note until August 24, and then his only reply was a counter query from the First Chief, asking whether the invitation had been issued in the names of their governments, or had been sent by the ministers as private citizens. Carranza told a correspondent for the *New York World* that he would reply to the note when he received assurances as to who had sent it. In any case, he said, "outside influences never have been and never will be beneficial in the arranging of any country's home affairs." Carranza cited the American civil war and Brazil's revolt against the monarchy in 1889 as instances of revolutions carried to their conclusion without foreign interference. He said that at any meeting the conferees must limit themselves to international matters, for he would countenance no intervention in internal Mexican affairs.[59]

By August 11 President Wilson had begun to show a turn of heart. He counseled the ministers not to "take for granted or insist on [the] elimination of Carranza." But the First Chief's failure to answer the mediators' note and his attitude as revealed in the *World* completely exasperated Wilson. He wrote bitterly to Lansing on August 31: "It is a great pity, but it is clear that nothing can be done either with or through Carranza. . . ."[60]

Carranza had nothing to lose by his continued procrastination. Each week that passed saw the further consolidation of the Constitutionalist authority throughout Mexico. When, on September 10, he finally gave his answer, all need for such a conference had disappeared. Carranza told Lansing and the Latin American ministers that he could not consent to any mediation by foreign powers in Mexican affairs. He stressed the strength of the Constitutionalist cause and said, quite logically, that to enter into "a deal" with the other factions would be to "renounce . . . the victory achieved at the cost of countless sacrifices. . . ." He remained appreciative of the labors of the ministers to attain peace, but he said he would meet with them only on the borders between Mexico and the United States and then to discuss solely international affairs.[61] He meant the recognition of his government as the *de facto* regime in Mexico. It was this last act which the government of the United States would not yet consummate.

In contrast to the intractable Carranza, Francisco Villa manifested toward the United States a docility which belied his passionate nature. It is ironical that while Wilson and Lansing sought means to eliminate Carranza, the one leader who stood for legally constituted government, order, and stability, they showed a strange affinity for Villa, the most lawless factional leader in the Mexican revolution. When Carranza insisted upon Mexico's sovereign right to settle her own problems, he was "disgusting" to Wilson. When Villa robbed, murdered, and raped, his actions were, while not condoned, at least observed with the tolerant attitude of an indulgent father toward his truant offspring. There is no indication that the United States ever seriously contemplated granting recognition to the Villista faction, much less to Villa himself. But it was symptomatic of the diplomatic myopia in Washington that Angeles was considered the most likely candidate for the provisional presidency. The worse Villa's spoliation became, the more the American government tried to find means to placate him. Wilson and Lansing were in the uncomfortable position in the summer of 1915 of recognizing that Carranza would triumph, while at the same time wishing to overlook that unpleasant truth, or even to delay or destroy the fruits of his victory.

Driven north by Obregón and confined to the states of Durango and Chihuahua, seeing his subordinates throughout the Republic surrender to the Constitutionalists, Villa's conduct toward property owners, especially foreigners, became increasingly harsh. On July 22 Carothers, now in El Paso, reported to Lansing that Villa was "becoming harder to deal with." Villa rationalized his defeats by attributing them to a loss of will to fight on the part of his underlings. But his greatest need was for more arms and ammunition. His actions in July and August 1915 are explicable only in the light of his search for dollars to purchase supplies in the United States. On July 20 a shipment of a quarter of a million cartridges arrived at El Paso consigned to the Division of the North. But when Villa could find no money to pay for them, the shippers threatened to sell the ammunition to the Constitutionalists instead.[62]

Frantically scrambling for revenues from any source, legitimate or otherwise, Villa levied confiscatory taxes on the cotton growers in the Comarca Lagunera and on the copper mining companies in Chihuahua. All producers of cotton were required to make a payment of five hundred dollars in gold for each section of one hundred hectares under cultivation. To replenish the badly depleted stores of his division, Villa tried to buy up food and other supplies in the territories still under his control. He offered in payment the fiat money printed by his government. But the merchants, well aware of the way the tide of revolution was running, refused to accept the Villista currency, which was by now worth, at the most, two American cents on the peso. Villa, no man to find a hindrance in legality, took whatever goods he needed without any compensation at all. Spaniards and Chinese especially suffered at the hands of the Villistas. Villa also ordered the mining companies in Chihuahua, which had almost ceased operations, to open their mines to produce copper he could exchange for dollars. And he seized and placed under the control of the Division of the North the foreign-owned power and light company in Chihuahua.[63]

Despite the provocations, Robert Lansing sent no admonitory messages to Villa, nor did he contemplate using force to protect American lives and property, as his administration was to do in March 1916. Instead, the Secretary of State proposed a scheme to make it possible for Villa to market his stolen cattle easily in the United States. In that way, Lansing hoped that Villa would find it unnecessary to confiscate American business properties in order to buy arms. On August 6 Lansing asked the Secretary of Agriculture, David F. Houston, to establish a meat inspection point on the Chihuahua border to facilitate the entry into the United States of Villista cattle. Lansing wrote: "This is a matter of profound importance at the present time, when this government is bending every effort to terminate the chaotic conditions in Mexico." Lansing sent a copy of this letter to Wilson and explained to the president that his proposal, if carried out, would give Villa a "legal" means of disposing of his cattle and thus "relieve his strained financial situation." [64]

Wilson was taken aback by Lansing's scheme, though he did

not countermand it. He wrote to his Secretary of State: "This message puzzles me a little." Should the American government, he asked, put Villa in a position to get money when he was at his weakest and on the verge of collapse? It was for this very reason that Lansing proposed the inspection station. "This will," he replied to the president, "relieve to a considerable measure, I believe, Villa's desperate financial situation, which has induced his arbitrary conduct." Houston acceded to Lansing's request, and on August 9, as the Latin American ministers met in Washington to propose mediation, Lansing made a further explanation of his policy to Wilson. He wrote: "We do not wish the Carranza faction to be the only one to deal with in Mexico. Carranza seems so impossible that an appearance, at least, of opposition to him will give us the opportunity to invite a compromise of factions. I think, therefore, it is politic for the time to allow Villa to obtain sufficient financial resources to allow his faction to remain in arms until a compromise can be effected." That Lansing was willing to prolong hostilities in Mexico with resultant loss of life and destruction of property, shows that the two principal aims of American policy in Mexico were at cross-purposes. Lansing wanted the elimination of Carranza more than he wanted peace.[65]

Probably Villa's strongest supporter in Washington was General Hugh Scott. They were personal friends, and Villa had attested his feelings for Scott after their meeting in January by sending him a hand-woven Mexican blanket. To placate Villa and to settle his troubles with the mining companies in Chihuahua, Wilson sent Scott to confer with Villa once more. On August 10 they met in El Paso, and Carothers was again their interpreter. Scott found Villa yielding and reasonable. He promised to restore the confiscated properties to their rightful owners. In their turn, the copper mine owners of the state offered to give Villa a thousand tons of coal for his trains to make up for the loss of the coalfields at Muzquiz to the Constitutionalists.[66]

At the conclusion of their meeting Villa authorized Scott to treat in his name for a three-month armistice. As had the Convention earlier, Villa proposed that during this period each faction should remain in control of the area it then occupied. Any faction which refused an armistice was to be cut off by the United States from all war supplies. Optimistically, Carothers telegraphed the Secretary of State that if Scott could see Obregón, González, and Zapata "on these matters, I am sure he could settle the whole problem." [67]

Scott was then asked by Wilson to seek a conference with Obregón, who was known to be in the North of Mexico, with the view of eliminating Carranza. The American consul general at Monterrey, Phillip C. Hanna, was instructed to ascertain "discreetly" whether Obregón would be willing to meet with Scott either at Laredo or Tampico "in a purely informal conference regarding the future welfare of Mexico." Such a conference, it was felt in Washington, might serve to drive a wedge between Obregón and Carranza. But this was not the Obregón of a year earlier, who had planned with Villa in Chihuahua the elimination of the First Chief. He was now completely loyal to Carranza, as was every other Constitutionalist commander. Obregón told the State Department that he could not go to Tampico or to the border, without Carranza's permission.[68]

While Lansing moved mountains to help Villa wage his unequal war against the Constitutionalists, the American government made no effort to hide its hostility toward Carranza. The wholesale pillaging in the North did not concern the Department of State as much as the alleged incitement by Carrancista authorities in Veracruz of a mob "to commit violence on foreigners." Ominously, Lansing requested Josephus Daniels on August 10 to order a portion of the American Caribbean fleet to Veracruz in a show of force against the government of Carranza. As a result, the Secretary of the Navy dispatched two battleships of the Fourth Division of the Atlantic fleet to the port. The official and published reason for this unfriendly act was to take Cardoso de Oliveira to New Orleans. The Brazilian minister had become ill and was returning to his own country. But the show of force was timed to coincide with the demands of the mediating powers that Carranza negotiate with the Conventionists. And it was intended as a reminder to Carranza of Washington's displeasure with him.[69]

With the passage of time, however, the evident superiority of the Constitutionalists had a sobering effect in Washington. When Carranza finally framed his reply to the ministers' note of August 11, the question of American support or displeasure was academic. Short of actual armed intervention similar to the seizure of Veracruz, nothing Wilson could do would change the course of the revolution. By September 12 even Lansing found Carranza's position in rejecting reconciliation "not unreasonable." While he felt that the American government could not sanction a conference with the Constitutionalists on "international matters," as Carranza had asked, since that would imply recognition of his regime, Lansing had "almost reached the conclusion that they are so dominant that they are entitled to recognition." [70]

Fortune had deserted Villa and no act of his own or of the American State Department could stem defeat. In the state of Coahuila the troops of Carlos Treviño occupied Saltillo to restore to the Constitutionalist First Chief his prized jewel. During August and early September Francisco Murguía's forces pushed north from Zacatecas through the state of Durango to capture Torreón, as the Villista garrison evacuated the city without firing a shot. The loss of Torreón deprived Villa of the key to his control of the cotton lands of Viesca and Parras. Confronted with inevitable defeat, many of Villa's generals, such as Pánfilo Natera, decided to make their peace with Obregón and seek absolution in the Constitutionalist camp. As Villa's empire crumbled, Lansing no longer seemed certain that a negotiated peace was necessary. He wrote to Wilson: "Are we bound to call a conference when only the defeated factions have accepted?" Lansing thought such a conference would serve no useful purpose.[71]

Nonetheless, representatives of the Convention assembled in Washington in the forlorn hope that the United States and the Latin American nations calling the conference might decide against recognizing Carranza. Roque González Garza headed a delegation of Villistas who passed through El Paso on September 17 on their way to the American capital. The once friendly González Garza was now suspicious and ill-tempered, for he had tasted the gall of total defeat. Carothers reported to Lansing that González Garza's "whole attitude . . . was a veiled threat that if they do not get what they feel is due them from the American government, Villa will begin hostilities against us with the hope that the whole country would rally to him in preference to Carranza." With remarkable prescience, in view of Villa's raid on Columbus, New Mexico, in the following year, Carothers told the Secretary of State that he feared the Villistas were preparing an attack on an American city, "immediately after they become convinced that their commission or González Garza can achieve nothing in Washington." [72]

Though the conference of American ministers renewed its sessions in Washington on September 18, it was a fiasco. The Constitutionalists sent no representatives, while the Conventionists, González Garza, Escudero, Díaz Lombardo, and Raúl Madero, arrived too late. Nor could the conferees agree among themselves on a common course to follow with the Mexican factions. The Brazilian ambassador to the United States, Domicio da Gama, steadfastly opposed dealing with any faction. He preferred to support a nonrevolutionary provisional government, headed by Iturbide, Lascuráin, or perhaps even the deposed Huerta. Lansing felt, however, that the Brazilian government would follow the lead of the United States, and he decided to confer separately with each of the factional representatives in Washington, Eliseo Arredondo for the Constitutionalists, and Enrique Llorente for the Convention. González Garza also met with the Secretary of State after his arrival in Washington. Unreasonably, Villa's representative was optimistic and expected to the last moment that the United States would lend its support to his faction.[73]

The ministers met again on October 9 and by now even da Gama saw that it was fruitless to oppose Carranza. On the following day the press was informed that recognition for the Constitutionalist faction was near, and on October 19 the United States designated Carranza's regime as the *de facto* government of Mexico. The Latin American countries which participated in the mediation conference fell in line with the decision of the United States. At the same time, to seal the victory of the Constitutionalists, President Wilson proclaimed an embargo on arms to all revolutionary groups in Mexico, other than the government of Carranza.[74]

In that moment the last faint hope of the Conventionist revolutionaries for ultimate victory was extinguished. González Garza returned to Texas an embittered man, refusing to enter Mexico so long as Carranza was its president. Felipe Angeles came home in the mistaken belief that he could be forgiven his opposition to the Constitutionalists. He erred grievously and paid with his life for that error. The government of Carranza tried Villa's "grey lieutenant" as a traitor and he was executed before a firing squad.

For Carranza the pacification of Mexico proved more difficult than the defeat of the Convention. The unregenerate Villa fought in the North as a leader of irregular guerrilla forces while Zapata held out in Morelos and maintained an enclave completely independent of Carranza's national government. The recognition of Carranza, though a most logical and necessary step, brought no peace to the unfortunate Republic.

A hard core of Conventionists in Toluca refused to concede the victory of the Constitutionalists. Through the summer and early fall of 1915 a rump assembly continued to meet, discussing and approving the remaining articles of the Program of Government. No longer supported by a great coalition of armies, the government of Lagos Cházaro could call upon few troops for its defense. There was a constant attrition of forces as many chiefs and their soldiers fled north or deserted to the Constitutionalists. Had Pablo González desired, he could have marched upon Toluca and easily dispersed the Convention. But with the sufferance of the Constitutionalist commander, Toluca was unmolested. On September 1 González sent Lagos Cházaro an ultimatum to evacuate the city by the middle of the month or expect an attack.[75] Yet the passing of the deadline saw no attempt by the Army of

Operations to oust the Conventionists. Instead the few troops who remained loyal to Lagos Cházaro made periodic, but weak, sallies in the direction of Mexico City. In one such venture on October 9 the forces of the Convention reached Las Cruces, only twenty miles from the capital. But their lack of artillery and shortage of ammunition caused the attack to bog down. At the end of the skirmish the Conventionists had virtually exhausted their ammunition. Worst of all, they had no means of replenishing their stores.[76]

It was at this moment that word reached Toluca of the approach from the west of Constitutionalist troops under Alfredo Elizondo. Unable to tarry further, the Convention voted to disband. On the following day, the delegates of Villa, protected by a column of troops, struck north in the hopes of finding their chief. The Conventionists had been completely isolated in Toluca since midsummer and knew nothing of the events in Washington. They were entirely ignorant, therefore, as they left Toluca, that the United States had now decided to accord recognition to their enemies.

The flight of Lagos Cházaro and the remaining Villista members of the Convention marked the final split between North and South. The men of Villa were not doleful as they bade farewell to their comrades from Morelos. Yet to leave Toluca at all was recognition of the failure of the cause for which they had labored so long. The Zapatistas crossed over to Cuernavaca, where they maintained the façade of a Conventionist government, continuing to decree agrarian legislation for the state of Morelos. When the Constitutionalists captured Cuernavaca early in 1916 the Zapatista delegates moved on to Jojutla. There, on May 16, 1916, after publishing their own version of the Program of Reform, they dissolved their Convention.[77] Until the death of Zapata in 1919 the agrarian reforms remained in effect. Haciendas were occupied by the military authorities. Lands were restored to the pueblos, and the state of Morelos was a Zapatista elysium of anarchism. Ruined haciendas, bullet-ridden town buildings, and wrecked sugar factories remain today as mute testimony to the attempt of Emiliano Zapata to bring earthly happiness to the dispossessed Indians of his state.

On October 10 the Villista Conventionists departed from Toluca for Ixtlahuaca, twenty-one miles to the north, where their column was to be joined by a brigade of Joaquin V. Casarín. With them went Benjamín Argumedo, ex-Colorado, ex-federal, and now ex-Zapatista, who preferred to cast his lot with the revolutionaries of the North, rather than remain with Zapata. Near Ixtlahuaca they were attacked by the troops of Elizondo. Most were able to escape, but many of the Conventionists, sorely pressed and despondent over their uncertain future, decided to submit to the Carrancistas. Among these was Juan Antonio Acosta, González Garza's chief of staff, who took with him a third of the 1,500 soldiers who had been counted upon to guard the marching column of civilians. Most of the remaining troops were unarmed, and all were disorganized and without discipline. From the state of Mexico the Villistas turned east, hoping to follow, in general, the route taken by Gutiérrez ten months earlier, through the no man's land of the Huasteca. They studiously avoided the rail lines, which were now under the control of their enemies.

During the next month and a half the dispirited band made its way north through the mountainous terrain of San Luis Potosí, Zacatecas, and Durango. The column was attacked frequently by Constitutionalist troops, and losses were heavy. There was a constant attrition as individuals and groups broke off to desert to the enemy or to return to their homes. No major engagements were fought, however, for the Conventionists sought to avoid trouble wherever possible. By the middle of December there was almost nothing left of the column. Giving up all hope, Federico Cervantes, who had become separated from the main body during one of the skirmishes, crossed the frontier to seek asylum in the United States. He was joined in Texas by several other Villista members of the Convention.

A few diehards still refused to concede the field to Carranza. Led by Lagos Cházaro, these straggled across Chihuahua into the mountains of the West. Like Gutiérrez in Dr. Arroyo, these

Conventionists fed upon fantasies of final victory over their enemies. Reinforced by the troops of Calixto Contreras and Canuto Reyes, who had left Villa, they planned to initiate a comeback for the Convention by attacking Torreón. On January 1, 1916, the forces of Argumedo, Contreras, and Reyes made a surprise attack on Lerdo and Gómez Palacios, ousting the Constitutionalist garrisons in those towns. The attack carried the troops of the Convention into Torreón, but lack of artillery support and the plaguing shortage of ammunition forced a cessation of the fire fight. Driven back into the mountains and faced with using hazardous guerrilla tactics, if resistance was continued, Lagos Cházaro decided to follow Cervantes into exile.

In the first month of 1916 the government of the Convention ceased to exist. In Texas Cervantes and three other Villistas, José G. Nieto, Alberto B. Piña, and Francisco R. Velázquez, penned a fervent, stirring obituary for the assembly. Reviewing the long history of the Convention, they spoke bitterly of those Carrancistas who had once sworn to uphold its banner, only to fall into betrayal. But though the Convention had now disappeared, "the Conventionist ideals have not died," they said. "In the mountains of the South and in the Center and North of the Republic, there are still patriots who will fight for these ideals." [78]

And they were right. Villa and Zapata fought on, though not with the results for which Cervantes and his companions in exile had hoped. The victory of Carranza and his Constitutionalist armies on the battlefield brought no similar triumph for the political ideals of the First Chief. Though Zapata died at the hands of a traitorous assassin and Villa made his peace with Obregón after 1920, the social reforms for which both had fought became the warp and woof of the real revolution. In 1916 and 1917 at Querétaro, the aspirations of Zapata and of the Convention were reflected in the radical provisions of the new constitution. And for the next twenty-five years Zapatista land reforms were the basis for the government's program of rural reconstruction. The inarticulate, militarily ineffectual Zapata accomplished in death what he could not win in life. His spirit lived on, and in a strange, illogical, but totally Mexican twist of fate, he became the greatest hero of the Revolution. In the hagiography of the Revolution the *caudillo* of Morelos continues to ride his white charger against an enemy, which is neither Constitutionalist, nor Conventionist, and therefore completely apocryphal.

As for Carranza, no similar legends arose to hallow his grave, though he too became the victim of an assassin's bullet. The Liberalism of the Constitutionalist First Chief was, after all, an anachronism in twentieth-century Mexico. The future belonged to the mentality of the Convention. Through Obregón, Calles, and above all Lázaro Cárdenas, the Revolution of the Convention of Aguascalientes became the Revolution of all Mexico. The men of Villa, who had fought and died at Torreón, Zacatecas, Celaya, and León, and the Zapatistas, who gave their lives defending Puebla or Mexico City against the Constitutionalists, had not done so in vain.

Bibliographical Note

        IT WOULD BE POINTLESS TO LIST THE GREAT NUMBER OF books consulted in the preparation of this manuscript, for so few were used to any extent. Secondary accounts of the period are often unreliable, as are the books written by participants in the Revolution upon which these secondary accounts are based. There is nothing in Mexico to compare with the studies of Madero made by Stanley R. Ross and Charles Cumberland. Too often the Mexican historian of the Revolution is a partisan of one or another of the various factions. He is a Carrancista or Zapatista first, and a historian second. He uses his own papers or recollections exclusively, for he is denied access to the papers of other factions or other historians. For this reason the work now being done by the Mexican and American scholars affiliated with the Colegio de México and supported by the Rockefeller Foundation in cataloging and collating materials on the Revolution is of extreme importance. There were three books, however, which I did find valuable, though even these must be used with care: Francisco Ramírez Plancarte, *La Ciudad de México durante la Revolución Constitucionalista;* Juan Barragán Rodríguez, *Historia del Ejército y de la Revolución Constitucionalista;* and Alfonso Taracena, *Mi vida en el vértigo de la Revolución Mexicana.*

    There were three main sources from which this study was written. Most important was the personal archive of General Roque González Garza in Mexico City. As president of the Convention, González Garza kept complete records of the business of the Convention's government, as well as correspondence with Villa, Zapata, and other revolutionaries.

The second was the collection of State Department papers in Washington's National Archives. There are materials there on the Mexican Revolution which are unobtainable in Mexico, especially in the post records and the 812 files (political affairs in Mexico) of the State Department. The historian who depends solely on the printed Foreign Relations papers misses the bulk of the records, and the most important part, at that. The third source consists of the newspaper collections of the Hemeroteca Nacional and the Biblioteca de México in Mexico City, the Library of Congress, and the University of Texas library. González Garza had stenographic notes of the debates in the Convention, but these had become waterlogged in a flood, so that most of the debates were reconstructed largely from the columns of *La Convención, El Monitor, El Pueblo,* and *El Liberal.* The *New York Times,* with its excellent index, is, of course, an indispensable aid in studying this period. And the *New York World* was useful in reflecting the view of the Wilson administration.

Of lesser importance, but nevertheless valuable, were the manuscript collections of the Library of Congress (the Wilson, Bryan, Lansing, and Scott papers), the personal papers of Antonio Díaz Soto y Gama and Vito Alessio Robles, and the Basave collection of the Biblioteca de México. And finally I must record my debt of gratitude to González Garza and Díaz Soto in submitting to personal interrogations on their participation in the Conventionist revolution. Without General González Garza's reminiscences, especially, and his papers, this book could not have been written.

Notes

CHAPTER 1

1. Juan Barragán Rodríguez, *Historia del Ejército y de la Revolución Constitucionalista* (México, 1946), I, 97–98.
2. *Ibid.*, 185.
3. *Ibid.*, 90.
4. Ramón Puente, *Vida de Francisco Villa contada por el mismo* (Los Angeles, 1919), 49–50.
5. *Ibid.*, 54–62.
6. Barragán Rodríguez, I, 206–211.
7. *Ibid.*, 212.
8. *Ibid.*, 367. Feliciano Gil, *Biografía y vida militar del General Alvaro Obregón* (Hermosillo, 1914), 20.
9. Barragán Rodríguez, I, 368–371.
10. Puente, 74.
11. *Ibid.*, 76–77. Barragán Rodríguez, I, 271.
12. Puente, 78.
13. John Reed, article in the *New York World*, April 12, 1914, 2T:1–5. Theodore C. Hamm to William Jennings Bryan, April 13, 1914, State Department Files of the National Archives, 812.00/11706. Unless otherwise indicated all correspondence of the Department of State will be from the 812.00 files and will be identified only by the slash number.
14. Reed, *New York World*.
15. *Ibid.*
16. Roque González Garza, *La Batalla de Torreón* (Torreón, 1914), 4.

17. Hamm to Bryan /11706.

18. Reed, *New York World*. See also his *Insurgent Mexico* (New York, 1914), 204 ff.

19. *Ibid.*

20. *Ibid.* Hamm to Bryan /11706.

21. González Garza, 5–30. Hamm to Bryan /11706. Puente, 83.

22. Reed, *Insurgent Mexico*, 140.

23. Guillermo Canales Montejano, *Historia militar de México* (México, 1940), 161–163.

24. Hamm to Bryan, April 19, 1914 /11703.

25. George C. Carothers to Bryan, April 9, 1914 /11461.

26. Barragán Rodríguez, I, 439–444.

27. Alfonso Taracena, *Mi vida en el vértigo de la Revolución Mexicana* (México, 1936), 265.

28. Barragán Rodríguez, I, 469.

29. *Ibid.*, 475–476.

30. *Ibid.*, 476.

31. *Ibid.*, 477. Puente, 85–86.

32. Barragán Rodríguez, 515.

33. Vito Alessio Robles, "Episodios de la Revolución," *Todo*, June 3, 1954, 12.

34. Barragán Rodríguez, I, 480–483.

35. Puente, 86. Taracena, 270. Alessio Robles, *Todo*, October 27, 1949, 13. Barragán Rodríguez, I, 517–520.

36. *Investigation of Mexican Affairs*, Senate Document 285, 66th Congress (Washington, D. C., 1920), I, 1771.

37. Francisco Villa, *Manifiesto a la Nación* (Chihuahua, 1914), 50.

38. *Ibid.*, 52–55.

39. Barragán Rodríguez, I, 533.

40. Felipe Angeles, *La Batalla de Zacatecas* (Chihuahua, 1914), 5–27. *El Sol*, June 27, 1914, 1:4–7.

41. Alessio Robles, "La Convención Revolucionaria de Aguascalientes," *Todo*, November 17, 1949, 14.

42. Barragán Rodríguez, I, 539. Taracena, 272.

43. Leon J. Canova to Bryan, July 2, 1914 /12462.

CHAPTER 2

1. Canova to Bryan, July 2, 1914 /12462.

2. Alessio Robles, *Todo*, December 1, 1949, 12–13.

3. Canova to Bryan /12462.

4. Barragán Rodríguez, I, 534, 565.

5. Carothers to Bryan, July 5, 1914 /12472.

6. Villa to Hugh Scott, July 6, 1914; Scott to Villa, July 6, 1914, Scott Papers in the Library of Congress, Box 16.

7. Alessio Robles, *Todo*, December 1, 1949, 12–13. *Papers Relating to the Foreign Relations of the United States, 1914* (Washington, D. C., 1922), 559–560.

8. Alessio Robles, *Todo*, December 1, 1949, 12.

9. Carothers to Z. L. Cobb, July 8, 1914 /12470.

10. Federico Cervantes, *et al.*, *La Convención Nacional Revolucionaria* (n.p., 1917), 31. A pamphlet which was originally written in the United States in January 1916.

11. Alessio Robles, *Todo*, December 8, 1949, 12–13.

12. See below, p. 152.

13. Canova to Bryan, July 14, 1914 /12501.

14. Marion T. Letcher to Bryan, July 25, 1914 /12614.

15. Tasker H. Bliss to Scott, July 18, 1914, Scott Papers, Box 16. Bliss to Lindley M. Garrison, July 20, 1914 /12559.

16. Bliss to Garrison /12559.

17. Cobb to Bryan, July 24, 1914 /12601.

18. Barragán Rodríguez, I, 581.

19. Carothers to Bryan, April 23, 1914 /11654.

20. Bryan to Carothers, April 24, 1914 /11654.

21. Canova to Bryan, July 6, 1914 /12429.

22. *El Sol*, July 5, 1914, 1:6; July 6, 1914, 1:4–7; July 7, 1914, 1:4.

23. *El Sol*, July 11, 1914, 1:4–7.

24. John R. Silliman to Bryan, July 10, 1914 /12469.

25. *Ibid.*

26. Baltasar Dromundo, *Emiliano Zapata* (México, 1934), 97.

27. Silliman to Bryan, July 19, 1914 /12522.

28. J. M. Cardoso de Oliveira to Bryan, July 22, 1914, Post Records (Mexico City), 1914/800. The records of the various diplomatic and consular posts are found in the Foreign Relations section of the National Archives. All of the documents used in this study were from folders marked 800 (political affairs). Hereafter these will be cited as PRMC (1914 or 1915).

29. William Canada (for Silliman) to Bryan, July 25, 1914 /12625.

30. *El Sol*, July 26, 1914, 1:1–5. Cardoso de Oliveira to Bryan, July 27, 1914 /12637.

31. Cardoso de Oliveira to Bryan /12637.

32. Silliman to Bryan, July 30, 1914 /12691.

33. *El Sol*, August 2, 1914, 1:1–3. Phillip C. Hanna to Bryan, August 2, 1914 /12780.

34. Hanna to Bryan, August 1, 1914 /12704.

35. Silliman to Bryan, August 1, 1914 /12700.
36. Silliman to Bryan, August 3, 1914 /12723.
37. Barragán Rodríguez, I, 587–588.
38. Cardoso de Oliveira to Bryan, August 1, 1914, PRMC (1914).
39. Cardoso de Oliveira to Bryan, August 4, 1914, PRMC (1914).
40. Silliman to Bryan, August 5, 1914 /12774. (No other name) McMillan to Sir Lionel Carden, August 5, 1914, PRMC (1914).
41. Frederick F. Funston to Agwar (Adjutant General, War Department), August 7, 1914 /12845.
42. Cardoso de Oliveira to Bryan, August 8, 1914, PRMC (1914).
43. Cardoso de Oliveira to Bryan, August 9, 1914, PRMC (1914).
44. Cardoso de Oliveira to Bryan, August 10, 1914, PRMC (1914).
45. Eduardo Iturbide, *Mi paso por la vida* (México, 1951), 127–139.
46. Cardoso de Oliveira to Bryan, August 13, 1914 /12834.
47. Cardoso de Oliveira to Bryan, August 13, 1914, PRMC (1914).
48. Hanna to Bryan, August 14, 1914 /12861.
49. *Foreign Relations* (1914), 586–587.
50. *El Sol*, August 15, 1914, 1:4–7. Alvaro Obregón, *Ocho mil kilómetros en campana* (México, 1917), 259. Iturbide, 142–143.

CHAPTER 3

1. *El Liberal*, August 19, 1914, 1:1; August 25, 1914, 1:6–7; August 27, 1914, 1:1–2; August 20, 1914, 1:1–2. Cardoso de Oliveira to Bryan, August 22, 1914 /12963. Cardoso de Oliveira to Bryan, August 25, 1914 /12901.
2. Canova to Bryan, August 29, 1914 /13039.
3. Canova to Bryan, August 27, 1914 /13013.
4. Canova to Bryan, August 27, 1914 /13020.
5. Canova to Bryan, August 29, 1914 /13039.
6. Dromundo, 98.
7. *El Liberal*, August 18, 1914, 5:5–6; 7:4. Dromundo, 98.
8. Milpa Alta Proclamation, August, 1914, PRMC (1914).
9. *Foreign Relations* (1914), 592.
10. *El Liberal*, August 28, 1914, 1:3–4.
11. Manuel W. González, *Contra Villa* (México, 1935), 363–368. J. W. Belt to Garrison, September 3, 1914 /13095. *El Liberal*, September 7, 1914, 3:1–2.
12. Belt to Bryan, September 3, 1914 /13068.
13. Belt to Garrison, September 3, 1914 /13095.
14. *El Liberal*, September 7, 1914, 3:3.
15. Canova to Bryan, August 22, 1914 /12960. *El Sol*, August 23, 1914, 1:1–2. *El Liberal*, August 22, 1914, 1:3.

16. Obregón, 270–274.

17. *Ibid.*, 275–276.

18. *El Liberal*, September 26, 1914, 1:1–2. Puente, 92. Taracena, 287. Villa, *Manifiesto*, 19–24. Alessio Robles, *Todo*, December 22, 1949, 12–13, 58.

19. *El Liberal*, September 26, 1914, 1:1–2. Barragán Rodríguez, II, 71.

20. Silliman to Bryan, September 5, 1914 /13116.

21. Lansing to Cardoso de Oliveira, September 17, 1914, PRMC (1914).

22. Silliman to Bryan, September 8, 1914 /13133.

23. Bryan to Cardoso de Oliveira, September 15, 1914, PRMC (1914).

24. Cardoso de Oliveira to Bryan, September 17, 1914, PRMC (1914).

25. Funston to Agwar, September 17, 1914 /13251.

26. Lansing to Cardoso de Oliveira, September 22, 1914, PRMC (1914).

27. *Mexican Herald*, September 14, 1914, 1:4.

28. Alessio Robles, *Todo*, January 12, 1950, 12. Puente, 93.

29. Obregón, 309–310.

30. Canova to Bryan, September 22, 1914 /13323.

31. Carothers to Bryan, September 19, 1914 /13237. Barragán Rodríguez, II, 78.

32. Obregón, 312. Barragán Rodríguez, II, 78.

33. Canova to Bryan, September 22, 1914 /13323.

34. Obregón, 314.

35. *Nueva Patria*, September 26, 1914, 2:4–7.

36. *Ibid.* Barragán Rodríguez, II, 84–87.

37. Canova to Bryan, September 21, 1914 /13247.

38. Villa, *Manifiesto*, 31–34.

39. *El Liberal*, September 26, 1914, 3:1–3. *Nueva Patria*, September 26, 1914, 6:6.

40. Canova to Bryan, September 25, 1914 /13326. Obregón, 317–318.

41. *El Paso del Norte*, October 4, 1914, 1:2–5.

42. Canova to Bryan, October 9, 1914 /27411.

43. Canova to Bryan, September 25, 1914 /13326.

44. Canova to Bryan, October 9, 1914 /27411.

45. *El Paso del Norte*, October 4, 1914, 1:2–5.

46. Obregón, 325–327.

47. Puente, 94.

48. Canova to Bryan, October 9, 1914 /27411.

49. Villa, *Manifiesto*, 7–29. *El Pueblo*, October 6, 1914, 6–7; 7:2.

50. Villa to Arrietas, September 23, 1914; Arrietas to Villa, September 24, 1914, Personal Archive of Roque González Garza. Hereafter these papers will be identified as Archives RGG.

51. Hamm to Bryan, September 27, 1914 /13429.

52. *Mexican Herald*, September 29, 1914, 1:1. Cobb to Bryan, September 27, 1914 /13304.

53. *El Liberal*, September 30, 1914, 3:4.

54. *Mexican Herald*, September 30, 1914, 1:1. Belt to Bryan, September 29, 1914 /13327.

55. *Nueva Patria*, September 27, 1914, 1:5; October 4, 1914, 1:6–7.

56. *Nueva Patria*, October 1, 1914, 1:4.

57. *Nueva Patria*, October 4, 1914, 6:2–5.

CHAPTER 4

1. Jorge Useta (Pseudonym for José Ugarte), *Impresiones de guerra* (Laredo, Texas, 1915), 67–68.

2. *Nueva Patria*, October 2, 1914, 1:1–3; 6:3–4.

3. *El Pueblo*, October 2, 1914, 6:4. Alessio Robles, *Todo*, February 2, 1950, 12.

4. *El Pueblo*, October 3, 1914, 1:1–2.

5. *Nueva Patria*, October 3, 1914, 4:3.

6. *Nueva Patria*, October 4, 1914, 4:2–3.

7. *El Pueblo*, October 4, 1914, 5:2.

8. *El Pueblo*, October 4, 1914, 5:2–5.

9. *Nueva Patria*, October 4, 1914, 4:5.

10. *El Pueblo*, October 5, 1914, 4:1–7.

11. *El Pueblo*, October 6, 1914, 6:3. Canada to Bryan, October 9, 1914 /13466.

12. *Nueva Patria*, October 6, 1914, 6:1–4. Belt to Bryan, October 6, 1914 /13399. *El Pueblo*, October 6, 1914, 7:2.

13. Bryan to Cardoso de Oliveira, October 1, 1914, PRMC (1914). Wilson to Bryan, October 2, 1914 /13407.

14. Cardoso de Oliveira to Bryan, October 5, 1914, PRMC (1914).

15. Bryan to Cardoso de Oliveira, October 7, 1914, PRMC (1914).

16. Silliman to Bryan, October 29, 1914 /13570.

17. Cardoso de Oliveira to Bryan, October 27, 1914, PRMC (1914).

18. Funston to Agwar, October 30, 1914, Funston War Diary, AGO file 2228507, National Archives.

CHAPTER 5

1. *La Convención*, December 16, 1914, 3:1.

2. Cobb to Bryan, October 11, 1914 /13463.

3. Alessio Robles, *Todo*, February 16, 1950, 12–13.

4. *El Liberal*, October 20, 1914, 1:1–2.

5. Villa to Felix A. Sommerfeld, October 12, 1914, Scott Papers, Box 16.

6. Alessio Robles, *Todo*, March 9, 1950, 12.

7. Francisco Ramírez Plancarte, *La Ciudad de México durante la Revolución Constitucionalista* (México, 1941), 107.

8. Canova to Bryan, October 19, 1914 /13531.

9. *El Liberal*, October 17, 1914, 3:3-6.

10. *Nueva Patria*, October 19, 1914, 1:1-2.

11. *El Pueblo*, October 20, 1914, 3:1-4.

12. Alessio Robles, *Todo*, April 27, 1950, 12-13. *La Convención*, January 7, 1915, 5:4; 6:1; January 12, 1915, 6:1.

13. Alessio Robles, *Todo*, April 6, 1950, 14.

14. *Foreign Relations* (1914), 611-612.

15. *La Convención*, January 15, 1915, 3:2-4.

16. Alessio Robles, *Todo*, May 18, 1950, 12-13.

17. Alessio Robles, *Todo*, May 25, 1950, 12-13.

18. *La Convención*, January 15, 1915, 6:1-3. Alessio Robles, *Todo*, June 1, 1950, 12, 66.

19. *La Convención*, January 16, 1915, 3:1-2.

20. Cobb (for Canova) to Bryan, October 28, 1914 /13619. *La Convención*, January 16, 1915, 4:2.

21. *La Convención*, January 16, 1915, 5:1.

22. Cobb (for Canova) to Bryan, October 28, 1914 /13619.

23. *La Convención*, January 16, 1915, 5:2. Ramírez Plancarte, 162.

24. *La Convención*, January 16, 1915, 5:4. Alessio Robles, *Todo*, June 15, 1950, 12-13.

25. *La Convención*, January 26, 1915, 4:1.

26. Ramírez Plancarte, 171-173. Alessio Robles, *Todo*, June 22, 1950, 12-13. *El Pueblo*, October 29, 1914, 1:6-7.

27. Carranza to Convention, October 23, 1914, Archives RGG.

28. Alessio Robles, *Todo*, July 6, 1950, 12, 58. Ramírez Plancarte, 184-189.

29. Alessio Robles, *Todo*, June 13, 1950, 20-21.

30. Ramírez Plancarte, 195-198.

31. *El Pueblo*, November 2, 1914, 1:5-6.

32. Cobb (for Canova) to Bryan, November 4, 1914 /13684.

33. Alessio Robles, *Todo*, August 10, 1950, 12-13. Taracena, 303.

34. Cobb (for Canova) to Bryan, November 2, 1914 /13657.

35. Cobb (for Canova) to Bryan, November 4, 1914 /13684.

36. Paulino Martínez to Emiliano Zapata, November 4, 1914, Magaña Collection. Copies of a few documents from the Gildardo Magaña collection are in the office of the Hispanic Foundation of the Library of Congress.

37. *El Liberal*, November 4, 1914, 3:1.

38. Barragán Rodríguez, II, 112-113.

39. Canova to Bryan, November 12, 1914 /27413.

40. *El Liberal*, November 5, 1914, 3:1.

41. Cobb (for Canova) to Bryan, November 8, 1914 /13714.

42. *El Liberal*, November 9, 1914, 1:1.

43. Silliman to Bryan, November 9, 1914 /13729.

44. Taracena, 307. Ramírez Plancarte, 224–226.

45. *El Sol*, November 11, 1914, 1:3–5. Alessio Robles, *Todo*, October 15, 1950, 14–15.

46. Silliman to Bryan, November 12, 1914 /13756. Cobb (for Canova) to Bryan, November 13, 1914 /13769.

47. Cobb to Bryan /13769.

48. *El Pueblo*, November 14, 1914, 1:1–3.

49. *El Sol*, November 16, 1914, 1:1–3.

50. *La Convención*, November 14, 1914, 1:3–4. *El Nacional*, December 1, 1914, 1:6–7.

51. *El Sol*, November 18, 1914, 1:5–7.

52. *El Sol*, November 21, 1914, 1:6–7.

53. Cardoso de Oliveira to Bryan, November 20, 1914, PRMC (1914). Lansing to Cardoso de Oliveira, November 21, 1914, PRMC (1914).

54. *El Sol*, November 21, 1914, 1:1–2. Cardoso de Oliveira to Bryan, November 20, 1914, PRMC (1914).

55. Cardoso de Oliveira to Bryan, November 22, 1914, PRMC (1914). Dromundo, 100.

56. Carothers to Bryan, December 16, 1914 /14061.

57. Cardoso de Oliveira to Bryan, November 10, 1914, PRMC (1914).

58. Canada to Bryan, November 11, 1914 /13755. *Foreign Relations* (1914), 625.

CHAPTER 6

1. *El Nacional*, November 27, 1914, 1:3.

2. *El Sol*, November 28, 1914, 1:1–4. Ramírez Plancarte, 255.

3. *El Nacional*, November 30, 1914, 1:5–7.

4. Villa to Zapata, December 1, 1914, Magaña Collection.

5. Carothers to Bryan, December 1, 1914 /14061.

6. Cobb (for Canova) to Bryan, December 7, 1914 /13974.

7. Canova to Bryan, December 8, 1914 /14048.

8. Canova to Bryan /14048. "Entrevista preliminar entre los generales Villa y Zapata," Typewritten notes by Gonzalo Atayde, Archives RGG.

9. Carothers to Bryan, December 16, 1914 /14061. Further details as to the names of the intended victims, etc., were furnished to me in personal conversation with Antonio Díaz Soto y Gama in the summer of 1954.

10. Carothers to Bryan /14061. *La Opinión*, December 7, 1914, 3:3–5; 4:1–4. Canova to Bryan, December 8, 1914 /14048.

11. *La Opinión*, December 7, 1914, 3:1. *El Monitor*, December 8, 1914, 1:6–7.

12. *La Opinión*, December 10, 1914, 1:6–7. *El Sol*, December 9, 1914, 1:3–5. *La Opinión*, December 18, 1914, 1:1–5.

13. *La Opinión*, December 10, 1914, 1:6–7; December 11, 1914, 1:5–7.

14. Cervantes, 48. Alessio Robles, *Todo*, November 30, 1950, 12–13. *El Monitor*, December 15, 1914, 1:1–2. *La Opinión*, December 13, 1914, 1:4.

15. Ramírez Plancarte, 281–282.

16. Silliman to Bryan, January 8, 1915 /14168. Canova to Bryan, December 16, 1914 /14097. Eulalio Gutiérrez, *Manifiesto*, January 13, 1915, Archives RGG.

17. Canova to Bryan, December 16, 1914 /14097. Canova to Bryan. December 17, 1914 /14122. *La Opinión*, December 16, 1914, 1:5–7.

18. Canova to Bryan, December 14, 1914 /14008.

19. Silliman to Bryan, December 15, 1914 /14019.

20. Martín Luis Guzmán, *Memorias de Pancho Villa* (México, 1951), 795. Puente, 97. Admittedly Guzmán's book represents an imaginative reconstruction of actual events. But his accounts have the ring of authenticity and can be accepted with a few reservations.

21. *El Monitor*, December 19, 1914, 3:1–2; December 22, 1914, 1:1–2.

22. Antonio I. Villarreal, *Immediate Causes of the Mexican Revolution* (n.p., n.d.), 18. A pamphlet published in the United States.

23. *El Sol*, December 23, 1914, 1:1–4.

24. Silliman to Bryan, December 23, 1914 /14070. Alessio Robles, *Todo*, December 28, 1950, 15.

25. *El Monitor*, December 28, 1914, 1:1. Alessio Robles, *Todo*, December 28, 1950, 15. Silliman to Bryan, December 29, 1914 /14104.

26. Guzmán, 818–821. Silliman to Bryan, December 29, 1914 /14104. Alessio Robles, *Todo*, December 28, 1950, 15.

27. Alessio Robles, *Todo*, January 4, 1951, 12–13.

28. *La Opinión*, January 1, 1915, 1:1–2.

29. Gutiérrez, *Manifiesto*, Archives RGG.

CHAPTER 7

1. *El Pueblo*, December 19, 1914, 3:4–5; December 22, 1914, 4:3.

2. *El Pueblo*, January 7, 1915, 1:2–6. Julio Cuadros Caldas, *Catecismo agrario* (Puebla, 1923), 17–26. *Documentos de la Revolución Mexicana* (México, 1945), 76–82.

3. *El Pueblo*, January 21, 1915, 5:1; February 10, 1915, 5:1–5; September 3, 1916, 1:1–4.

4. Barragán Rodríguez, II, 211.

5. *El Pueblo*, January 6, 1915, 1:3–4.

6. Barragán Rodríguez, II, 202. Gutiérrez to Obregón, January 7, 1915; Obregón to Gutiérrez, January 12, 1915 /14247.

7. Silliman to Bryan, January 9, 1915 /14173. Silliman to Bryan, January 12, 1915 /14188. *La Opinión*, January 12, 1915, 1:1; January 13, 1915, 6:6–7. Silliman to Bryan, January 13, 1915 /14195.

8. Gutiérrez, *Manifiesto*, Archives RGG.

9. *La Opinión*, January 14, 1915, 1:3–5.

10. *La Opinión*, January 14, 1915, 6:3–5.

11. Silliman to Bryan, December 11, 1914 /13944.

12. Canada to Bryan, December 13, 1914 /13997.

13. Carothers to Bryan, December 19, 1914 /14044.

14. Scott to Charles E. Rushmore, January 19, 1915; Scott, Memorandum to the Secretary of War, January 17, 1915, Scott Papers, Box 17.

15. Scott to Garrison, January 2, 1915; Maytorena to Scott, January 3, 1915, Scott Papers, Box 16.

16. Scott to Palmer C. Ricketts, January 21, 1915; Scott to Wood, January 27, 1915; Villa to Maytorena, January 9, 1915, Scott Papers, Box 17.

17. The signed agreement is in Box 16 of the Scott Papers.

18. Scott, Memorandum to the Secretary of War, January 29, 1915, Scott Papers, Box 17.

19. Bliss to Scott, January 13, 1915; Scott, Memorandum to the Secretary of War, January 29, 1915, Scott Papers, Box 17.

20. F. D. H. (No other identification) to L. D. Ricketts, February (?), 1915, Scott Papers, Box 17.

21. Barragán Rodríguez, II, 177.

22. Personal conversation with Roque González Garza in the summer of 1954.

23. *El Monitor*, January 19, 1915, 1:5–7.

24. Roque González Garza, Manifesto No. 1, January 16, 1915, Archives RGG.

25. Gutiérrez to Villa, January 16, 1915, Archives RGG.

26. Conferencia telegráfica, January 16, 1915, Archives RGG.

27. *Decretos de la Convención* (México, 1915), 4–5. *La Opinión*, January 17, 1915, 1:6–7. *El Monitor*, January 17, 1915, 1:1–7; 3:1–2.

28. *La Opinión*, January 19, 1915, 1:5; 5:4; January 20, 1915, 1:6–7; 3:3. *Decretos de la Convención*, 9–10.

29. *La Opinión*, January 20, 1915, 3:5; January 24, 1915, 1:7. *Decretos de la Convención*, 17–19.

30. Roberto M. y Martínez to González Garza, January 24, 1915, Archives RGG.

31. Conferencia telegráfica, January 17, 1915, Archives RGG.

32. Gaston Schutz to Bryan, January 30, 1915 /14347. Wilbert L. Bonney to Bryan, February 1, 1915 /14349.

33. Villa to Zapata, March 18, 1915, Archives RGG. Francisco Naranjo, *Diccionario biográfico revolucionario* (Mexico, 1935), 18.

34. Martínez to González Garza, January 25, 1915; González Garza to Villa, January 25, 1915, Archives RGG.

35. Vasconcelos, *La Tormenta*, 278–287. Vasconcelos to Bryan, March 24, 1915 /15106.

36. *Mexican Herald*, March 24, 1915, 1:5. Naranjo, 37. Cobb to Bryan, April 3, 1915 /14772.

37. *El Monitor*, January 24, 1915, 3:1; January 26, 1915, 1:1–3; 3:3–6.

38. González Garza to Villa, February 2, 1915; Conferencia telegráfica, January 20, 1915; Villa to González Garza, January 21, 1915, Archives RGG.

39. Villa to Zapata, March 18, 1915, Archives RGG. *Mexican Herald*, February 24, 1915, 1:3.

40. Barragán Rodríguez, II, 227–228.

41. *La Opinión*, January 27, 1915, 1:1. González Garza to Villa, February 2, 1915; Villa to González Garza, January 27, 1915, Archives RGG.

42. *La Opinión*, January 28, 1915, 1:1–5.

43. Sinopsis de los principales asuntos tratados por la Soberana Convención Revolucionaria, Archives RGG.

CHAPTER 8

1. *La Opinión*, January 31, 1915, 1:2–3.

2. *Mexican Herald*, February 2, 1915, 1:1; February 7, 1915, 1:4.

3. Cardoso de Oliveira to Bryan, February 3, 1915 /14346. Lansing to Silliman, February 6, 1915 /14346.

4. *Mexican Herald*, February 2, 1915, 1:1. Cardoso de Oliveira to Bryan, February 3, 1915 /14346.

5. Cardoso de Oliveira to Bryan, February 5, 1915 /14353.

6. *Mexican Herald*, February 5, 1915, 1:1; February 6, 1915, 1:1.

7. Silliman to Bryan, February 6, 1915 /14356. Silliman to Bryan, February 6, 1915 /14385.

8. *La Convención*, April 25, 1915, 5:1–3. This periodical was not published in Cuernavaca, but the debates were recorded at a later date when the Convention returned to Mexico City.

9. *Mexican Herald*, February 7, 1915, 1:1. Silliman to Bryan, February 12, 1915 /14385.

10. *Historia gráfica de la Revolución* (México, n.d.), II, 919.

11. *Mexican Herald*, February 11, 1915, 1:4; February 12, 1915, 1:1–2.

12. Silliman to Bryan, February 12, 1915 /14385.

13. Rosendo Salazar and J. G. Escobedo, *La pugna de la gleba, 1907–1922* (México, 1923), 84–89.

14. *Ibid.*, 93–95.

15. *La Prensa*, February 8, 1915, 1:6–7.

16. *Mexican Herald*, February 18, 1915, 1:4.

17. Salazar and Escobedo, 95–96.

18. *El Pueblo*, February 18, 1915, 1:1. Salazar and Escobedo, 99.

19. Silliman to Bryan, February 16, 1915 /14402.

20. Silliman to Bryan, March 16, 1915, PRMC (1915).

21. *Mexican Herald*, February 13, 1915, 1:2.

22. *El Pueblo*, February 15, 1915, 1:4; February 21, 1915, 1:3–4. *Efemérides Galván* (México, 1926), 588–589. *Mexican Herald*, February 16, 1915, 1:5.

23. *Mexican Herald*, February 19, 1915, 1:5.

24. *Mexican Herald*, February 20, 1915, 1:1.

25. *La Prensa*, February 19, 1915, 1:4.

26. *Mexican Herald*, February 21, 1915, 1:1.

27. *Mexican Herald*, February 21, 1915, 1:2.

28. *Mexican Herald*, February 22, 1915, 1:1. Ramírez Plancarte, 325–336.

29. From a personal conversation with Canon Jesús García Gutiérrez in 1950.

30. *Mexican Herald*, February 23, 1915, 1:1–2.

31. *Mexican Herald*, February 23, 1915, 1:5; March 1, 1915, 1:4.

32. *Mexican Herald*, February 27, 1915, 1:1–3. Silliman to Jesús Urueta, March 1, 1915, PRMC (1915).

33. Cardoso de Oliveira to Bryan, March 2, 1915 /14472.

34. *Mexican Herald*, March 4, 1915, 1:1–2. Cardoso de Oliveira to Bryan, March 4, 1915 /14500.

35. *La Prensa*, March 4, 1915, 1:1–2. Silliman to Bryan, March 3, 1915 /14494.

36. Cardoso de Oliveira to Bryan, March 2, 1915 /14472. *Mexican Herald*, March 4, 1915, 1:1–2. Cardoso de Oliveira to Bryan, March 4, 1915 /14500.

37. Cardoso de Oliveira to Bryan, March 6, 1915 /14515.

38. Lansing to Cardoso de Oliveira, March 6, 1915 /14501. Cardoso de Oliveira, "Important Notice," March 6, 1915, PRMC (1915). Wilson to Bryan, March 6, 1915 /14504½.

39. Bryan to Cardoso de Oliveira, March 7, 1915, PRMC (1915). Cardoso de Oliveira to Bryan, March 7, 1915 /14519.

40. Lansing to Bryan, March 8, 1915 /14664½.

41. Silliman to Bryan, March 10, 1915 /14550.

42. Wilson to Carranza, March 11, 1915 /14573.

43. *Mexican Herald*, March 10, 1915, 3:4; March 11, 1915, 1:4–7; 3:5.

44. Barragán Rodríguez, II, 237.

45. *Mexican Herald*, March 13, 1915, 1:4.

CHAPTER 9

1. Villa to Zapata, March 18, 1915, Archives RGG.

2. González Garza to Gustavo Baz, February 23, 1915; González Garza to Alfredo Cuarón, February 23, 1915, Archives RGG.

3. Decree of Roque González Garza, February 2, 1915; González Garza to Municipal President of Jojutla, February 17, 1915, Archives RGG. *Decretos de la Convención*, 21.

4. Zapata to González Garza, February 9, 1915, Archives RGG.

5. González Garza to Zapata, February 10, 1915, Archives RGG.

6. González Garza to Baz, February 11, 1915, Archives RGG.

7. *Decretos de la Convención*, 24.

8. González Garza to Villa, February 28, 1915, Archives RGG.

9. Taraceña, 336.

10. "Declaración a los habitantes de la Ciudad de México," February 26, 1915; Decretos de la Convención, February 18, 1915; Sinopsis de los principales asuntos, Archives RGG.

11. González Garza to the Convention, February 19, 1915, Archives RGG.

12. González Garza to Antonio Díaz Soto y Gama and Otilio Montaño, February 21, 1915, Archives RGG.

13. Montaño and Díaz Soto to González Garza, February 24, 1915, Archives RGG.

14. *La Convención*, May 29, 1915, 7:3; 8:3; 9:1; 10:4; May 31, 1915, 3:1–4; 4:2; 5:1–3. *Decretos de la Convención*, 26–27.

15. González Garza to Zapata, March 10, 1915, Archives RGG.

16. Juan M. Banderas to González Garza, February 19, 1915, Archives RGG.

17. *La Convención*, May 26, 1915, 2:2. González Garza to secretaries of the Convention, February 23, 1915; González Garza to Zapata, February 24, 1915, Archives RGG.

18. Santiago Orozco to González Garza, February 27, 1915; González Garza to Orozco, March 2, 1915; Zapata to González Garza, March 3, 1915; González Garza to Zapata, March 8, 1915, Archives RGG.

19. González Garza to Villa, March 4, 1915, Archives RGG.

20. *La Convención*, March 24, 1915, 7:1–3.

21. Wilson to Bryan, March 18, 1915 /14665½.

22. Duval West, Report to the Secretary of State, May (?), 1915, 111.70 /W52 /42a.

23. González Garza to Amador Salazar, March 11, 1915, Archives RGG. *Mexican Herald*, March 16, 1915, 1:1.

24. Gildardo Magaña to González Garza, March 13, 1915; González Garza to Magaña, March 14, 1915, Archives RGG.

25. Ramírez Plancarte, 403–404.

26. *Mexican Herald*, March 17, 1915, 1:1–2; March 18, 1915, 1:5; March 19, 1915, 1:2; March 20, 1915, 1:2–4.

27. *El Monitor*, March 22, 1915, 1:5–7; 2:2–3.

28. *El Monitor*, March 24, 1915, 1:1–2. *Mexican Herald*, March 24, 1915, 1:1–2. *El Monitor*, March 25, 1915, 1:5–7; 2:5–6; March 26, 1915, 1:5–7; 2:3; March 28, 1915, 1:4–6; 2:1–2.

29. Baz to González Garza, March 22, 1915, Archives RGG.

30. González Garza to Villa, March 22, 1915; Villa to González Garza, March 23, 1915, Archives RGG.

31. González Garza to Villa, March 24, 1915, Archives RGG.

32. Cardoso de Oliveira to Bryan, March 26, 1915, PRMC (1915).

33. Villa to González Garza, March 27, 1915, Archives RGG.

34. Decree of the Convention, March 27, 1915, Archives RGG. Barragán Rodríguez, II, 440–447.

35. *Mexican Herald*, March 29, 1915, 1:4. Manuel Palafox to González Garza, March 28, 1915, Archives RGG.

36. Santiago Orozco to González Garza, March 29, 1915; González Garza to Orozco, March 30, 1915, Archives RGG.

37. González Garza to Villa, March 28, 1915; Villa to González Garza, March 28, 1915; González Garza to Francisco Estrada, March 29, 1915; Estrada to González Garza, March 30, 1915; Andrés Pérez to González Garza, March 29, 1915, Archives RGG

38. Zapata to González Garza, March 29, 1915; González Garza to Zapata, March 29, 1915, Orozco to González Garza, March 29, 1915; González Garza to Orozco, March 29, 1915; González Garza to Zapata, March 31, 1915; Zapata to González Garza, April 1, 1915, Archives RGG.

39. Palafox to Chief of the Division of National Railroads, March 30, 1915, Archives RGG. Cardoso de Oliveira to Bryan, March 29, 1915; Bryan to Cardoso de Oliveira, March 29, 1915, PRMC (1915).

40. *Mexican Herald*, March 30, 1915, 1:1–2.

41. *Foreign Relations* (1915), 683. Silliman to Bryan, April 5, 1915 /14794.

42. Cobb (for Carothers) to Bryan, April 6, 1915 /14795.

43. González Garza to Zapata, April 2, 1915; Zapata to González Garza, April 3, 1915; González Garza to Zapata, April 3, 1915; Zapata to González Garza, April 4, 1915; Villa to González Garza, April 4, 1915; González Garza to Villa, April 3, 1915, Archives RGG. *New York Times*, April 7, 1915, 5:2–3; April 8, 1915, 5:3.

44. Barragán Rodríguez, II, 224.

45. From a personal conversation with Roque González Garza in the summer of 1954.

46. Canales Montejano, 187–188. Barragán Rodríguez, II, 271–275.

47. *New York Times*, April 9, 1915, 1:4; April 10, 1915, 4:2–3; April 12, 1915, 5:2.

48. Barragán Rodríguez, II, 280–281.
49. *New York Times*, April 12, 1915, 5:2.
50. Canales Montejano, 189. Barragán Rodríguez, II, 286–296. *New York Times*, April 17, 1915, 1:3.
51. *New York Times*, April 18, 1915, 6:1–2.
52. J. R. Ambrosins to Arthur Constantine, April 23, 1915, Archives RGG. Canales Montejano, 189. Barragán Rodríguez, II, 296.
53. Barragán Rodríguez, II, 354.
54. *New York Times*, April 20, 1915, 1:4.

CHAPTER 10

1. *New York Times*, April 8, 1915, 5:4. González Garza to Villa, April (?), 1915, Archives RGG. *Historia gráfica de la Revolución Mexicana*, II, 942.
2. West to Bryan, April 10, 1915 /14832. Wilson to West, April 12, 1915 /14832.
3. West, "Report."
4. West to Bryan, April 19, 1915 /14890. Bryan to Cardoso de Oliveira, April 22, 1915 /14890.
5. González Garza to secretaries of the Convention, May 12, 1915, Archives RGG.
6. Eufemio Zapata to (No other name) García, April 28, 1915, Archives RGG.
7. *Decretos de la Convención*, 36. Statement of González Garza to the press (no date), Archives RGG.
8. Antonio Díaz Soto y Gama expressed the opinion in 1954 that Palafox had always been a "scoundrel."
9. Veyan, Jean y Cia. to González Garza, April 3, 1915, Archives RGG.
10. González Garza to Zapata, April 7, 1915, Archives RGG.
11. The original signed document is in the Archives of González Garza. See also the *Mexican Herald*, May 7, 1915, 1:2 and *El Monitor*, May 7, 1915, 1:5; 2:7.
12. Amador Salazar to González Garza, April 22, 1915; González Garza to Salazar, April 25, 1915, Archives RGG.
13. Baz to González Garza, April 24, 1915; González Garza to Baz, April 28, 1915, Archives RGG.
14. *El Monitor*, April 24, 1915, 1:2; 2:4–6; April 25, 1915, 2:4–7.
15. *El Monitor*, April 30, 1915, 1:4.
16. *El Monitor*, May 1, 1915, 1:1–2; 2:3–4.
17. *Mexican Herald*, May 3, 1915, 1:1. Also from a personal conversation with González Garza in 1954.
18. Zapata to González Garza, May 2, 1915; González Garza to secretaries

of the Convention, May 3, 1915; González Garza to Zapata, May 3, 1915, Archives RGG.

19. *La Convención*, May 3, 1915, 1:4. *Mexican Herald*, May 4, 1915, 1:3.

20. *Mexican Herald*, May 4, 1915, 1:3; 2:6.

21. *Mexican Herald*, May 5, 1915, 1:5; 2:4; May 7, 1915, 2:2–3.

22. Zapata to González Garza, May 4, 1915, Archives RGG. Personal conversation with González Garza in 1954.

23. Zapata to the Convention, May 8, 1915 /15085.

24. Barragán Rodríguez, II, 335.

25. *El Monitor*, May 8, 1915, 1:1–3. *Mexican Herald*, May 8, 1915, 1:1. Message of González Garza to the people of Mexico, May 7, 1915, Archives RGG. Antonio Barona to González Garza, May 7, 1915; Barona to González Garza, May 8, 1915, Archives RGG.

26. *Mexican Herald*, May 8, 1915, 1:6–7. *El Monitor*, May 8, 1915, 1:3–5.

27. Zapata to González Garza, May 10, 1915, Archives RGG.

28. *El Monitor*, May 5, 1915, 1:2–3, 2:4–5.

29. *El Monitor*, May 8, 1915, 2:5.

30. *El Monitor*, May 7, 1915, 1:1–2.

31. *El Monitor*, May 8, 1915, 1:1–2; 2:3–4.

32. *El Monitor*, May 9, 1915, 2:3.

33. Ramírez Plancarte, 423–427.

34. *El Monitor*, May 18, 1915, 1:1–2.

35. *El Monitor*, May 20, 1915, 1:5–7; 2:3–4.

36. *Mexican Herald*, May 21, 1915, 1:1–2; 2:3. *El Monitor*, May 21, 1915, 1:3. Ramírez Plancarte, 452–455.

37. *La Convención*, May 22, 1915, 1:2–3.

38. *El Monitor*, May 22, 1915, 1:2–3; 8:1. *Mexican Herald*, May 22, 1915, 1:3.

39. *El Monitor*, May 22, 1915, 1:6; 2:1–2. Cardoso de Oliveira to Bryan, May 22, 1915, PRMC (1915). *Mexican Herald*, May 22, 1915, 1:3.

40. *Mexican Herald*, May 25, 1915, 1:6–7. *La Convención*, May 25, 1915, 12:3–4. Translation of Cicero taken from Louis E. Lord, *The Speeches of Cicero* (London, 1946), 15.

41. *El Monitor*, May 26, 1915, 2:3.

42. *El Monitor*, May 26, 1915, 2:6. *Mexican Herald*, May 26, 1915, 1:6–7.

CHAPTER 11

1. West, "Report."

2. *New York Times*, May 26, 1915, 5:3; May 29, 1915, 1:3; 6:2–4.

3. *New York Times*, May 29, 1915, 6:2–4.

4. *New York Times*, May 30, 1915, 4:1.

5. *New York Times*, June 3, 1915, 4:3. *Lansing Papers*, 1914–1920. In *Foreign Relations of the United States* (Washington, D. C., 1940), II, 532–533.

6. Woodrow Wilson, *The New Democracy* (New York, 1926), I, 339–340.

7. *Lansing Papers*, II, 534–535.

8. *Foreign Relations*, (1915), 698.

9. González Garza to Governors and Military Commanders, June 1, 1915, Archives RGG. Eufemio Zapata to González Garza, June 1, 1915, PRMC (1915).

10. Zapata to González Garza, June 3, 1915; González Garza to Zapata, June 4, 1915, Archives RGG.

11. *Mexican Herald*, June 3, 1915, 1:2; June 4, 1915, 1:3. Ismael Palafox to Cardoso de Oliveira, June 3, 1915, Archives RGG.

12. Cardoso de Oliveira to Bryan, June 6, 1915, PRMC (1915).

13. "Secret session of the Convention, June 5, 1915," PRMC (1915). "Secret session of the Convention, June 5, 1915," /15735. These two accounts differ slightly, but not substantially, and were evidently prepared by different persons.

14. *Mexican Herald*, June 6, 1915, 1:1; 2:2. *El Monitor*, June 6, 1915, 1:1–2; 3:3–4.

15. Ramírez Plancarte, 495–497. Barragán Rodríguez, II, 362.

16. Barragán Rodríguez, II, 324, 344–346.

17. Silliman to Lansing, June 11, 1915 /15202. *Foreign Relations* (1915), 705–707.

18. *Foreign Relations* (1915), 703–704. Carothers to Lansing, June 19, 1915 /15490.

19. *Lansing Papers*, II, 535.

20. *Foreign Relations* (1915), 715–716, 718–719.

21. *Lansing Papers*, II, 536.

22. *Mexican Herald*, June 10, 1915, 1:1–2.

23. Ramírez Plancarte, 486–487. *La Convención*, June 10, 1915, 1:1–4.

24. *Mexican Herald*, June 11, 1915, 1:3–4; 1:6–7; June 12, 1915, 1:4.

25. *Mexican Herald*, June 13, 1915, 1:2.

26. Almazán to González Garza, May 12, 1915, Archives RGG.

27. Barragán Rodríguez, II, 358.

28. *La Convención*, June 15, 1915, 1:3–4; 12:3.

29. *El Renovador*, June 17, 1915, 6:3. *Mexican Herald*, June 17, 1915, 1:1–2. Ramírez Plancarte, 498–499.

30. *Foreign Relations* (1915), 715. *El Renovador*, June 18, 1915, 4:1.

31. *Mexican Herald*, June 19, 1915, 2:1.

32. *Mexican Herald*, June 20, 1915, 1:4; June 26, 1915, 1:1.

33. *Mexican Herald*, June 26, 1915, 1:6–7; June 27, 1915, 1:4–5; 1:6–7.

34. *El Renovador*, June 23, 1915, 1:6–7. Canada to Lansing, June 24, 1915 /15299. Ramírez Plancarte, 500–505. *El Mexicano*, July 16, 1915, 1:1–4.

35. Ramírez Plancarte, 508.

36. *Mexican Herald*, July 6, 1915, 1:7; 2:2.

37. *El Renovador*, July 8, 1915, 2:2–4.

38. Cardoso de Oliveira to Lansing, July 11, 1915, PRMC (1915). *Foreign Relations* (1915), 723–724. *Mexican Herald*, July 10, 1915, 1:6–7.

39. *Foreign Relations* (1915), 724. Silliman to Lansing, July 14, 1915 /15438.

40. *Mexican Herald*, July 11, 1915, 1:1–2. Barragán Rodríguez, II, 361. González, *Contra Villa*, 328.

41. Cardoso de Oliveira to Lansing, July 15, 1915 /15459. *El Mexicano*, July 16, 1915, 1:6–7.

42. *Mexican Herald*, July 18, 1915, 1:1–2; 1:4.

43. Taracena, 353.

44. González, *Contra Villa*, 342–349. Cervantes, 69–70. *El Mexicano*, August 4, 1915, 1:1; 2:1–3.

45. Barragán Rodríguez, II, 395.

46. *Foreign Relations* (1915), 724.

47. *Mexican Herald*, July 19, 1915, 1:1–2; July 20, 1915, 1:1; July 21, 1915, 1:5–6.

48. Cardoso de Oliveira to Lansing, July 22, 1915 /15953.

49. *Foreign Relations* (1915), 732. Cobb (for Carothers) to Lansing, August 1, 1915 /15613.

50. Barragán Rodríguez, II, 390.

51. *Foreign Relations* (1915), 732. González, *Contra Villa*, 358–359.

52. Wilson to Lansing, July 2, 1915 /15409.

53. *Lansing Papers*, II, 538–539.

54. Eduardo N. Yturbide [sic] to Lansing, July 1, 1915 /15553.

55. *Lansing Papers*, II, 539–541.

56. Argentina, Brazil, Chile, Bolivia, Uruguay, and Guatemala.

57. *Lansing Papers*, II, 542–544. Ministers of Latin American countries to all factions in Mexico, August 11, 1915 /16115. *El Mexicano*, August 10, 1915, 1:6–7.

58. Enrique C. Llorente to Lansing, August 19, 1915 /15826. *Foreign Relations* (1915), 740–742.

59. Silliman to Lansing, August 24, 1915 /15894. *El Mexicano*, August 30, 1915, 1:6–7.

60. Wilson to Lansing, August 11, 1915 /15753½. Wilson to Lansing, August 31, 1915 /16017½.

61. *El Mexicano*, September 11, 1915, 1:1–2.

62. Carothers to Lansing, July 22, 1915 /15518. Cobb to Lansing, July 22, 1915 /15519.

63. Carothers to Lansing, August 5, 1915 /15658. Carothers to Lansing, August 10, 1915 /15718.

64. *Lansing Papers*, II, 545–546.

65. *Ibid.*, 546–548.

66. Carothers to Lansing, August 10, 1915 /15717. Carothers to Lansing, August 10, 1915 /15718. Carothers to Lansing, August 12, 1915 /15739.

67. Carothers to Lansing, August 10, 1915 /15717.

68. Lansing to Hanna, August 13, 1915 /15717. W. L. Bonney to Lansing, August 20, 1915 /15864. Scott to Lansing, August 14, 1915 /15963. Scott to Lansing, August 16, 1915 /15779.

69. Lansing to Wilson, August 10, 1915 /15736a.

70. *Lansing Papers,* II, 550–551.

71. Luis F. Bustamante, *Ebano a Torreón* (Monterrey, 1915), 74–77, 117. Taracena, 357. *Lansing Papers,* II, 552.

72. Carothers to Lansing, September 17, 1915 /16219.

73. Lansing to Wilson, September 18, 1915 /16344½a. As late as 1954 González Garza told me that they had expected to gain American recognition, and he was still bitter about the decision of Lansing to recognize Carranza's regime.

74. *Foreign Relations* (1915), 767, 771.

75. *El Mexicano,* September 1, 1915, 1:1.

76. The following account of the last days of the Convention is taken primarily from Federico Cervantes' pamphlet, published in the United States. See above.

77. According to Antonio Díaz Soto y Gama.

78. Cervantes, 114.

Index

273, 276, 277, 286; confers with
Carranza, 57
Carothers, George C., consul and
special agent, 23, 26, 31, 46, 70,
104, 106, 134, 162, 219, 222, 283,
285, 286; appointed special agent,
36; interview with Carranza, 36–
39; relations with Villa, 40–41;
confers with Maytorena, 160; de-
scribes Villa's desperation, 262;
forecasts Villa's raid, 288
Carranza, Jesús, Constitutionalist
general, 27, 53; capture of San
Luis Potosí, 49
Carranza, Venustiano, First Chief of
the Constitutionalist Forces, 14, 44,
54, 122, 127, 182, 193; opposes
Huerta, 8; named First Chief, 9;
personality, 9–10, 46, 90–91; Plan
of Guadalupe, 9; ejection from
Coahuila, 11, 15; in Sonora, 15;
in Chihuahua, 16, 18; relations
with Villa, 18, 26–34, 37–39, 40,
41, 75, 84–85; saves Chao's life,
27; telegraphic conference with
Villa, 31; accepts Villa's "resignation," 31; shuts off Villa's coal, 34;
lack of popularity, 36–37; interviewed by Canova and Carothers,
37–39; political principles, 42, 43,
64, 71, 151; rejects Pact of Torreón, 43; American recognition, 45,
288–289; relations with Wilson, 46,
99, 263, 282; refuses to send delegates to Niagara Falls, 46; demands
unconditional surrender, 49–51; refuses to see delegates, 53; relations
with Zapata, 56, 63, 64, 65, 66,
67, 68; confers with Cardoso de
Oliveira, 57; to be provisional president, 58, 61–62, 69–70, 83; arrives
in Mexico City, 61; foreign diplomats, 61; relations with American
government, 68, 97–98; summons
Convention, 70; refuses Wilson's
demands, 74; cuts communications
with Villa, 78; Villa withdraws
recognition, 79; addresses Convention, 90–91; resigns, 91; government in Mexico City, 97; refuses
guarantees, 98–99; relations with
Convention, 102–103; invited by
Convention, 104; "disposed to retire," 115; resignation accepted,

116–117; leaves Mexico City, 120;
ultimatum to Convention, 122; opposes Gutiérrez, 123; in rebellion,
123; concession, 124; gives guarantees, 130; occupies Veracruz, 131;
additions to Plan of Guadalupe,
151–152; Veracruz Decrees, 152;
Liberal reforms, 152–153; orders
recapture of Puebla, 154; rejects
American interference, 159–160; orders Obregón to take Mexico City,
177; remains in Veracruz, 180; ig-
nores foreign diplomats, 181; pact
with Casa del Obrero Mundial,
187–188; releases priests, 192; rejects neutralization of Mexico City,
219; rebuffs West, 228; reaction to
Wilson's note, 261–262; "Manifesto
to the Mexican People," 261–262;
orders González to capture Mexico
City, 267; refuses to return to Mexico City, 278; rejects mediation,
281–282; granted American recognition, 289; death, 293
Carrera Torres, Alberto, refuses to
join Gutiérrez, 174–175
Cartwright, W. D., proposes plan to
Scott, 163
Casa del Obrero Mundial, joins
Obregón, 185–188; pact with Carranza, 187–188; attacks Catholics,
191
Casarín, Joaquín V., Conventionist
officer, 291
Casta, José, delegate to Convention,
236
Castellanos, José, delegate to Con-
vention, 212
Castro, Cesáreo, Constitutionalist gen-
eral, 37, 181, 222, 224–225
Catholic Church, attacked by Obre-
gón, 188–192
Catholic Party, opposes Madero, 6;
supports Huerta, 7
Ceballos, Ciro B., Carrancista editor,
10, 104, 106
Cedillo, Emilio, delegate to Conven-
tion, 89
Cedillo, Saturnino, refuses to join
Gutiérrez, 174–175
Celaya, Battle of, 220–226
Ceniceros, Severino, Villista officer,
33, 79
Centennial celebration, 1

Díaz, Encarnación, Zapatista officer, 202

Díaz, Félix, *cuartelazo*, 5, 7

Díaz, Porfirio, dictatorship, 2; re-elected in 1910, 3; exile, 4

Díaz Lombardo, Miguel, Villista official, 42, 70, 177, 288

Díaz Soto y Gama, Antonio, delegate to Convention, 66, 107, 112, 113, 118, 125, 186, 205, 206, 212, 213, 241, 246, 272; Milpa Alta declaration, 65–66; personality, 109, 153; addresses Convention, 109; refuses cabinet post, 143, 265–266; eulogizes parliamentary government, 157; attacks Gutiérrez, 169; opposes Palafox's dismissal, 234–235; attacks González Garza, 240, 245, 249, 250; supports Committee of Public Safety, 242–243; anticlericalism, 244; attacks Wilson's note, 259–260; attacks Villistas, 265

Diéguez, Manuel, Constitutionalist general, 142, 177

Division of the North, 13, 16, 22, 34, 69, 150, 253; captures Saltillo, 29; captures Zacatecas, 32; marches on Mexico City, 125, 126, 127, 129; leaves Mexico City, 143; campaign in the West, 177; northern campaign, 214; defeat at Celaya, 220–226; defeat at León, 261

Education, reforms by Convention, 243–244

Eguía Lis, Rafael, Zapatista general, 271

Election of 1910, 3

Election of 1914, 47

Elizondo, Alfredo, Constitutionalist general, 198, 201, 290

Embargo of arms, American, 44, 289

Escudero, Francisco, Villista official, 177, 288

Estrada, Agustín, Villista general, 143, 172, 177, 217; defeats Aguirre Benavides, 173

Estrada, Francisco, Villista general, 218; murder, 241

Estrada, Roque, Constitutionalist official, 89

Fabela, Isidro, Constitutionalist official, 10, 16, 48, 51, 52, 71, 98, 99, 120, 127, 129

Federal forces, 10, 13, 17, 19, 23, 25, 26, 50, 54, 55; relations with Madero, 6–7; surrender of Mexico City, 58

Fierro, Rodolfo, Villista officer, 144, 145, 147, 148, 177, 275, 277

First Chief; *see* Carranza, Venustiano

Fletcher, F. F., American admiral, 72

Flores Magón party, 42

Foreign diplomats, 127; ignored by Carranza, 181; protest to Carranza, 193

Frontier violations, 158, 161

Fuller, Paul, Wilson's agent, 66, 67; interviews Carranza, 71–72; with ABC ministers, 280–281

Funston, Frederick, occupation of Veracruz, 99; asks delay in evacuation, 73–74

Galván, Leobardo, Zapatista officer, 86, 89

Gama, Agustín, Zapatista official, 170

Gama, Domicio da, Brazilian minister, 288

Gama, Valentín, Minister of Commerce, 143

Garay, Rafael, murder, 207

García Aragón, Guillermo, executed by Zapata, 139, 144

Garrison, Lindley M., Secretary of War, 44, 73

Garza Cárdenas, Luis de la, Villista official, 177

Gavira, Gabriel, Constitutionalist officer, 276

Gómez, Rodrigo, Minister of Justice, 143, 166, 170

Gómez Palacio, capture by Villa, 22–23

González, Onésimo, delegate to Convention, 89

González, Pablo, Constitutionalist general, 15, 27, 28, 30, 37, 47, 120, 123, 124, 137, 140, 171; supports Carranza, 119; defends Tampico, 151; ultimatum to Convention, 268; attacks Mexico City, 270–271, 273–274; enters Mexico City, 274; leaves Mexico City, 275; returns to Mexico City, 278; ultimatum to Lagos Cházaro, 289